Learning and Developme Practice

Kathy Beevers and Andrew Rea

D0246211

The Chartered Institute of Personnel and Development is the leading publisher of books and reports for personnel and training professionals, students, and all those concerned with the effective management and development of people at work. For details of all our titles, please contact the publishing department:
tel: 020 8612 6204
e-mail: publish@cipd.co.uk
The catalogue of all CIPD titles can be viewed on the CIPD website:
www.cipd.co.uk/bookstore

Learning and Development Practice

Kathy Beevers and Andrew Rea

Chartered Institute of Personnel and Development

Published by the Chartered Institute of Personnel and Development,
151, The Broadway, London, SW19 1JQ

This edition first published 2010

Typeset by 4Word Ltd, Bristol

Printed and bound in the UK by the Charlesworth Group, Wakefield

British Library Cataloguing in Publication Data
A catalogue of this publication is available from the British Library

ISBN 9781843982616

Chartered Institute of Personnel and Development, CIPD House, 151, The Broadway,
London, SW19 1JQ

Tel: 020 8612 6200

E-mail: cipd@cipd.co.uk Website: www.cipd.co.uk

Incorporated by Royal Charter. Registered Charity No. 1079797

Contents

List of Figures and Tables

Acknowledgements

We owe a big thank you to:

Andrea Young, John Rodwell, Steven Cartwright, Suzanne Copley, Linda George, Steven Wilson, Janet Medcalf and all the other brilliant people who contributed their thoughts and ideas to this book.

And to Kirsty Smy, Ruth Lake and Robert Williams for their support and publishing expertise.

How to Use This Book

Welcome to *Learning and Development Practice*. Whatever your aim in reading this book, we hope you will find it an enjoyable and worthwhile investment of your time.

WHY READ ANY FURTHER?

The book is designed to give you a sound introduction to practical learning and development (L&D), whilst also providing some key theories and models you can use to develop your practice.

You may be reading this book because you work in L&D and want to know more, or you may be preparing for an L&D role. Equally, you might be working towards a qualification – one of the CIPD qualifications in L&D, or another qualification for L&D professionals

Whatever your reason, we have set out to write a text that is both practical, and developmental and which will support you if you are working towards a qualification.

The book is practical in that it reflects the realities of working within L&D. We are both practitioners and passionate about training and wanted the book to include real experiences, tips and advice from practising trainers. We have therefore called on colleagues and contacts and included their contributions as quotes or case studies or used them to inform certain areas of text.

Development is provided through a mix of explanation and input as well as the numerous case studies and examples which bring the text 'to life' and illustrate how people have applied the ideas we discuss. The text also includes reflective activities, practical tips, and suggestions for putting learning into practice. There is a mix of approaches in the book – and we hope that there is something for everyone.

Finally, the book is written to support the content of current qualifications for trainers and L&D professionals, particularly the CIPD Foundation Certificate in Learning and Development. As you will see, the chapters reflect the units of this qualification and the content will guide you through the required learning for each unit and support you towards achievement of your qualification. More indirectly, the book also supports other CIPD and national qualifications in Learning and Development

WHAT IS IN THE BOOK?

The book is composed of nine chapters and a final section containing 12 Essential Learning Pages.

THE CHAPTERS

The nine chapters each cover a different aspect of L&D practice.

The first three chapters explore three essential aspects of being an L&D professional – ensuring your own professional development, understanding how L&D contributes to organisational success and managing L&D information effectively.

At the heart of the book are four chapters which follow the training cycle – learning needs analysis, designing learning activities, delivering learning activities and evaluating learning activities.

Ref to ELP 1– Training Cycle

The remaining two chapters are about coaching in the workplace and mentoring in the workplace – two increasingly popular interventions and increasingly essential skill areas for trainers.

Each chapter follows the same broad structure:

- chapter objectives and an introduction
- a short section on why the subject is important – and why L&D practitioners need to know about and understand it
- a section clarifying the meaning of the subject – definitions and practical meanings, and how the subject differs from other similar practices
- a main section giving practical advice about how to carry out the subject – this section, with the sub-heading 'In practice' is the main part of each chapter
- a final 'What next' section giving suggestions about how you could experiment with and extend your learning in the subject area
- a chapter summary and reading/resource references.

THE ESSENTIAL LEARNING PAGES (ELPs)

The ELPs are a series of pages explaining key ideas in learning and development. They have been provided separately because:

- Some important theories and models are relevant to several of the chapters and, rather than keep repeating the information, we have provided a full explanation in the ELP and then made reference to it from the relevant chapters. Each time one of the models or theories is mentioned in a chapter we simply talk about how it applies in that particular context.
- Some learners may want to read more about the models and theories they encounter in the chapters, or refer to them at times, and the ELPs provide a handy source of useful further information for you to refer to whenever you need it.

WHERE TO START?

Are you a logical reader – are you reading this section now because you naturally started at the beginning? Or are you more of a dipper – you've had a look around, read a few of the things that struck you as interesting and now have happened to find this page? Or maybe you are a focused reader – there are certain things that you want to get from this book, and you are reading this page to find out how to meet those needs?

There is no requirement for you to work through the book 'chapter by chapter'. Each chapter stands alone as material about a particular topic and, while the chapters are presented in a logical sequence, they can be read separately or in any order you choose.

The ELPs are referred to in the chapters where they fit into the text, but they also stand alone as reference material for you to access as and when you require them.

In short – use the book in whatever way suits you best. The book is written to assist you and your learning. We hope it will inform your practice, assist your continuing development and, most of all, add to your enjoyment of being a L&D professional.

Kathy and Andrew

NOTE FOR CIPD STUDENTS AND TUTORS

If you are a tutor who has adopted this book as your core text or a CIPD student who has purchased this text, you can access the accompanying online resources:

- www.cipd.co.uk/tss: for tutor resources that will assist with course design and delivery, including a Lecturer's guide, lecture slides and case studies
- www.cipd.co.uk/sss: for student resources including self-test questions, annotated web-links and activities

Learning and Development Practice

The content of this CIPD certificate is covered as follows:

Learning and Development Practice unit	Learning and Development Practice chapters
Developing yourself as an effective L&D professional	Chapter 1: Developing yourself as an effective L&D professional ELP 3, 5, 6
Understanding organisations and the role of human resources	Chapter 2: Understanding organisations and the role of human resources
Recording, Analysing and Using L&D Information	Chapter 3: Recording, Analysing and Using L&D Information ELP 8
Delivering learning and development activities	Chapter 4: Delivering learning and development activities ELP 3, 7, 12
Undertaking a learning needs analysis	Chapter 5: Undertaking a learning needs analysis ELP 2, 3, 4, 5, 7
Preparing and designing learning and development activities	Chapter 6: Preparing and designing learning and development activities ELP 1, 2, 3, 4, 7, 8, 9, 11
Evaluating learning and development activities	Chapter 7: Evaluating learning and development activities ELP 1, 11, 12
Developing mentoring skills for the workplace	Chapter 8: Developing mentoring skills for the workplace ELP 2, 10
Developing coaching skills for the workplace	Chapter 9: Developing coaching skills for the workplace ELP 10

Walkthrough of textbook features and online resources

HOW TO USE THIS BOOK (PAGES IX–XII)

The opening section explains the rationale behind the book and its innovative structure. Dip in and out of the chapters or read the book cover to cover, depending on your learning style.

UNIT CHAPTERS

The first nine chapters focus on different aspects of learning and development practice and reflect the units of the CIPD's Learning and Development Practice certificate.

ESSENTIAL LEARNING PAGES

The second part of the book covers key ideas in learning and development practice. Each ELP looks at a different theory or model, giving you control over how much depth you go into.

Ref to ELP 7 –
Principles of
adult learning

CROSS-REFERENCES

Marginal cross-references within the unit chapters will point you in the direction of relevant Essential Learning Pages, helping you to apply the theories and models to different contexts.

CHAPTER INTRODUCTIONS

Concise chapter introductions outline the structure of each chapter and the topics covered.

LEARNING OUTCOMES

At the beginning of each chapter a bulleted set of learning outcomes summarises what you can expect to learn from the chapter, helping you to track your progress.

LEARNING OUTCOMES

When you have read this chapter you should be able to:

- explain why developing yourself as an L&D professional is essential
- identify professional requirements of L&D roles
- define your customers and their requirements
- describe key aspects of delivering an effective L&D service
- explain the concept and process of continuing professional development and produce your own CPD records
- discuss key factors to consider when selecting activities for your own development.

CASE STUDIES

A number of case studies from different sectors and countries will help you to place the concepts discussed into a real-life context.

CASE STUDY 1.1

DEVELOPMENT AS AN L&D PRACTITIONER

Prior to taking on the role of Employee Development Officer for an international organisation which owns a number of ports across the world, I had been working in a Further Education college. The culture change was fascinating. In my new role, my first training role with such a large private sector organisation I was part of a small team, delivering development programmes for all managers and employees (approx 2,500 people) across one site.

My new role was primarily to deliver an off-the-shelf programme from an American organisation. I was trained to deliver

a change in senior management, eventually abandoned the programme and adopted a more tailored approach. This included:

- a complete needs analysis for one of the specialist departments within the organisation
- design and delivery of training for a specific group of team leaders
- design and delivery of a competence-based programme for a group of future team leaders within the operational areas of the business.

Training staff worked alongside

REFLECTIVE ACTIVITY

How do you know what is required of you at work?

And where and how is the information stated?

What about your job title?

REFLECTIVE ACTIVITIES

Questions and activities throughout the text encourage you to reflect on what you have learnt and to apply your knowledge and skills in practice.

WHAT NEXT

DEVELOPING YOURSELF

Below are some activities to help further your learning from this chapter:

1 Have a look at the HR Profession Map at www.cipd.co.uk and particularly at the interactive self-assessment tool My HR Map.

2 Review your function's approach to service delivery. Consider:
   – Who are all the customers you deal with?

WHAT NEXT?

Take your learning of a topic to the next level by exploring some of the ideas within the What Next? sections, placed towards the end of each chapter.

CHAPTER SUMMARIES

At the end of each chapter, the chapter summaries are designed to consolidate your learning and pull out key points for you to remember.

EXPLORE FURTHER

BOOKS:

Covey, S.R. (1994) *The seven habits of highly effective people: Powerful lessons in personal change*. London: Simon & Schuster.

Goleman, D. (1996) *Emotional intelligence: Why it can matter more than IQ*. London: Bloomsbury Publishing PLC.

Dryden, W. and Constantinou, D. (2004) *Assertiveness step by step (overcoming problems)*. London: Sheldon Press.

ON-LINE GUIDANCE RELATING TO CIPD HR MAP (INCLUDING PROFESSIONAL AREAS OF LEARNING AND TALENT DEVELOPMENT AND SERVICE DELIVERY AND ACCESS TO MY HR MAP):

EXPLORE FURTHER

Explore further boxes contain suggestions for further reading and useful websites, encouraging you to delve further into areas of particular interest.

ONLINE RESOURCES FOR STUDENTS

- Self-test questions – identify areas in need of further development

- Annotated weblinks – click through to a wealth of up-to-date information online

- Advisory notes – hints and tips to help you through the CIPD certificate

- Additional activities – practical tasks to help consolidate your learning

- Extended case studies – read around the cases that really grabbed you

Visit **www.cipd.co.uk/sss**

ONLINE RESOURCES FOR TUTORS

- Lecturer's Guide – practical advice on teaching the CIPD certificate using this text including a few additional activities for you to use with students

- PowerPoint slides – build and deliver your course around these ready-made lectures, ensuring complete coverage of the CIPD certificate

- Additional case studies – for you to use with students in seminars or lectures

Visit **www.cipd.co.uk/tss**

CHAPTER 1

Developing Yourself as an Effective Learning and Development Practitioner

INTRODUCTION

This chapter begins with a look at what is required of L&D professionals and how L&D roles are specified. We discuss the CIPD HR Profession Map and how we can use it to assess our professional development needs. We then move on to look at how we deliver our L&D service, considering: who are our customers, how well do we meet their needs and what can we do to improve our service delivery. In the final section of the chapter we look at the concept of Continuing Professional Development (CPD) and give some practical tips on how to complete a CPD Record and select activities for professional development.

LEARNING OUTCOMES

When you have read this chapter you should be able to:

- explain why developing yourself as an L&D professional is essential
- identify professional requirements of L&D roles
- define your customers and their requirements
- describe key aspects of delivering an effective L&D service
- explain the concept and process of continuing professional development and produce your own CPD records
- discuss key factors to consider when selecting activities for your own development.

BEING AN EFFECTIVE L&D PRACTITIONER

The L&D profession is a wonderful profession to belong to. As a career it offers constant variety, the satisfaction of seeing the results of your work, recognition in many different forms – and endless opportunities for learning.

Of course, the profession is not without its challenges, frustrations and occasional upsets, but in our experience trainers love their work.

Learning and development roles are rarely a 'first career'. Often we spend a few years developing expertise in a technical area or operational role and then move gradually towards helping others to gain the same expertise. This creates a sort of natural selection, in that it is the people who have a natural interest in helping others learn who move gradually into formal L&D roles.

There was a time, perhaps, when being able to do a technical role yourself and having an interest in helping others learn was enough for you to be deemed capable to pass your skills and knowledge on to others. This is no longer the case. Learning and development has become a profession, with its own body of professional knowledge and professional standards. As well as being skilled in the subject areas we teach, train or tutor, we must also be skilled in the technicalities of identifying learning needs, designing, delivering and evaluating learning, and have a clear understanding of the organisational contexts in which we work.

An effective L&D practitioner knows what is required of them and enjoys building their capability to meet the requirements. Once they have developed a sound base of essential skills and knowledge they continue to seek new learning, experiment with new approaches and keep renewing their abilities as learning and development professionals.

UNDERSTANDING L&D ROLES AND REQUIREMENTS

How do you know what is required of you at work? We would suggest that there are at least two sets of requirements which affect what you do and how you do it:

1 organisational job or role descriptions and internal competence frameworks

2 professional specifications and standards.

ORGANISATIONAL SPECIFICATIONS

Most people working for an organisation will have a job description which sets out the essential requirements of their role. This may be supplemented by further information, about the skills, knowledge and experience required (for example in a person specification at the recruitment stage) or an internal competence framework which details the abilities and behaviours required of different roles within the organisation.

There are many variations of L&D roles; you may, for example, be involved in:

- identifying learning needs and planning learning activities
- designing learning activities and materials
- delivering and evaluating learning activities
- providing one-to-one training or coaching
- assessing and reviewing learning progress
- supporting line managers to train their staff
- advising people in the organisation about L&D
- maintaining L&D information systems
- designing or supporting e-learning/technology/enabled learning

- organising learning programmes, schemes or events
- monitoring training expenditure and budgets.

Learning and development job titles include: Trainer, L&D Consultant, Training Advisor, Training Consultant, Business Partner – and some more specific ones, such as Assessor, Instructor or Qualification Adviser, where the actual role may extend beyond the specific meaning of the title.

Your L&D role will depend on a number of factors including the type and size of your organisation and the sector you work in. You might be directly employed by the organisation you provide training for working within their L&D or training function, or you might work for a training provider, delivering training services to a range of different organisations. You might also be an independent trainer offering your services directly to organisations or working through an agency or training association who arranges the work for you. In a smaller organisation you may well be 'the training function'.

Along with an overall description of the requirements of your job, it is likely that you will have specific objectives to meet – individual performance objectives or key performance indicators (KPIs) which extend aspects of your work role into measurable activities. For example you may be required to deliver a particular number of programmes or support specific work projects or bring about a specific level of improvement in staff performance.

REFLECTIVE ACTIVITY

How do you know what is required of you at work?

Where and how is the information stated?

What about your job title – how well does it reflect your job role?

How do you describe your job to your friends and family?

PROFESSIONAL DEFINITIONS AND STANDARDS

The Chartered Institute of Personnel and Development (CIPD)

The CIPD is the professional body for 'those responsible for the management and development of people within organisations' in the UK. The CIPD's 135,000 members include people who work in or are studying towards HR/Personnel roles, as well as those involved in Learning, Development and Training (44 per cent).

The CIPD has developed a specification of the activities, knowledge and behaviours required by the different HR roles with its overall remit. This specification is known as The HR Profession Map and it is available on the CIPD website.

The map divides the HR arena into 10 professional areas, each further divided into four bands. It also includes eight key behaviours considered essential to the HR profession.

Figure 1.1 The HR Profession Map

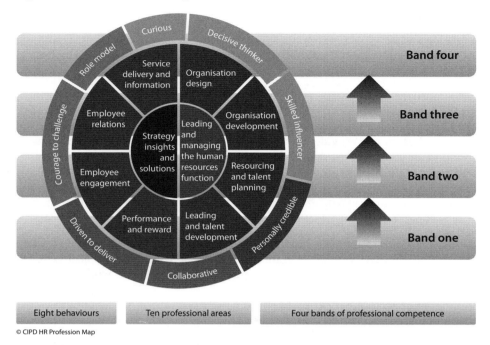

© CIPD HR Profession Map

The 10 professional areas

Of the 10 areas of HR activity, the first two, as listed here, are considered 'key areas' because they extend across all the other eight.

The 10 areas are:

- strategy insights and solutions
- leading and managing the human resources function
- organisation design
- organisation development
- resourcing and talent planning
- **learning and talent development**
- performance and reward
- employee engagement
- employee relations
- service delivery and information.

Each area has an extended definition to clarify the key requirements of people who work in that area. For example the requirement of '**learning and talent development**' professionals is defined as:

ensuring that people at all levels of the organisation possess and develop the skills, knowledge and experiences to fulfil the short- and long-term ambitions of the organisation and that they are motivated to learn, grow and perform.

The four bands

Each of the 10 professional areas is further divided into four bands, defining the different levels of work activities and responsibility within the area. Figure 1.2 below is an extract from the **learning and talent development** pages.

There is also a useful section within the information on bands, entitled Transitions, which explains how we can move, or prepare to move, from one professional band to the next.

The eight behaviours

The behaviours describe how work activities should be carried out.

The behaviours are:
- decisive thinker
- skilled influencer
- personally credible
- collaborative
- driven to deliver
- courage to challenge
- role model
- curious.

Different combinations of the eight behaviours link to each professional area. For example the behaviours deemed essential for people working within **learning and talent development** (at band 2) are:
- driven to deliver
- personally credible
- curious.

Whilst we have explained the HR map in brief here, this is no substitute for you actually trying out the map. There is a lot of information about the map on the CIPD website, and members can access the interactive My HR Map self-assessment tool. This tool will help you to clarify the requirements of your role, assess your capabilities against requirements and plan your career progression and professional development.

Figure 1.2 Extract from Learning and Talent Development (Bands)

What you need to do (activities)

	Band 1	Band 2	Band 3	Band 4
6	Implements systems and processes that measure the efficiency of third-party suppliers, and the expected return of the learning and training interventions.	Works with third-party providers to monitor service levels and give timely feedback. Uses the relationship with third parties to gain new insights on the external marketplace. Develops processes that measure the expected return of the learning and talent development interventions.	Manages third-party learning and talent development suppliers against agreed standards, contracts or service-level agreements.	Negotiates and manages major third-party contracts for the delivery of learning and training services, establishing reasonable costs and high standards of execution. Sets and manages appropriate metrics to track delivery.
7	Processes and captures data from learning and talent development events to support the evaluation of initiatives in the immediate and longer term.	Develops, pilots and evaluates learning and talent development initiatives for effectiveness, business relevance and cost. Ensures measures are relevant and understood by managers.	Leads the development of business cases for learning and talent development initiatives and works to ensure the delivery of stated benefits using participant feedback, tracking metrics and expected return analysis.	Creates and leads the business case for learning and training including costs vs. benefits considerations. Designs metrics that track the business benefit and is able to demonstrate expected return and value created.
8	Supports instructional design experts in the development of programmes, and researches and analyses the cost of the most appropriate delivery channels.	Works with subject matter experts and takes the instructional design lead in the development of programmes. Recommends the most appropriate delivery channel.	Works with subject matter experts and takes the instructionl design lead in the development of major programmes across the organisation. Recommends the most appropriate delivery channel.	Takes the lead in the design and delivery of critical learning and talent development interventions.
9	Supports the delivery of learning and training programmes, managing delegate lists, joining instructions and evaluation process.	Facilitates internal learning events and workshops, delivering content as appropriate.	Facilitates internal learning events and workshops, delivering content as appropriate.	Facilitates executive leadership learning events and workshops, delivering content as appropriate.
10	Manages organisation learning management or training records system and highlights retraining requirements in safety-critical skills and areas of compliance.	Engages with managers and employees to ensure that the organisation is in compliance at all times with relevant training legislation.	Keeps abreast of local and international legislative changes that may impact learning and talent development, eg HSE, food hygiene training and legal training.	Establishes systems and processes to ensure that staff are adequately trained and regularly retrained in safety-critical skills and other compliance issues in accordance with local legislation.
11	Informs and advises staff and management on the elements of the development infrastructure and how the whole system is intended to operate.	Advises and coaches managers in the optimal use of the development infrastructure, challenging them to agree personal development plans with staff.	Leads the detailed design and management of a section of the development infrastructure, eg apprentices, graduates, managers, executives and front-line staff.	Leads the design of a development infrastructure, including career paths/maps, capability frameworks, technical ladders for each technical discipline and contribution level (eg individual contributor, supervisor, manager, leader, executive).

Other standards for the learning and development profession

Lifelong Learning UK (LLUK), the Sector Skills Council for Lifelong Learning, has also developed specifications and standards for their sector. These include a framework of qualifications for teachers, tutors and trainers working within the FE system, and a number of National Occupational Standards (NOS). The 'FE system' primarily refers to colleges and college staff, working with learners in a further education setting, but also encompasses some trainers working within government-funded adult and work-based learning contexts.

The qualifications for new teaching staff entering the FE system include:

- Preparing to Teach in the Lifelong Learning Sector (PTLLS)
- Certificate in Teaching in the Lifelong Learning Sector (CTLLS)
- Diploma in Teaching in the Lifelong Learning Sector (DTLLS).

Like the CIPD qualifications, each qualification is composed of a number of units specifying the skills and knowledge required by the target group. The LLUK units specify the skills and knowledge required to operate as a teacher, trainer or tutor within the lifelong learning/FE system.

Finally, in 2009, LLUK revised the National Occupational Standards for Learning and Development which also provide a specification of the required activities and capabilities of different learning and development roles. Previous versions of these standards have provided the basis of National Vocational Qualifications in Learning and Development and have been embedded within a range of other trainer qualifications. The Learning and Development NOS also include the standards for NVQ Assessors and Verifiers. At the time of writing, only the new standards for assessors and verifiers have been converted into qualifications, but this may be extended across the remainder of the Learning and Development NOS in due course.

REFLECTIVE ACTIVITY

What does being a 'professional trainer' mean to you?

What makes you a 'professional'?

EFFECTIVE DELIVERY OF THE L&D SERVICE

Whatever your role within learning and development, you will be involved in providing a service to customers. Being effective as an L&D professional means not just providing a high quality service in terms of your training abilities – but also delivering your service efficiently and in a way that meets your customer's needs.

The HR map definition of Service Delivery is:

> ensures that the delivery of service and information to leaders, managers and staff within the organisation is accurate, efficient, timely and cost-effective and that human resources data is managed professionally.

Whilst this book is particularly focused on the development of training skills, particularly chapters 4–9, it is appropriate here to spend a little time exploring the skills of effective service delivery – and how you might develop these further. Here are some of the things you need to consider.

KNOW YOUR CUSTOMERS AND THEIR REQUIREMENTS

> If you're not serving the customer, you'd better be serving someone who is.
>
> Karl Albrecht

Knowing who our customers are, and what they expect from us, is key to how we deliver our service.

The role of L&D is not necessarily to serve an organisation's 'end users' or 'external customers'. It is about making sure that those end users are served by people who have the knowledge skills and behaviours needed to do their jobs successfully. So, our direct customers are usually the staff within an organisation who want and need to develop their capabilities. This takes us back to the definition of learning and development within the CIPD HR map:

> ensuring that people at all levels of the organisation possess and develop the skills, knowledge and experiences to fulfil the short- and long-term ambitions of the organisation and that they are motivated to learn, grow and perform.

However, our customers are likely to extend beyond just the learner groups we work with. For example Figure 1.3 below is a spider-gram showing how a trainer (Richard) working in a regional office of a government department identified his customers. Richard's remit is to deliver induction for new staff, technical and generic training for operational staff and some 'first-line management' training for team leaders.

As you can see from the spider-gram, Richard has identified five customers or customer groups. He summarises their needs and expectations from him, as:

- Learner groups including new staff, staff and team leaders require/expect:
  - training that is designed, organised and delivered professionally, that will enable them to fulfil their job role
  - information and advice about learning activities so that they can make their own choices about learning
  - fair access to training and learning activities
  - accurate information about learning activities so that they can be available and prepared for learning
  - support to transfer learning into the workplace

Figure 1.3 Identifying customers

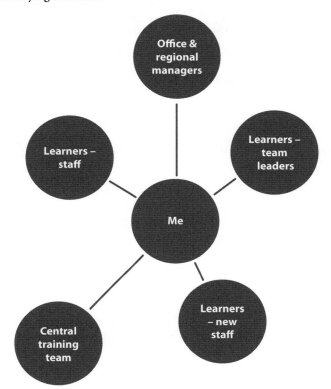

- support with any difficulties they have in developing themselves for their job role
- occasional representation to managers about the need for learning opportunities.

● Managers in the region require/expect:
  - staff who are able to fulfil their job role and so fulfil the organisation's targets
  - training that is delivered efficiently and within budgets
  - training that is delivered with the minimum of disturbance to the business.

● Central team require/expect:
  - training delivered in line with organisational requirements
  - information about training delivered in the region
  - information on current and future learning needs and skills gaps
  - lessons learned, evaluation info and improvement suggestions.

In some ways, Richard could also have considered the external customers of the organisation as his customer – although this would not be a direct relationship. Some would also say that Richard's line manager and colleagues are also his customers. However here Richard has focused on the direct customers of the service he delivers.

REFLECTIVE ACTIVITY

Who are your customers?

What do they need/expect from you?

COMMUNICATE, COMMUNICATE, COMMUNICATE!

Keep your communications with customers effective by thinking of the following factors.

Know your objective

Even the simplest of communications has a purpose. If you are not clear yourself about what you are trying to say, then your communication will also be unclear.

Consider the needs of the recipient

Relevant information will include:

- the types and amount of information they need from you
- their preferred method of communication and the channels available for them to reply
- how much they already know about the subject – so that you can pitch your communication at the right level and use the right language and technical-speak, for example
- whether or not they are likely to agree with your communication and how they are likely to react to your message.

Choose your medium

This depends on much more than just your personal preferences for communicating. An e-mail might be the easiest for you – but is it the most effective for the objective that you need to achieve? Other communication options might be: face-to-face meetings, conversations, group bulletins, telephone calls, conference calls, presentations, texts and electronic postings.

Whilst e-mails allow people to access information in their own time and provide a written record of a communication, they can be impersonal and open to interpretation. Sometimes a telephone call or face-to-face meeting is more appropriate to clarify and discuss details or address more sensitive matters.

"As someone who is quite 'task focused' I recognised that my e-mails sometimes came over as a bit stern or unfriendly to recipients who are more 'people focused'. I tend to go straight into the main purpose of the communication, forgetting any of the 'opening words' that make an e-mail friendlier and more engaging for the reader.

Now, I still focus on writing the main purpose of the e-mail first (whilst it is clear in my thoughts), but before I send it I go back to the beginning and think about the recipient a bit more – and maybe add some more personal or sociable opening words . It doesn't take much – just a 'how are you doing' or 'I hope X project is going well' can make the e-mail more balanced and avoid it sounding too stern or impersonal."

Presentations and formal meetings have their place for formal communications – and can add weight to a message – but can be disruptive and costly in terms of time away from the workplace. Texts are great for informal messages within well established relationships, but may be inappropriate for business communications and communications with certain customer groups. Group bulletins and electronic postings are useful for non-urgent information and for delivering a consistent message to large numbers of people.

The main factor is to choose the best method for the purpose and to make sure that the style of communication is congruent with the message. In face-to-face and spoken communication, for example, make sure that your body language, facial expressions, and tone of voice, all convey the same thing. As well as choosing the right words to use, you have to look and sound like you mean it.

Check for receipt and understanding

Good communicators always make sure that their message has been received and understood. In face-to-face communication we can check out the body language and facial expressions of our audience. In telephone communications we can monitor the questions we are asked, or ask questions ourselves to gauge the level of understanding. For important written communications we may ask for responses or compile a list of frequently asked questions.

The true meaning of a message is what is received, rather than what is sent.

If you are interested in developing your relationship building or communication skills – you might find topics such as Emotional Intelligence, Assertive Behaviour, Non-violent Communication or some aspects of Neuro-Linguistic Programming (NLP) of interest.

An example NLP approach aimed at enhancing communication skills concerns 'thinking styles'. Three pairs of thinking styles are identified as 'away from and towards', 'global and detail' and 'procedures and options'.

Away-from thinkers are motivated to take action when it will get them away from the things that they do not want. Your message should refer to penalties, current problems and potential dangers.	Towards thinkers are motivated to take action when it will move them towards things that they do want. Your message should refer to rewards, solutions and achievements.

Global thinkers understand things when they can see the bigger picture. Your message should include overall concepts and link to bigger themes and messages.	Detail thinkers understand things when they know the ins-and-outs of the details. Your message should include practical examples and referenced detail.
Procedures thinkers like to follow instructions and processes. Your message should include step by step procedures and protocols to follow.	Options thinkers like to make their own decisions. Your message should include the choices that are available and the level of individual empowerment that people have.

If you recognise any of these thinking styles in your customers or colleagues, you could try adjusting your message to fit their style – and see if this adds to the quality of your communications with them.

ESTABLISH POSITIVE WORKING RELATIONSHIPS

Building good working relationships with your customers will help you and them get what they need from the relationship and manage things more easily when there are problems or difficulties. Some good relationships will happen by accident, through natural rapport, but others may need working on. Some steps in building a good working relationship are:

Make an active effort to build the relationship

Decide which relationships are important and commit to actively working on them. You can build rapport through taking a genuine interest in the other person, and finding out a little about their situation, their motivations, their likes and dislikes. Let them know a little about you too – it is a two-way relationship.

Take time to understand customer needs and preferences

Listen to them and establish what is important to them. Keep clarifying what they need from you and from your function. Ask them to tell you if you do something that they are unhappy with, before it becomes a big issue.

Set clear and realistic expectations of what you can provide

Be clear about what you can and cannot provide. It may be tempting to agree to more than you can deliver, but this will only cause trouble later. Ultimately you will gain much more professional respect by being honest about what can and cannot be achieved and setting realistic expectations.

There may be guidance already in the organisation to inform how you deliver your service to customers. Your organisation may have a customer service policy or service standards for external customers which could inform how you serve internal customers. Or you establish service level agreements or service contracts with customers. Perhaps your performance objectives specify the standards of service you are required to provide. Having clear guidelines for your work will help you make quicker decisions about what you can and cannot provide and help you to set realistic expectations with customers.

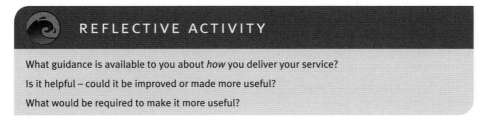

REFLECTIVE ACTIVITY

What guidance is available to you about *how* you deliver your service?

Is it helpful – could it be improved or made more useful?

What would be required to make it more useful?

DELIVER THE SERVICE

Meet expectations

Having agreed what you will provide – provide it as agreed. The best way to maintain good relationships with your customers is to consistently provide the service they are expecting from you. This builds up customer's confidence in you and is the basis of all good working relationships.

Keep customers well informed

Let customers know what you are going to do, what you have done, what is still to do, when it will be done, etc, etc. Keeping customers informed will prevent them becoming concerned that things are not going to plan. Information is important when things are going well but even more important when there are difficulties. If ever you cannot fulfil requirements, maintain trust by telling customers about the potential problems as soon as possible, explaining why problems have arisen and offering the best solutions you can.

Manage your time and workload

Getting everything done on time can be difficult and we often have to prioritise our work, according to key work objectives and project timelines. A useful tool to help us think about our work priorities is the Time Management Matrix, which was popularised by Dr Stephen Covey, in The Seven Habits of Highly Effective People (1992).

To use the matrix, you first need to classify your tasks in terms of how important they are and how urgent they are:

- An important task is one that helps you achieve your main objectives, or moves you forward in an important direction. It is probably something you want to spend time on and do particularly well.

- An urgent task is one that has to be done to meet a deadline. The nearer you get to the deadline, the more urgent the job becomes.

You can then 'plot' tasks on the two scales of the matrix – and so identify four quadrants or categories of tasks. How you approach your different tasks can then be guided by which quadrant they sit in.

Figure 1.4 Time management matrix

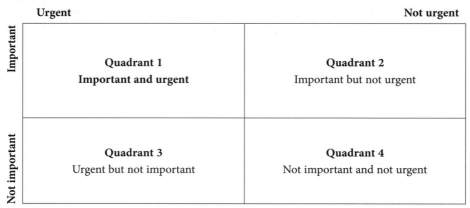

Quadrant 1: Important and urgent

These are your top priorities and should be done first. However you should try to avoid tasks moving into this quadrant by planning important work ahead.

Quadrant 2: Important but not urgent

You should start working on these as soon as you can. Plan in advance how you will address them and start 'chipping away' at them whenever you have some time. Because they are important, they should not be left to the last minute, when you may have to compromise your standards. Try to keep making small contributions to these tasks before the deadline so that you avoid the pressure and compromises of them becoming urgent.

Quadrant 3: Urgent but not important

You will have to do these tasks quickly because there is a deadline, but do not spend too much time on them. Get them out of your way quickly or if possible delegate them to someone who is capable and that you can trust.

Quadrant 4: Neither important nor urgent

There are three ways to deal with these:

1 Do not do them at all if they are a waste of time.

2 Delegate them.

3 Forget about them until they are nearer to the deadline.

If you are managing your workload well, the majority of your time will be spent on Quadrant 2 activities. If your time is taken up with Quadrant 1 activities then you are constantly fire-fighting and probably not achieving a great quality of work. If you are spending your time on Quadrant 3 and 4 tasks, then you may be neglecting important work for tasks that you find easier or more immediately interesting. It is probably a good time to review and re-consider your priorities.

> "Providing a service to your clients should not make you a servant to their every wish. It's about valuing and respecting the people expertise you bring and working in equal partnership to meet the organisation's needs."
>
> Steven Cartwright, Customer Service Consultant, With a V Ltd

Balance conflicting customer needs

Sometimes the different needs of customer groups can conflict. For example learners may want extra time to complete their learning, but managers want to minimise time away from the workplace, or staff may want to undertake a qualification but the organisation has decided not to sponsor the type of qualification the staff member is seeking, or your learners would like you to be in one place supporting them, whilst your manager needs you to be somewhere else covering a different activity.

Ideally, there will be an underpinning policy or procedure to help you deal with such situations – for example a Learning and Development Policy covering sponsorship of staff qualifications or specifying staff's entitlement to training and development – and if there is not then this is an area you could usefully help develop.

If there is no obvious guidance, then grade or levels of power in the organisation may come into play with managers being able to make the final decisions. However, often there is a way of meeting both needs to some extent – and offering something to either party, whilst explaining why you cannot fully meet either's needs is often the best way forward.

In the examples above, you may be able to negotiate a compromise between managers and staff on the actual time spent away from the workplace for learning, or you may be able to refer the person wanting to study a qualification not sponsored internally to other funding sources, and also link them to a mentor in the organisation who could support them with their qualification.

However much we try to meet our customers' needs there will be times when we have to explain that a need or request cannot be met. As long as we do this professionally and sensitively it may be our best solution. Knowing when to bring a situation to a close and move on to other things is an essential aspect of managing our time to best meet the needs of all our customers.

Address problems, complaints and difficulties

"In the middle of difficulty lies opportunity."

Albert Einstein

If you have already taken time to: establish customers' needs, build a positive working relationship with them and communicate regularly and effectively, you will have done much to avoid problems arising.

However, things do go wrong sometimes and have to be addressed – they rarely 'just go away'. Before attempting to resolve a problem it is important to be sure that it is your place to solve it – consider whether an issue should be referred to someone else, for example, or be escalated up the management line.

The classic approach to problem solving is to:

- clarify the problem – taking into account the views of different parties
- identify the options for solving the problem
- establish the relative advantages and disadvantages of the various options
- agree the preferred option with those involved and implement the option.

At such times it is very helpful to have organisational policies and procedures, or even legislation, to refer to. We have policies and procedures so that everyone knows what is expected or accepted in certain circumstances and these are an obvious source of help in clarifying problems and identifying solutions. Service level agreements are also very useful as they remove the subjectivity from an issue – either an agreement was met or not.

Remember that you do not have to come up with a solution yourself. Problem solving is about finding solution options, from talking to others and reviewing relevant documentation, and establishing the best solution from the options available.

The way you handle problems and complaints will have a big impact on the outcome. If you can stay calm, avoid becoming defensive and focus on finding the best solution to the problem, you will get a much better response than if you argue, speak aggressively or behave unprofessionally yourself.

"If you find dealing with customer problems difficult or you have a tendency to over-promise, you might find an Assertive Behaviour workshop useful. Assertiveness is not about being 'bossy' but is about finding a balance between your needs and the needs of the people you are working with, and expressing this clearly and confidently."

Keep reviewing the service

Hopefully problems will only form a very small part of your relationship with your customers but, do not wait for feedback – or complaints – take the initiative and keep checking if customers are getting the service they need. Keep reviewing, keep evaluating and keep making use of the information collected to develop and improve the service.

Exceeding customer expectations

We started this section with 'meet expectations' – an essential of good service delivery. However, if we can find ways of sometimes exceeding expectations we can give our customers an even better experience, whilst demonstrating our commitment to providing a great service.

Here are some wide-ranging examples of great customer service in a learning and development context:

- staying late to help someone finish a project in time for their deadline
- preparing a pack of material and a promise of a one-to-one coaching session for someone who was unable to attend a training event
- following up an enquiry from a learner, even though it is officially outside your remit
- adapting training events to meet learners needs – on the day – if the intended content is not the most suitable
- basing your advice about learning purely on what is best for the learner – even if that means promoting someone else's service rather than your own
- providing silly prizes within a training course to make it a bit more fun – especially if it is a tough subject or session
- being courageous in telling someone when you think that what they are doing is not in their best interests or in the interests of their team
- recognising when learners or managers are under pressure and doing something, beyond your remit, to help without being asked
- sending out a quick and timely summary of agreements made in a meeting or of some notes you made which would be helpful to others
- providing electronic copies of handouts and important flip-chart pages immediately after the event
- providing something a little bit special with the refreshments during a training session – it is amazing how much goodwill can be generated by providing a cake for afternoon break!

> "Arriving at a training event on a cold winter morning, we were greeted with bacon sandwiches – great customer service! Except for the vegetarians who they had forgotten about – not so great customer service!"

REFLECTIVE ACTIVITY

What great service have you received – in any aspect of life?

Can you transfer any of these ideas to your own service delivery?

MANAGING YOUR OWN DEVELOPMENT

> "Learning is ongoing – you can learn from every interaction – it is one of the true joys in life and is free."
>
> Terry Hart, HR Director

CONTINUING PROFESSIONAL DEVELOPMENT

Continuing professional development (CPD) is the action we take to maintain, update and grow the knowledge and skills required for our professional role. As the name suggests, it is an ongoing commitment, lasting for as long as we remain within our profession.

As L&D professionals, our knowledge is our product. If we are not knowledgeable in our subject areas or we do not know how to support and facilitate learning, then how can we help others or contribute to our organisations? CPD is an essential investment in our career and doubly important to us if we are to role model the commitment to learning and development we expect from others. Undertaking CPD and keeping an appropriate record of it is a requirement of membership of the CIPD and of most other professional bodies.

There are many reasons why we are motivated to learn new things. The fact that we are in this profession suggests that we are already enthusiastic learners. CPD requires us to focus a part of our learning specifically on areas that are related to our profession – but L&D is a very wide field, and there are very few things we can learn that do not contribute in some way to our abilities to help other people with their learning.

REFLECTIVE ACTIVITY

What motivates you to learn?

What was the last learning activity you undertook?

How did this contribute to your abilities as an L&D practitioner?

The benefits of developing ourselves are boundless – not just for us but also for our learners, the organisations we work in or with, and the L&D team or function we are a part of. Some of the potential benefits are shown in Table 1.1 below.

Undertaking continuing professional development is not just about setting personal development objectives and fulfilling these, it is also about reflecting on our learning and applying it to our working life. We should also record our learning activities and reflections to capture our progression as learners and also to demonstrate our commitment to CPD to other parties.

The concept of CPD reflects both the Training cycle and the Learning cycle. It follows the Training cycle in that we need to identify our learning needs, find

Ref to ELP 1– Training cycle

Table 1.1 Potential benefits of CPD

Benefits for you:	Benefits for your learners:
• enhanced reputation and job satisfaction • increased confidence and self esteem • improved career prospects and employability • improved professional status • development is a transferable skill.	• better quality training • up-to-date advice and information • training that employs new approaches and methods • training that better meets needs • greater confidence in the training provided for your organisation.
Benefits to your L&D function:	Benefits to the organisation:
• enhanced reputation • more likely to be seen as credible and reliable and to become a trusted partner in the business • more influence with key stakeholders • a more exciting learning environment and opportunities to learn from each other.	• staff who can do the job • more likely to achieve evolving organisational goals • managers can be confident that staff skill levels are compliant and up-to-date with requirements • improved employee engagement • enhanced external reputation.

learning to meet these needs, access the learning and then evaluate how well our learning needs have been met – and then start again with the next learning need.

Ref to ELP 2–
Experiential
learning cycle

CPD also follows the Learning Cycle in that it requires us to reflect on our experiences, find new ideas and ways of doing things, and experiment with our new ideas – and then start again reflecting on our new experience.

Let's have a closer look at some key features of CPD:

1 CPD includes an element of planning and an element of recording and reflecting. You may already have a 'development plan' at work or you may want to devise your own.

2 Planning your CPD is important to ensure that you take a strategic approach to your professional development and include everything needed to meet your professional requirements. You might link your development plan to a performance review cycle at work, or it might be something you do on an annual, or more frequent, basis.

3 You will need to set SMART objectives for your development so that you can measure your progress towards, and eventual achievement of, your objectives.

4 You should review your progress towards objectives regularly and ensure you stay 'on track' – particularly for learning objectives that are compliance or qualification related.

5 As well as planning your CPD you should also record and reflect on your CPD and consider how you will make use of your learning. If you can get into the habit of recording your reflections as you go along it will be easier and more useful to you.

SMART

Specific – be clear about what you want to achieve; what is the actual result or outcome that you want?

Measurable – how will you know that you have achieved? What will you see, hear and feel that will tell you that you have achieved?

Achievable – the objectives in your plan should be realistic and achievable steps to take you closer to your overall ambitions.

Relevant – your objectives should be steps to larger career and personal aspirations, not just random pieces of learning.

Time-bound – each outcome should have an achievable end-date – ideally within the timescale of your CPD planning period.

---

6 The way you record your CPD reflections is up to you – although some suggested formats are provided below and more are available on the CIPD website.

7 There are likely to be learning activities and learning experiences that you have not planned but which are relevant to your overall development and that you want to include in your CPD record. That is fine – it is your record to use as is most useful to you.

8 You may need to make your CPD record available to other parties occasionally – but it is usually acceptable to provide a reduced or summary version if you are uncomfortable about revealing the full document.

In our experience, different people like different formats of CPD plans and Records and there is no 'one size fits all'. Most seem to opt for a table style of document (as in the examples below) although CIPD has also produced some questionnaire style templates which some also find useful.

The table style documents usually landscape and have column headings such as those in tables 1.2–1.5.

Table 1.2 CPD plan format – Example 1

What I want to achieve	How I will achieve it	Info/resources required	Review date	Outcome

Table 1.3 CPD plan format – Example 2

Objective	Action required	Outcome

Table 1.4 **CPD reflective record format – Example 1**

Key dates	What I did	Why	What I learned	How I'll use it

Table 1.5 **CPD reflective record format – Example 2**

Date	Event/experience/activity	Reflections on learning & how I will use it

There are several examples of completed CPD plans and records on the CIPD website and lots of relevant materials to support you in the CPD process.

Figure 1.5 is an example from an L&D practitioner (and CIPD student) CPD record. Here the first column is used to link activities to the learner's Personal Development Plan (PDP).

Figure 1.5 Extract from a CPD record for an L&D practitioner

PDP ref	Experience/Activity	Reflections on learning and how I will use it
4	Attended second 'Certificate in Learning & Development Practice' workshop	Got an overview of the full L&D role and realised it is wider than I had thought. Made me aware of some of the areas I still have to learn. I recognised that I need further development in undertaking a learning needs analysis and designing training. Feel more confident about delivery and evaluation. I also need to think more about our organisational objectives – and would like to develop my coaching skills further. We did some self-assessments and I scored highly in communication skills, and supporting other people's learning. This makes me feel more confident about my abilities. I realised that I do contribute to the organisation in lots of ways – but don't always make these explicit – or even recognise it myself sometimes.
	Team meeting (May 5th)	We began the process of setting team objectives for next year. We did a review of what we need to do more of, what we need to change, and what we need to stop doing. I ran a session on our organisational goals and how these cascaded down into what our team has to achieve. Everyone said this was really useful and helped them see how they fit in to the big picture. Preparing for this session has made me so much more aware of my role and my contribution to the organisation – and I can use it towards my qualification.
	Read '59 Seconds' by Richard Wiseman	Really enjoyed this – and loads of learning in it. Particularly liked the ideas about how to be persuasive – and how to be more creative (will try out the group dynamics idea and the upside down arrow picture) and the general philosophy that so much can be achieved in such a short time or in small ways.
3	Completed A1 portfolio & had professional discussion	The final 'piece' of my assessment was a professional discussion with my assessor, which went well. There are just a couple of 'loose ends' to tie up and then I will have finished. I should have completed this sooner – I can assess now without having things countersigned all the time and be more decisive when I give J or L feedback on their work. I will be able to use my learning from the A1 in other types of assessment too. I now have a clearer idea of different assessment methods and how to plan for and implement them. I also feel more confident about how I give feedback having been observed doing this and discussed my approach with . . . .

CHOOSING SELF-DEVELOPMENT ACTIVITIES

There will be a number of practical factors impacting on your choice of development activity, including:

- costs
- availability
- time scales.

Beyond these factors it is good to get a balance of learning across:

Maintenance and development needs

What you need to keep refreshed and up-to-date against what will be new areas of learning for you.

Specialist subjects and training skills/knowledge

If you train in a particular subject area you will need to maintain your technical abilities and knowledge, as well as developing your skills and knowledge as a trainer.

Performance requirements and personal aspirations

As well as the learning you have to undertake for your job and professional requirements, you may also have personal aspirations or long terms plan you want to prepare for.

Different learning methods

Ref to ELP 3 – Learning styles

Even if you have a preferred learning style it is important to involve yourself in a range of different approaches. Challenge your preferences sometimes – maybe opting for a highly participative learning activity, even though you would normally choose to learn through researching or reading – and develop your other styles in doing so.

> "The way we communicate has changed significantly over the years and whether you have a fear of, or fascination with, social networks, they should be embraced as they are shaping the way we manage our personal development and the impact this has on our personal reputation management."
>
> Karen Waite, Director, Leap Like a Salmon Ltd

Left brain and right brain

Ref to ELP 6 – Left brain, right brain

Ref to ELP 5 – Multiple intelligences

If work-related development needs are very logic-based and left-brained you could balance this by undertaking some more right-brained 'creative and artistic' development activities.

Established content and leading edge

Whilst there is a vast amount of current and established learning content essential to our professional development, being aware of some leading-edge developments can greatly enhance career prospects. New ideas relating to learning are emerging from all kinds of fields including neuroscience (how the brain works), psychology (how people behave) and technology (developments in mobile technology, new models of learning communities and ongoing developments in virtual learning environments).

Serious and fun

Sometimes it does us good to do some light-hearted development that may appear to have little professional connection but could just 'light a spark' of a future learning direction or at least be a good stress reliever. Who knows what attending a 'juggling skills workshop' could lead to – you *will not know* unless you try!

As an L&D practitioner you will be aware of the many types of learning activity available and there are further descriptions and discussions of these in later chapters of this book (particularly Chapter 4: Undertaking a Learning Needs Analysis and Chapter 5: Designing Learning and Development Activities).

Some methods to consider for your development may include:

- attending a training event
- attending a conference or exhibition
- reading books, articles or blogs
- job shadowing
- academic learning
- IT enabled learning
- reflecting on work events
- being coached
- having a mentor
- taking part in a project
- action learning sets
- attending networking events.

Before undertaking any of these activities, ask yourself 'what is my objective for doing this, what do I want to learn?' Having completed the activity, ask yourself 'What did I learn and how will I use it?'

Finally, remember that undertaking your CPD is itself a development activity. Writing down your goals and planning how you will address them will give you a much greater chance of achieving them. Recording and reflecting on your development activities will consolidate and enhance the learning you get from them. Your CPD Record is a symbol of your commitment to your own learning and something you can be very proud of.

WHAT NEXT

DEVELOPING YOURSELF

Below are some activities to help further your learning from this chapter:

1 Have a look at the HR Profession Map at www.cipd.co.uk and particularly at the interactive self-assessment tool My HR Map.

2 Review your function's approach to service delivery. Consider:
   – who are all the customers you deal with?
   – what those customers expect of you?
   – how close you come to meeting their expectations?
   – what else you could do?

3 Arrange meetings with your key customers and use those meetings to discuss and agree the levels of service that you will both provide.

4 Re-visit your CPD documents or set some up if you do not currently have any. Remember that there is a range of support materials, guidance and further information about CPD on the CIPD website.
   – Do you have a comprehensive professional development plan?
   – Are you recording and reflecting on your development?
   – Do you have personal goals and aspirations?
   – What do you do each day, week or month towards your goals?

5 Have a look at other professional organisations and institutes – what CPD methods do they use?

6 Consider the case study below – what do you think about Jackie's experiences? Do you agree with her learning points?

CASE STUDY 1.1

DEVELOPMENT AS AN L&D PRACTITIONER

Prior to taking on the role of Employee Development Officer for an international organisation which owns a number of ports across the world, I had been working in a Further Education college. The culture change was fascinating. In my new role, my first training role with such a large private sector organisation, I was part of a small team, delivering development programmes for all managers and employees (approx 2,500 people) across one site.

My new role was primarily to deliver an off-the-shelf programme from an American organisation. I was trained to deliver the materials provided by the American company – which involved learning how to deliver workshops via a script supported by exercises, workbooks and videos. This was a completely different approach to what I had been used to before.

On delivering the programmes, I found that the groups I worked with were quite resistant to the approach being taken – it could be described as a 'sheep-dip approach', ie everyone getting the same training whether they needed it or not. As this feedback continued, we started to be more flexible with the materials and, after a change in senior management, eventually abandoned the programme and adopted a more tailored approach. This included:

- a complete needs analysis for one of the specialist departments within the organisation
- design and delivery of training for a specific group of team leaders
- design and delivery of a competence-based programme for a group of future team leaders within the operational areas of the business.

Training staff worked alongside operational staff to both design and deliver the programmes. Looking back on the experience, I can see that the first 'sheep-dip' programme did have some results in terms of skills development and encouraging cross-organisational working. The original objective had been behavioural change from a top-down management style to a more collaborative and consultative style – but this was only achieved in small areas and, with hindsight, was not necessarily appropriate for the working environment.

Moving to a more tailored approach meant that each area of the business felt involved in identifying and meeting their learning needs and therefore the individual learners and their managers were more engaged with the process and it was embedded in day-to-day working. Learning took place on-and off-job and was felt to be more relevant and appropriate.

The key learning for me was:

- Learning and development activity is not just limited to delivering training.
- If individual learners are not aware of why they are attending training courses, they are unlikely to engage fully. This makes the trainers' lives more difficult and the learners are less likely to implement any learning back in the workplace.
- Off-the-shelf training packages can work and when time is of the essence can be very useful, however it is unrealistic to expect to change the culture of an organisation by delivering workshops that are perceived as irrelevant by the learners!
- As an L&D professional working within an organisation it is vital to understand the business of the organisation, to get to know key people, to spend time in operational areas in order to understand the culture of the organisation and to work alongside technical and operational experts to deliver programmes of learning that are relevant and appropriate.
- L&D professionals should not be 'precious' about what they do. It is perfectly possible for operational staff to make excellent trainers and to deliver on-the-ground HR services to their teams. The role of the L&D team should be to support, guide and advise; to offer specialist services when they are required and to develop the skills of those people who are 'on the ground'.

Jackie Clifford, Clarity Learning & Development

SUMMARY

This chapter has explored:

Why developing yourself as an L&D professional is essential

- Self-development is an aspect of 'being a professional'.
- Knowledge is our product; we need to be up-to-date with our subject areas and our knowledge of how to help other people learn so that we can contribute to our organisations.

- The commitment to self-development is a prerequisite for membership of our professional institute.

Different professional specifications of L&D roles

- L&D roles are specified in the CIPD HR Professional Map.
- L&D roles are captured in the CIPD L&D qualifications.
- L&D roles are also captured in the Learning and Development National Occupational Standards.

Customers and their requirements

- It is important to know who our customers are and what they need from our service.
- Customers of the L&D service are often 'internal customers'.
- We should consider how we communicate with customers and how we can best meet their needs.
- We should only agree what we can realistically deliver, and then should deliver what we have agreed.
- It is important to keep reviewing service delivery and to check that we are meeting customer requirements.
- Sometimes, at least, we should exceed our customers' expectations.

Continuing professional development

- CPD is the action we take to maintain, update and grow the knowledge and skills required for our professional role.
- CPD is about planning our development, reflecting on our learning and recording it.
- Our CPD records should detail the learning we have undertaken, what we have learned and how we will use our learning.

Factors which affect the selection of activities for our own development

- Choosing development activities depends on some practical factors, like cost, time and availability, but also on what we specifically want from our learning.
- We need to maintain our specialist subject knowledge, our training skills and our understanding of the business.
- We should consider maintenance and development needs, performance requirements and personal aspirations, left and right brain activities, different learning methods and some new learning content.

EXPLORE FURTHER

BOOKS:

Covey, S.R. (1994) *The seven habits of highly effective people: Powerful lessons in personal change.* London: Simon & Schuster.

Goleman, D. (1996) *Emotional intelligence: Why it can matter more than IQ.* London: Bloomsbury Publishing PLC.

Dryden, W. and Constantinou, D. (2004) *Assertiveness step by step (overcoming problems).* London: Sheldon Press.

WEBSITES:

On-line guidance relating to the CIPD hr map (including professional areas of learning and talent development, service delivery and access to my hr map):

www.cipd.co.uk/hr-profession-map

On-line guidance relating to national occupational standards for learning & development:

www.lluk.org/national-occupational-standards.htm (select learning & development (2010) standards)

On-line information and national standards for customer service:

www.instituteofcustomerservice.com

On-line guidance and materials relating to cpd:

www.cipd.co.uk/cpd

On-line communities and social media channels:

www.cipd.co.uk/communities

www.cipd.co.uk/podcasts

www.cipd.co.uk/news/blogs

www.linkedin.com/cipdmember

www.twitter.com/CIPD

www.facebook.com/CIPDUK

CHAPTER 2

Understanding Organisations and the Role of Learning and Development

INTRODUCTION

The chapter begins with a short consideration of why understanding the organisation is a critical aspect of any L&D practitioner's role. It goes on to look at organisations from a number of different angles and considers different factors that shape and characterise them. We also explore some popular ways of analysing organisations and some different ways of categorising and describing them – including type, structure and culture. The chapter then moves on to look in general terms at the role of HR, before focussing specifically on the L&D function and its role in supporting organisations to fulfil their goals and purpose.

LEARNING OUTCOMES

When you have read this chapter, you should be able to:

- explain the importance of understanding organisational context
- describe and explain vision, mission, values and strategy statements
- use at least two methods for analysing factors which impact on organisations
- discuss key factors which characterise organisations
- describe different HR functions and how they support organisations
- explain how the L&D function contributes to the achievement of organisational plans and goals.

WHY ORGANISATIONAL CONTEXT IS IMPORTANT

For some learning professionals, the over-riding focus of their work is the needs of individual learners. This may be the case for lecturers and tutors, who operate within the further education system, for example. However, for L&D professionals who are employed or contracted by an organisation for the purpose of developing staff within that organisation, there is a double focus – the needs of the individual learner and the needs of the organisation. Both are equally important and must be balanced.

Learning initiatives based wholly on the needs of individuals may overlook the business priorities, pressures and constraints of the overall organisation. So however successful they may appear in terms of learner satisfaction, they may well fail in the key purpose of the learning and development function – 'to ensure that people at all levels of the organisation possess and develop the skills, knowledge and experiences to **fulfil the short- and long-term ambitions of the organisation** and that they are motivated to learn, grow and perform'.

Equally, an initiative based wholly on the organisations purpose, that does not consider the wider needs and preferences of the learners involved, and does not '**motivate them to learn, grow and perform**', is also likely to be ineffective, and to fail in the key purpose of the learning and development function.

If L&D is to be effective it is essential that, whatever mix of internal and external provision it includes, it does not operate in isolation from 'the business' but works in partnership with it, aligning L&D activities to organisational goals and strategy.

> "The biggest change anticipated over the next five years is a closer integration of learning and development activity with business strategy (65 per cent)."
>
> The CIPD Learning & Development Survey (2009)

WHAT DOES THIS MEAN FOR THE L&D PROFESSIONAL?

To fully serve the organisation L&D professionals must first understand it.

This need to understand the organisation requires us to operate outside the confines of the L&D department or team and involve ourselves in the wider context of the whole organisation.

At some levels, this is about being able to influence organisational strategy, whilst at other levels it is about being aware of strategic objectives and ensuring these are the drivers of learning activity.

It requires us, as L&D practitioners, to align individual and team learning needs with overall organisational requirements, work alongside managers to identify best learning solutions and provide learning and development activities which balance the needs of stakeholder groups and help drive the organisation forwards.

In the rest of this chapter we will explore some practical ways for developing a greater understanding of organisations, how they work and what makes each one unique.

> "Both public and private sector organisations are increasingly focused on how expenditure will improve the business, reduce costs or increase revenues. Learning and development specialists need to understand the drivers of business, speak the language of business, and hold their own at the decision-making table more than ever before."
>
> Andrew Choi, Executive Director, Mid Yorkshire Chamber of Commerce

UNDERSTANDING ORGANISATIONS – IN PRACTICE

THE ORGANISATION AS A SYSTEM

One way to understand organisations is to view them as simple systems, with *inputs*, *transformation processes* and *outputs*.

Inputs might be raw materials, money, labour, knowledge, information.

Processes might be manufacturing, teaching, cooking, baking, healing, caring, constructing.

Outputs could be particular goods or services, waste products, information, profits, wages, or even learned skills and behaviours.

For example, the main elements of a food processing factory might be those shown in Table 2.1.

Table 2.1 **Inputs → processes → outputs: food processing factory**

Inputs	Processes	Outputs
	Measuring	
Raw Ingredients	Mixing	Chilled Ready Meals
Labour	Cooking	Wages
Premises	Refrigeration	Profit
Energy	Packing	Waste Products

Whilst a similar analysis for a small training consultancy company might be as shown in Table 2.2.

Table 2.2 **Inputs → processes → outputs: training consultancy company**

Inputs	Processes	Outputs
	Communicating	
Knowledge	Writing	Enhanced Capabilities
Labour	Teaching	Qualifications
Learning Materials	Coaching	Learning Resources
Money	Assessing	Wages/Profits
	Advising	
	Selling	

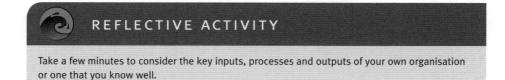

REFLECTIVE ACTIVITY

Take a few minutes to consider the key inputs, processes and outputs of your own organisation or one that you know well.

We can take this analysis a stage further by looking at what happens around the immediate environment of the organisational system. For example, who are the organisation's suppliers, key partners (eg advisers, manufacturing, service or delivery partners) and perhaps most importantly of all, the organisation's customers?

Figure 2.1 The immediate environment

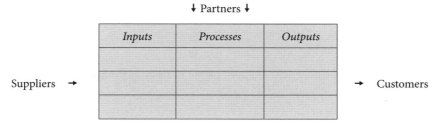

VISION, MISSION AND VALUE STATEMENTS

As organisations, and the contexts in which they operate, have become more complex and competitive, there has been an increased emphasis on clarifying organisational purpose, in the form of Vision, Mission and Value Statements. This clarification has several purposes including:

- demonstrating organisational transparency and openness – 'who we are, what we do, what we stand for'

- creating the 'start point' for the focus and drive of the organisation

- positioning the organisation in 'the market' and clarifying its 'uniqueness' amongst the competition

- enabling others to quickly understand the organisation and gauge how far it aligns with their own values

- attracting and engaging staff who are likely to be aligned with the organisation's values

- attracting and engaging customers and building brand loyalty.

Whilst the term 'values' seems to have a common and standardised meaning within corporate statements, 'vision' and 'mission', along with other terms such as 'goals', 'purpose' and sometimes 'strategy', are often used interchangeably or in different ways by different organisations. The term 'goals' can be used generally to cover any combination of these areas, whilst 'vision statement', 'mission statement' and 'value' statement can be defined as follows.

Vision statement

The vision statement of an organisation is a future based ideal of what the organisation intends to become. It is intended to be motivational by painting a picture of a desired state for people to work towards.

> "An aspirational description of what an organisation would like to achieve or accomplish in the mid-term or long-term future. It is intended to serve as a clear guide for choosing current and future courses of action."
>
> BusinessDictionary.com

For example:

Our vision – The Energy Saving Trust

Our vision for the future is that every home is a low carbon home and everybody leads a low carbon lifestyle.

Vision – Toyota Trucks USA Division

To become the most successful and respected lift truck company in the US.

Mission statement

The word 'mission' typically means purpose, vocation or intended task and so a mission statement is a formal written statement of an organisations key purpose.

> "An official statement of the aims and objectives of a business or other organisation."
>
> *Collins Concise Dictionary*

> "A written declaration of a firm's core purpose and focus which normally remains unchanged whereas business strategy and practices may frequently be altered to adapt to changing circumstances."
>
> BusinessDictionary.com

This is best illustrated by exploring some examples:

Mission statement – Marks and Spencer

We sell clothing, food and homeware and we work hard to provide our customers with the highest quality products, service and shopping environments.

Mission statement – Harley-Davidson

We sell dreams through the experience of motorcycling – by providing to motorcyclists and to the general public an expanding line of motorcycles, branded products and service in selected market segments.

Our goal – J Sainsbury PLC

At Sainsbury's we will deliver an ever-improving quality shopping experience for our customers with great products at fair prices. We aim to exceed customer expectations for healthy, safe, fresh and tasty food, making their lives easier everyday.

Value statements

Value statements are a declaration of the main life, business or behavioural principles which reflect the 'character' of the organisation and which underpin and guide the way it undertakes its activities.

Here are two examples:

Our values – J Sainsbury PLC

Five principles at the core of our business:

- The best for food and health
- Sourcing with integrity
- Respect for our Environment
- Making a positive difference to our community
- A great place to work.

Our values – Orange

Friendly
We take the time to listen. We treat everyone as individuals.
We enjoy working and succeeding together.

Honest
We are open. We say what we do and we do what we say.
We are happy to share

Straightforward
We are direct and easy to understand. We keep things simple.
We focus only on what's important.

Refreshing
We are brave. We dare to do things differently, to find a better way.
We give colour to all that we do.

Dynamic

We are passionate, confident and focused on the future.

We push the boundaries. We make a difference to people's lives.

REFLECTIVE ACTIVITY

Look at the vision, mission and value statements of an organisation you know well. To what extent do those statements show in the actual work of the organisation?

How do the L&D functions of the organisation reflect and 'live' the vision, mission and values?

BUSINESS STRATEGY AND OBJECTIVES

Strategy is:

> "A particular long term plan for success."
>
> *Collins Concise Dictionary*

In order to achieve their vision and mission, organisations usually need to take specific action in a specific direction. Business strategy is about determining the high level detail of the direction and action to be taken. Whilst some organisations may declare an overarching permanent strategy (eg to grow the business), strategy is more usually time-bound, and determined in relation to particular circumstances.

> The term 'strategy', originally a military term, is derived from the ancient Greek *strategos* and *strategia* meaning 'generalship' or the command of an army.

> H. Igor Ansoff is generally credited with bringing the term into the business arena in his book *Corporate strategy* (1965).

Organisational strategy can involve a whole range of projected organisational activity, for example:

- expanding or reducing the size of the organisation
- developing new products and services
- discontinuing certain products and services
- re-focusing of services or specialisation
- consolidation of existing products, services or practices
- particular development of existing products or services
- developing or moving into new markets or client groups
- organisation re-structuring
- addressing specific current issues or failures

- acquisitions, mergers and partnerships
- changed supply chain arrangements
- transformation of image or market position
- changed ethical, environmental or customer relations approaches
- changed financial or funding approaches.

When broad strategic aims or goals have been determined, these can be broken down into more specific objectives, and ultimately more detailed business plans.

The statement from Tesco plc below is one example of how organisational strategy has been broken down into more specific objectives.

OUR STRATEGY – TESCO PLC (2010)

Tesco has a well-established and consistent strategy for growth, which has allowed us to strengthen our core UK business and drive expansion into new markets.

The strategy to diversify the business was laid down in 1997 and has been the foundation of Tesco's success in recent years.

The objectives of the strategy are:

- to be a successful international retailer
- to grow the core UK business
- to be as strong in non-food as in food
- to develop retailing services such as Tesco Personal Finance, Telecoms and Tesco.com
- to put community at the heart of what we do.

For fuller details see www.tescoplc.com/plc/about us/strategy.

When the overall aim and purpose of the organisation are clear (vision and mission), and there are key strategic aims to be achieved, the role of the HR and L&D function is to create and implement the policies and practices that will enable the achievement of the business within the stated values.

USING ANALYSIS MODELS

Exactly what a particular organisation determines as its strategy will depend on a number of factors, both internal and external to the organisation. Internal factors might include: the organisation's stage of life-cycle – a new organisation is likely to require different strategies to a more established one, organisational size, structure, culture and management style, financial resources and projections or stability of funding sources, and current business results, successes and failures. External factors might include, for example: competitor activity, sector activity, political context, demographic and social trends and national and legal requirements.

There are a number of analysis models to help organisations identify key factors and determine best strategies. These include SWOT Analysis, PEST or PESTLE

Analysis, Michael Porter's 'Five Forces Model, Igor Ansoff's 'Product-Market Matrix' and Boston Consulting Group's 'Boston Matrix'. We will consider the first two of these below.

SWOT analysis

SWOT stands for: Strengths, Weaknesses, Opportunities and Threats.

Strengths and weaknesses are generally factors that are existing and **internal** to the organisation. Strengths are the things that an organisation is good at and which help it to achieve its goals. Weaknesses are the things that are less good and may get in the way of the organisation's success.

Opportunities and threats are generally factors that are **external** to the organisation and may not yet have come about. These are factors which could still help or hinder organisational success and need to be considered as the subject of specific future action. Opportunities are those things that an organisation could take advantage of to help towards achievement. Threats are factors which may require action to avoid them, or to prepare for them, in order to limit any adverse impact on the business.

A SWOT analysis can be applied to a department or business function, such as the Learning & Development function, as well as to the whole organisation.

The following is an example of a SWOT carried out by a family-owned independent department store in a regional town centre:

Strengths	Weaknesses
Good local reputation	Lack of a 'budget' range
Loyal customers	No on-line presence for customer orders
Long serving/well trained staff	Poor range of menswear
Only local supplier of key fashion brands	Seen by non-customers as a store for 'older' women
Excellent relationships with suppliers	
Buyers and managers understand the customer base	Buyers not skilled at negotiating discounts with suppliers
Recently refurbished ground floor	
Opportunities	**Threats**
Pedestrianisation and regeneration of town centre	Competition from out of town developments
New coffee shops opening in town	Staff leaving to work at new out of town store
Local competitor closing down	Disruption caused by pedestrianisation of town centre
Well known fashion brands looking for in-store concessions	Supermarkets selling budget schoolwear

PEST analysis

PEST provides another simple framework for highlighting factors which might impact on the organisation and so help identify appropriate strategic directions.

PEST stands for Political, Economic, Social and Technological. Occasionally the model is written as PESTLE where L = Legal and E = Environmental, however these areas are often already covered in political, economic and social considerations.

Political factors to consider might include:

Current and predicted legislation
European legislation
Regulatory bodies
Pressure groups
Funding policies
Election activity/potential changes of national or local government

Economic factors might include:

The economy – international, national and local
Global trends
Inflation
Predicted trends
Labour supply
Wage rates

Social factors might include:

Demographics
Labour supply/skills shortages
Lifestyle trends and fashions
Ethical issues
Consumer trends
Major events
Religious and cultural influences

Technological factors might include:

Information and communications systems
Service delivery developments
Competitor IT advantages
Product life-cycle or longevity
Automisation of labour processes
Staff capability and skills shortages
Buying and lifestyle behaviour

The PEST analysis (simplified version) for a regional training company specialising in the public sector might include:

Political	Economic
Introduction of the Common Assessment Framework (CAF)	Budget restrictions within client organisations and the need to achieve best value
Personalisation of Care Budgets	Increased use of tendering for the most 'economically viable' solution
Requests for training to support compliance issues	Increased competition from training companies offering discounted deals
Increased focus on partnership working	
Number of authorities looking for sole or preferred providers	
Social	Technological
Changing work patterns that challenge the practicality of the 'one-day' training course	Opportunity to provide on-line and blended learning
Increased requests to provide alternatives such as translation, large print, alterations to meet cultural needs etc	Increased acceptance of conference calling (Skype etc), on-line collection of data (surveys etc)
Increased expectation that training links directly to CPD	Increased marketing via own website and through social/business networking (LinkedIn, Facebook, Twitter, etc)

Some commentators feel it is more useful to undertake a PEST analysis before a SWOT analysis as the PEST analysis will bring out factors which can then be considered as potential threats or opportunities.

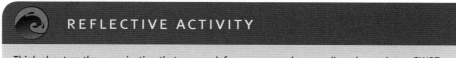

REFLECTIVE ACTIVITY

Think about an the organisation that you work for, or one you know well, and complete a SWOT and a PEST analysis. What factors are likely to have the biggest impact on the organisation? What will need to be tackled by L&D?

STAKEHOLDERS

An organisational analysis would not be complete without a consideration of the organisation's stakeholders.

Stakeholders, as the name indicates, are people who have some kind of interest in the organisation or business and how it is run. Sources disagree as to whether the name derives from the act of placing a stake in a particular area of land, particularly during the times of the gold-rush or from the act of being the third party holder of a betting stake until the outcome of the bet was known.

Stakeholders might, for example, be owners, directors, managers, staff, customers, suppliers, donors, neighbours, local community. Their interests could be financial or about the availability and quality of goods and services or about the way in which the organisation conducts its business, for example its environmental approach.

There are a number of useful models and stakeholder mapping grids available to help us analyse stakeholders and their interest in an organisation. One of the most widely used is the Stakeholder Interest-Influence Grid, which encourages us to consider the strength of a particular stakeholder's interest as well as the amount of influence the stakeholder can exert on the organisation (Figure 2.2).

In plotting stakeholders against the two axes, they are loosely divided into four boxes or groups and the model gives an indication of how to interact with stakeholders in each of the 4 groups (Figure 2.3).

Figure 2.2 Stakeholder Interest-Influence Grid – 1 (Letters represent particular stakeholders)

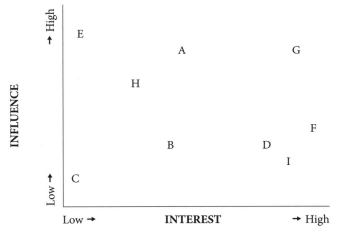

Figure 2.3 Stakeholder interest-influence Grid – 2

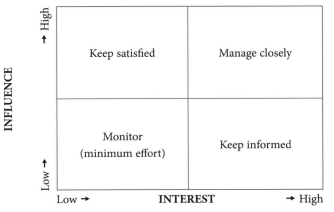

At a high level, an organisation might use stakeholder analysis to help it communicate or interact with its stakeholders in different ways.

Organisations will also consider their different stakeholder groups when making strategic decisions – either proactively by consulting with them or reactively by considering the impact certain decisions will have on them.

DIFFERENT TYPES OF ORGANISATION

It is difficult to find one single way of classifying organisations which encompasses everything, as each organisation has its own diverse nature and set of dimensions. However there are several ways in which organisations can be, and are, classified.

Legal Status – in legal terms, organisations might be categorised as sole-traders, partnerships, co-operatives, limited companies or public limited companies (for more detailed information see www.companieshouse.gov.uk)

Financial factors – organisations can be defined by how they are funded and how they use their funds. For example, whether they sit within the public (government funded) or private sector? Whether they seek to make a profit or simply cover their operational costs (not-for-profit organisations)? Whether profits raised are for shareholders or for all workers (co-operatives) or for social purposes (social enterprises)? Whether workers are paid or not (voluntary organisations)?

Organisation size – organisations which employ less than 10 people are often referred to as 'micro', with those which employ 10–49 employees as 'small', 50–249 employees as 'medium' and over 249 as 'large'. The term 'small–medium enterprise' therefore relates to an organisation which employs between 10 and 249 employees.

Geographical reach – larger organisations with bases in other countries may be referred to as multi-nationals or global organisations, depending on their spread. However, as smaller and virtual organisations extend their reach of operations across the globe these titles have become more blurred.

Of course, organisations can also be classified by the sector in which they sit, for example, construction or health and social care, and by the nature of their business, such as manufacturer, retailer, service provider, regulator, etc.

All of these factors will have an influence on the culture of an organisation and the ways in which it carries out its activities and this is discussed further in the sections below.

Functions, structure and culture

The functions within an organisation will depend on the organisation type and purpose; for example we would expect a commercial business to have a sales and marketing function but would be less likely to find this in a local authority service organisation, such as a residential care provider, although as the basis of operation between public and private organisations blurs this may not always be the case.

Typical functions we might find within organisations include:

Finance or Accounts – responsible for managing the financial aspects of an organisation; invoicing; managing cash-flow; monitoring business expenditure; preparing financial reports.

Purchasing or Procurement – ensuring the availability of necessary supplies and resources required for the organisation to fulfil its purpose. Negotiating and managing best value.

Research and Development – responsible for researching new developments in the market; designing and developing new products and services and improving current ones; ensuring the currency and sustainability of the business' products and services.

Production or Operations – managing and ensuring the effective manufacture of an organisation's products or delivery of services.

Sales and Marketing – responsible for finding, developing and sustaining markets for the organisations products and services and selling, directly or indirectly, to the organisations customers.

Distribution – responsible for ensuring products reach customers in line with sales contracts, managing distribution channels and operations.

Customer Services – responsible for customer liaison and dealing with customers requests, enquiries and complaints. Maintaining customer satisfaction, and developing customers' relationship with the organisation.

Human Resources and Learning and Development – with specialist responsibility for 'people issues' such as recruitment, payroll and training (see below).

Admin (Back Office) and IT – managing, processing and recording organisational information and activity and providing administrative support to other functions.

Presenting these functions separately like this suggests that they naturally exist as discrete departments within organisations. In many cases they do exist like this allowing clear role definitions, efficient use of resources and the build-up of expertise and specialism. However it is not always the case and depends substantially on the size, type and culture of the organisation in question.

Smaller organisations are unlikely to have the resources to operate highly delineated organisational structures and are more likely to have cross-over between functions and roles. Someone who is responsible for product sales, for example, may also be responsible for the distribution of the goods they sell and the related ongoing customer service. Equally someone in a small organisation may be responsible for selling, contracting for and providing a particular service.

Size though is not the only factor here and some larger organisations may tend towards more informal structures and more fluid overlap between different functions. There are good business reasons why organisations may be structured in other ways than a simple functional basis. For example it might make better business sense to arrange and sub-divide organisations in terms of service or product ranges, geographical location, or even market segment (for example a publishing company may divide itself in terms of its 'schools market' and its 'general public market'), with each sub-division having its own localised versions of the different organisational functions.

Structural arrangement of an organisation links strongly to organisational culture – the way the organisation is led, the level of formality within the organisation, the amount of autonomy enjoyed by workers and the way people within the organisation generally interact.

Charles Handy in *Understanding organisations* (1985), developing Roger Harrison's work, discusses four types of organisational culture and related structure (Figure 2.4)

Figure 2.4 Organisational culture and structure

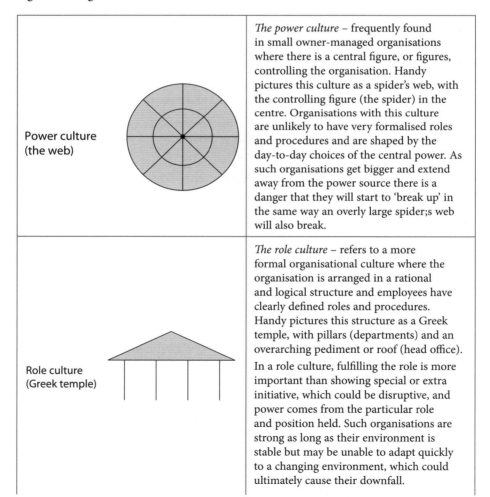

Power culture (the web)	*The power culture* – frequently found in small owner-managed organisations where there is a central figure, or figures, controlling the organisation. Handy pictures this culture as a spider's web, with the controlling figure (the spider) in the centre. Organisations with this culture are unlikely to have very formalised roles and procedures and are shaped by the day-to-day choices of the central power. As such organisations get bigger and extend away from the power source there is a danger that they will start to 'break up' in the same way an overly large spider;s web will also break.
Role culture (Greek temple)	*The role culture* – refers to a more formal organisational culture where the organisation is arranged in a rational and logical structure and employees have clearly defined roles and procedures. Handy pictures this structure as a Greek temple, with pillars (departments) and an overarching pediment or roof (head office). In a role culture, fulfilling the role is more important than showing special or extra initiative, which could be disruptive, and power comes from the particular role and position held. Such organisations are strong as long as their environment is stable but may be unable to adapt quickly to a changing environment, which could ultimately cause their downfall.

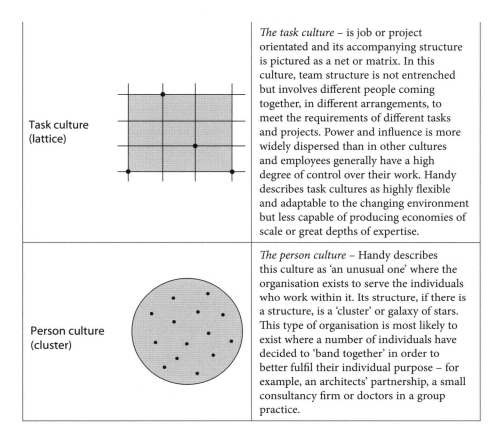

Task culture (lattice)	*The task culture* – is job or project orientated and its accompanying structure is pictured as a net or matrix. In this culture, team structure is not entrenched but involves different people coming together, in different arrangements, to meet the requirements of different tasks and projects. Power and influence is more widely dispersed than in other cultures and employees generally have a high degree of control over their work. Handy describes task cultures as highly flexible and adaptable to the changing environment but less capable of producing economies of scale or great depths of expertise.
Person culture (cluster)	*The person culture* – Handy describes this culture as 'an unusual one' where the organisation exists to serve the individuals who work within it. Its structure, if there is a structure, is a 'cluster' or galaxy of stars. This type of organisation is most likely to exist where a number of individuals have decided to 'band together' in order to better fulfil their individual purpose – for example, an architects' partnership, a small consultancy firm or doctors in a group practice.

Organisational culture may be strong, easily identified, recognised and upheld by people within the organisation or weak and hard to define. It may also differ between different areas or departments of an organisation, depending on leadership style and all the factors discussed above.

Both Charles Handy and Roger Harrison wrote further works on organisational culture, and Harrison has designed a survey instrument which organisations can use to assess and analyse their own culture as experienced by employees.

Senior managers may think they are the ones who set and lead the culture of an organisation. And to some extent, especially if there are well communicated Vision, Mission and Values, this may be true. This is often known as the 'espoused' culture.

It is also useful to know about the 'underlying' culture, or 'the way that things are around here'. This is more about a learned set of behaviours that are common knowledge to all employees and which represent the reality of the culture.

A third level, or strand, is the 'perceived' culture – how people outside the organisation view it.

It is really useful for the internal L&D professional to understand these different types of culture, so that the espoused culture can be supported and promoted, the underlying culture can be acknowledged and responded to, and the perceived culture challenged and made more realistic.

THE WIDER HUMAN RESOURCES FUNCTION

Over the last 50 years HR has seen many changes. The Personnel function has slowly shifted in name to HRM and Staff Training to HRD or more commonly Learning and Development. Whilst traditional responsibilities of the Personnel and Training Department remain, many new areas of work have evolved and been added to the HR remit within organisations.

Areas of the HR function might include:

Recruitment and Selection – ensuring the organisation has enough people of the right calibre and profile to fulfil the labour needs of the organisation, including job definition, description and advertising; management of the selection of personnel; processing of recruitment requirements, such as references, legal checks, contracting, and, often, induction to the organisation.

Employee Reward – ensuring pay and salary schemes effectively balance the needs of the organisation and its employees; formerly often known simply as payroll or wages department, but the remit has now widened to include all aspects of employee reward, such as pension schemes, childcare and travel vouchers, fitness schemes, bonuses and special rewards. This function is sometimes also referred to as 'compensation and benefits'.

Employee Relations – maintaining a healthy and constructive relationship between the organisation and its employees and avoiding factors which might impact negatively on operations, including managing negotiations between the organisation and employee representation, such as trade unions; dealing with conflict issues within the workforce; advising or representing on redundancy exercises and discipline and grievance matters.

Employment Law– ensuring organisational compliance with national and international employment legislation, including advising managers and other HR professionals on legal requirements; checking or creating compliant operational policies; assisting in employment relations issues and employment tribunals.

Health and Safety – helping to ensure the safety and well-being of people at work, including providing specialist advice on working conditions and working arrangements; monitoring and ensuring a safe workplace; ensuring employee safety and promoting employee well-being.

Organisation Design/Organisation Development – organisation design is primarily about creating and maintaining an organisational structure which best supports achievement of organisational goals. Organisation development is about ensuring ongoing organisational effectiveness and sustainability, and designing, planning and managing the change processes involved in this.

Employee Engagement – concerned with the level of alignment, connection and commitment employees feel to the organisation and particular area of work. This supports low staff turnover, quality of work performance and employee satisfaction levels.

Talent Management – concerned with identifying, recruiting, developing and retaining people with the key skills and abilities required by the organisation and who are seen to be of the highest value to the organisation.

Knowledge Management – the identification of areas of knowledge that are crucial to the organisation and the development of systems and processes for maintaining, sharing and making best use of it within the organisations operations.

As with other functions in the organisation, the structural position of HR depends on the type of organisation in which it sits. However there have also been prevailing – largely economic – trends which have influenced arrangements, either centralising, de-centralising, or out-sourcing the HR function. We have also seen the development of more shared service arrangements, where organisations such as governmental departments, combine their HR resources into a single centralised HR service.

Along with changes in terms, activity and structure, the relationship between HR and the rest of the organisation has also shifted. Once relatively isolated functions which undertook aspects of people management not required of managers, both Personnel and L&D have gradually moved towards the business, becoming partners with managers and advisors and facilitators of manager-led human resource practices.

Indeed, the title 'Business Partner' is now frequently applied to HR and L&D professionals working alongside the business areas, providing advice and services to support the achievement of business plans and goals.

THE LEARNING AND DEVELOPMENT FUNCTION

"As the owner of a children's nursery, it is extremely important for me to ensure that all my staff are trained to a high standard, not only in terms of ensuring that I am able to provide the best possible care to the children we look after, but also to help put parents at ease in the knowledge that they are leaving their children with people who are able to provide a safe, loving, caring and nurturing environment for them."

Carol Armstrong, Owner/Partner, Early Steps Nursery, Bathgate

As automation and communication processes develop it is increasingly difficult for organisations to offer unique products and services. Instead it is often how they deliver their products and services that gives any uniqueness and that enables them to gain competitive advantage. More than ever, therefore, the quality of performance of the people delivering products and services is crucial to organisational success.

This factor has heightened the importance of L&D over the last few decades and increased the contribution we can make to the achievement of organisational goals and business objectives.

At the beginning of this chapter, we said that the Learning and Development function has a key responsibility to ensure that people at all levels of the organisation possess and develop the skills, knowledge and experience to fulfil the short and long term ambitions of the organisation.

How the L&D function undertakes this responsibility depends partly on how it is arranged. Whilst some organisations have a wholly internal L&D team delivering all staff training and learning internally, and some have no internal training function at all, allowing line managers to buy in training as needed, it is now more typical for organisations to have a combination of internal and external provision.

This approach allows the use of specialists for particular areas of learning, whilst still having the benefits of an internal function which knows the business in some depth and can co-ordinate learning across the organisation to best meet organisational needs. This approach also requires L&D professionals to undertake wider roles. They must be expert in identifying needs and establishing best solutions, able to negotiate the provision of solutions with external providers and be effective monitors of training provision.

Debate continues as to how much L&D is part of an integrated HR function or whether it stands alone as a separate function within the organisation. To a great extent the debate is academic and the positioning of L&D depends on the type, size and specific arrangement of each organisation.

There are some advantages and disadvantages of both positions, and, as the needs of the organisation change, so too will the structure and positioning of L&D.

Integrated with HR – Advantages	Stand alone L&D – Advantages
'Strength in numbers' – HR and L&D are a unified force in the 'people' side of the business.	L&D can be tailored to the individual functions that it supports.
Can offer a one-stop-shop for all people needs.	Allows L&D to be regarded as a profession in its own right, rather than a subset of HR.
Can build a combined professional reputation and work in partnership across the business.	Can allow for more specialist interventions.
	L&D can build a deeper understanding of the parts of the business that it supports.
Integrated with HR – Drawbacks	Stand alone L&D – Drawbacks
Can become a 'generalist' function and lack specialist knowledge.	Could be a disjointed approach with a lack of corporate focus.
Could be slow to respond to needs of some smaller departments.	May result in inconsistency of coverage.
Might be seen by some employees as 'too corporate'.	May be disproportionately affected by budget cuts.

As with other HR functions, L&D has seen a shift over the last few years, towards greater partnership with line managers – either working with them to meet team and individual learning needs or assisting them to develop their own skills as coaches or learning facilitators. This was highlighted, and further predicted, in the 2008 CIPD Learning & Development Survey which stated:

> Indeed, the crucial role of line managers highlighted in previous surveys is reinforced this year, with the majority being involved in determining learning and development needs (86 per cent) and half predicting line managers will have greater responsibility for learning and development over the next five years (49 per cent).

Particular ways in which we can support line managers in the delivery of learning processes include:

- working with line managers to identify their team's learning needs
- providing and co-ordinating learning opportunities which are integrated with the workplace, involving managers and including approaches such as work based learning, computer-based (at-desk) learning, coaching and mentoring
- training and supporting managers to be coaches and mentors and helping managers to develop confidence in these processes
- involving managers in the review and assessment of individual learning
- supporting performance management processes and influencing the alignment of individual objectives with organisational goals.

Whether working directly with learners or via the management line, the key purpose of L&D to 'ensure that people at all levels of the organisation possess and develop the skills, knowledge and experiences to fulfil the short and long-term ambitions of the organisation and that they are motivated to learn, grow and perform', remains constant.

Fulfilling this purpose will always involve us in a number of key activities:

- promoting the benefits of learning
- establishing organisational requirements and priorities
- identifying capability gaps
- determining learning and development requirements and objectives
- designing effective and resource-efficient ways to meet learning objectives
- organising, delivering and facilitating learning and development activities which support organisation goals
- measuring the effectiveness of learning and development and ensuring objectives are met
- ensuring the capability of the L&D function through continued professional development.

Each of these key activities, along with coaching and mentoring, is explored in more depth in the further chapters of this book.

UNDERSTANDING ORGANISATIONS

1. Consider and describe your organisation's size, type, and structure. How is it similar to the models discussed in this chapter, and in what ways does it differ? What are the advantages and drawbacks of those differences?

2. What is the espoused culture of your organisation? And how does that differ from the underlying and perceived cultures? How can the work of your function (or you personally) affect those cultures?

3. Consider how the L&D function is positioned and organised within your organisation. Why is it positioned this way – and do you envision it changing in the future? How does the L&D function in your organisation differ from other organisations you are aware of?

4. Identify some learning and development activities within an organisation, you are involved in or know about, and explain how the activities link to organisational goals and how they support the achievement of these.

5. Analyse the key factors likely to impact on a specific organisation, in the next year, and in the next five years? How can the L&D function support your organisation to successfully meet these factors?

6. Have a look at the case study below and consider:

   – how Pathfinders' values impact on their L&D practice?
   – what benefits come from Pathways' aim to be: 'an employer of choice, providing high quality employment linked to individual learning pathways, which promotes high-quality care and high personal satisfaction'

     • for the staff they employ?
     • for the company itself?
     • for the residents of the home?
     • for other stakeholders?

CASE STUDY 2.1

CORPORATE VALUES AND L&D ACTIVITY

Dr Angela Nall, General Manager, Pathfinders Neurological Care Centre, Nottinghamshire

Pathfinders is registered with the Care Quality Commission as a 44 bed residential nursing home specialising in complex neurological conditions. The home provides long stay care, respite care, slow stream rehabilitation, stabilisation, and end of life care.

One of the four aims (or values) of Pathfinders is 'to be an employer of choice, providing high quality employment linked to individual learning pathways, which promotes high quality care and high personal satisfaction'.

The home is in Ollerton, North Nottinghamshire, a former mining area that has seen a slow and patchy regeneration. A number of the population have a low educational standard or level of literacy/ numeracy, and many employees arrive at Pathfinders with low learning and career expectations.

Pathfinders' approach to staff development is described by Angela as:

> All job applicants are tested at interview on literacy and numeracy skills, additionally they are scrutinised during induction week when there are various tests and assignments to complete. People who would make good staff members but lack sufficient numeracy and/or literacy skills are asked to join the literacy course that is led by our training partner.

All staff sign up to a learning contract as part of their terms of employment. Every single member of staff must sign up on the NVQ route (2 to 4), including myself.

The home comprises four units of 11 beds and each unit has its own specialism. Staff are assigned to a unit based on their general aptitude and then they develop a personal development plan based on how they measure up to the skills and knowledge required for that unit. They are given the opportunity to change to other units to learn different skill sets and to increase the flexibility of the home.

We plan to open a Care School later in 2010 so that each new entrant follows an apprentice style core skills learning programme that will sit alongside their NVQ commitment.

We have an award ceremony each year celebrating the success of employees in their learning and development.

Through our Spring Board Programme we encourage staff to pursue higher education and currently have four members of staff who have 'sprung' from our internal training into nursing training and one who has started occupational therapy training.

SUMMARY

This chapter has explored:

The importance of understanding organisational context

- The role of L&D is to help the organisation achieve it is aims.
- To be successful and influential, L&D needs to see the big picture as well as the detail.

The value of mission, values and strategy statements

- A vision statement describes the outcome an organisation aspires intends to achieve and the mission statement sets out its key purpose.
- Strategy statements are the plans for achievement of the vision and mission.

Popular methods for analysing organisational context

- SWOT analysis helps us to understand the internal and external factors which could affect the success of an organisation.
- PEST analysis helps to define the factors which will have an impact on the operation of an organisation.
- Understanding the needs and interests of stakeholders helps us to understand the different ways in which an organisation is being influenced.

Key factors which characterise organisations

- Organisations might be characterised in terms of their size, type, legal status, structure, culture, or the functions that are carried out within the organisation.

Hr Functions and how they support the organisation

- Key HR functions include recruitment and selection, reward, employee relations and health & safety.
- HR can work as a function within the organisation or as a partner to the business.
- HR makes sure that the organisation recruits the right people and rewards, manages and retains them effectively so that the organisation can fulfil its purpose.

Contribution of L&D to the achievement of organisational goals

- L&D is responsible for ensuring that an organisation has the ongoing capability to deliver its goals (in terms of the skills, knowledge and behaviours of the people within the organisation).
- L&D supports line managers to fulfil business plans and goals.
- L&D provides effective learning opportunities to meet the needs of learners and the organisation.
- L&D needs to understand the whole context of the organisation in order to fulfil its role.

EXPLORE FURTHER

BOOKS:

Ansoff, I. (1988) *Corporate strategy*. 2nd edn. London: Penguin.

Currie, D. (2006) *Introduction to human resource management: a guide to personnel practice*. London: CIPD.

Handy, C. (1993) *Understanding organisations*. 4th edn. London: Penguin.

Harrison, R. and Stokes, H. (1992) *Diagnosing organizational culture: instrument*. San Francisco USA: Jossey Bass.

Martin, M., Whiting, F. and Jackson T. (2010) *Human resource practice*. 5th edn. London: CIPD.

Porter, M. (2004) *Competitive advantage*. New edn. New York USA: Free Press.

WEBSITES:

Free (or partially free) on-line access to SWOT and PEST tools:

http://businessballs.com

Partially free on-line access to analysis, time management and problem-solving techniques:

www.mindtools.com

CHAPTER 3

Recording, Analysing and Using Learning and Development Information

INTRODUCTION

This chapter begins with a justification of the need to keep records about the people who work in organisations. We go on to look more specifically at the information required by the L&D function, and how it is used. We explore a range of systems for recording and using information, and the legal and other constraints which govern this. Finally we consider some important factors affecting the presentation of information and some techniques for presenting information effectively.

LEARNING OUTCOMES

When you have read this chapter, you should be able to:

- justify and explain the need to maintain records and information
- discuss different types of L&D information and how these can be used
- describe different systems for recording, analysing and using L&D information
- explain the legal constraints affecting the use of information in organisations
- present information in different formats to meet different needs.

THE NEED TO MAINTAIN RECORDS AND INFORMATION

We live in the 'information age' and to be effective in our work practice, and our lives generally, we all have to be competent in the management of information. This is particularly important for organisations, both for the benefits to be gained from the effective use of information and for reasons of compliance and good practice.

One of the key organisational reasons for collecting information is to meet legislative and regulatory requirements. For example, organisations need to demonstrate compliance with Minimum Wage, Working Time, Time Off for Training, Equality, and Health and Safety legislation as well as meeting

HMRC requirements for recording tax, national insurance, and pension related information.

This requires organisations to collect and maintain a range of HR and L&D information, such as:

- employee personal details
- employment contracts
- employee attendance records
- payroll and reward info
- employee performance info
- health and safety records
- attendance records
- discipline or grievance issues
- performance (appraisal) records
- training records.

However, even if compliance and regulation did not place such demands on organisations, there are other reasons why the collection and analysis of relevant information and data is to an organisations advantage.

Knowing about the workforce enables an organisation to make informed decisions about future activity. Information can inform ongoing recruitment needs, reward and well-being policies, employee engagement activities and the ongoing planning of training and development. It can also be used to inform the organisation's wider operational and service plans and to assist decisions about how best to develop the business.

Ultimately, information about the people in organisations can contribute to wider industry, sector and national knowledge about the workforce and help inform decision-making beyond the organisation.

MAINTAINING AND USING L&D INFORMATION

Information requirements within an L&D function will include:

- specific information about the types of training opportunities that are available
- records of the training activity that has been undertaken.

However, there is also a wider need for information about the organisation(s) and learners we are working with and the financial and legal context of our work. Table 3.1 considers some different types of information that may be collected and used by an L&D function.

Table 3.1 Information relevant to learning and development

Type of Information	Key Uses
Organisational information Operational plans, project plans and business objectives – current and future Related policies and procedures	• Informs L&D priorities and planning • Informs how L&D activities are delivered • Defines policy and procedural requirements
Financial information Budgets and spending priorities, costs of delivered L&D activities, price information for training related expenditures (eg venues, travel, external providers)	• Informs ongoing L&D planning • Informs design and purchase of L&D • Essential information for management of L&D budget and expenditure control • Enables effective use of budget and resources
Personnel /learner information Numbers and profiles of learners, personal, location and contractual details governing work arrangements	• Informs logistical arrangements for L&D activity • May inform design of L&D and delivery methods
Employee performance reviews Individual performance and development review (appraisal) records, showing learning needs identified within the review process	• Informs L&D priorities and planning • Enables effective targeting of training budget and resources • Patterns might indicate other problems in the organisation which L&D can address
Specific learning needs information Information gathered from specific needs analysis, maybe in relation to a new product, service or business development	• Informs design of L&D activities • Enables appropriate delivery of L&D for different learner groups • Identifies areas of strength and weakness and best deployment of staff • Can inform strategic objectives and timescales for achievement
Individual L&D records Record of learning needs identified (performance review documentation), L&D activity undertaken, outcomes of L&D activity where relevant (eg assessment outcomes, marks, grades)	• May be necessary to confirm compliance with organisational or legal requirements • Confirms individual competence, capability or eligibility for role • Supports claims for qualifications, licences and other professional requirements • May be necessary for audit by external awarding or funding bodies
Records of available L&D opportunities Types of learning available, practical information including costs, timing, availability, entry requirements, target audience, intended outcomes	• Essential for learners, and their managers, to make choices about learning • Essential for learners to be able to prepare for learning
Specific information about tailored L&D projects and activities – objectives, requirements, deliverables, intended outcomes	• Essential for communication purposes with project sponsor or stakeholders • Essential for review and evaluation purposes

Summary records of L&D delivered Overall 'delivery' of learning and development services and activity – what, where and when	• Informs ongoing L&D planning • Essential for monitoring against L&D plans and service level agreements • Essential for updating stakeholders • Supports ongoing L&D budget negotiations • Informs best deployment of personnel
Outcomes of L&D delivered Specific quantitative outcomes of L&D and qualitative information from evaluation activity, including learner and customer feedback	• Informs ongoing L&D planning • Informs ongoing design of L&D • Essential for monitoring against L&D plans and service level agreements • Essential for updating stakeholders • Supports ongoing L&D budget negotiations • Informs best deployment of personnel • Patterns might indicate problems in other areas or aspects of the organisation

The information we collect will include both qualitative and quantitative information, as shown in the following boxes.

Quantitative information	**Qualitative information**
Quantitative information is about facts, things that can be measured, ie quantities.	Qualitative information is less 'absolute' and more about qualities than quantities.
For example, it could be about the amount of L&D activity, the costs of activities, or numeric outcomes of training events.	It might be opinion based, for example what someone thought about a particular activity or how successful they thought it was.
An example of quantitative information is that '84 people attended in-house health and safety training in March 2010'.	An example of qualitative information is that 'learners did not find the health and safety training *very* relevant to their job roles'

REFLECTIVE ACTIVITY

What information do you collect and keep to support your work?

Why do you keep this specifically? How is it useful?

MANAGING L&D INFORMATION – IN PRACTICE

INFORMATION SYSTEMS

Systems used for recording and managing information are many and varied – from a simple filing cabinet with a hanging file for each staff member, into which paper based copies of attendance certificates are placed, through to sophisticated and comprehensive, multi-access, computer based Learning Management Systems.

The simple filing drawer has its advantages; it is easily accessed, easily understood and has no dependence on technology for usage. However, it misses out on the many benefits easily available from computerised information management systems and would probably only be useful within a very small organisation.

Computerised systems

More typically, many organisations make use of standard office software – such as word processing, databases and spreadsheets.

Databases can be particularly useful for keeping individual L&D records. Data entry screens can be set up so that data-fields align to the organisations particular information needs and contexts and, once entered, data can be retrieved in an array of different formats to meet different needs. Detailed information can be accessed about individuals or converged into a range of summary reports covering all or selected individuals within the database.

Figure 3.1 shows an example of a database used to record staff training details.

The kind of information and reports we could access from a database that has been set up in this way might include:

- staff who have received particular types of training
- staff who need particular types of training
- numbers and profiles of people who have received particular training
- amounts of training provided to different teams or business areas
- caseloads of coaches or mentors and trainer workloads
- all training undertaken in a particular period
- training undertaken by an individual employee and outcomes of their assessments.

Spreadsheets are equally useful for managing L&D information. A typical example of this might be a spreadsheet set up as a training matrix, showing team members listed down a side axis and required training activities along the top axis. Relevant cells can then be populated to show *who* has undertaken *what* training. Such a document might be further extended to show skill levels reached, assessment outcomes gained or renewal dates. (Some examples of a similar document to this – skills matrices – are included in Chapter 4: Undertaking a learning needs analysis.)

A different example of using a spreadsheet is described in the following box:

SPREADSHEET USE: INTERNAL CHARGING

An L&D function within a medium sized organisation, with a system of internal charging between business units, uses a simple spreadsheet to keep a record of activities.

Spreadsheet column headings include: course titles, various cost headings, attendees, payback required for individual attendees, and the resulting financial gains or losses of each course.

This information is used to provide a regular return to a central accounting function where financial adjustments are made to business unit budgets.

Spreadsheets require some familiarity to manipulate and make best use of the many facilities, but can be particularly useful for numerical information, such as training expenditure, as calculations can be easily embedded into columns of data. For example, the spreadsheet in Figure 3.2 has been set up to record and calculate aspects of an L&D budget.

Word processing: along with databases and spreadsheets, many organisations also make use of word processing features to record or present L&D information. An example is shown in the box on the following page.

Figure 3.2 Spreadsheet to record a learning and development budget

EXTRACT FROM AN INTERNAL VERIFICATION (IV) PLAN AND RECORD

A small organisation that provided vocational qualifications was asked to provide the External Verifier of their Awarding Body with an 'IV Sampling Plan and Record', showing the frequency and type of internal verification activity across a cohort of candidates.

The centre chose to provide this information in a very visual way, as a 'table', showing:

- which units candidates had achieved
- which units the IV had planned to verify
- which candidate units had actually been verified, and how.

The plan can be seen in Figure 3.3.

Figure 3.3 IV sampling plan and record

IV: Roger Taylor   **Assessor:** Bridget Marshall   **Group:** Core trainer (Group 1)   **Page** 1/3

ID	Candidate	Status	G3 (IA)	L6	L7	L10	L17	IV Undertaken
64	Linda Balmforth	Started 06.01.10	Ach 24.03.10	Ach 04.04.10				G3 & L6 sampled & IV/Candidate meeting 15.04.10 See IV report
99	Mary Sharpe	Started 06.01.10	Ach 12.04.10		Ach 24.03.10			G3 & L7 Unit sampled 15.04.10 See IV report
100	Christine Hunt	Started 06.01.10	Ach 24.03.10					G3 Unit sampled 15.04.10 See IV report
101	Ruth Milner	Started 06.01.10	Ach 24.03.10		Ach 04.04.10			Evidence not available on 15.04
102	Rita Beckton	Started 06.01.10						
103	Linda Firth	Started 17.01.10	Ach 19.04.10	Ach 19.04.10				G3 Unit sampled 15.04.10 See IV report

KEY: Ach = Unit achieved, ■ = Planned IV sample

All of the above approaches to using information require a certain amount of IT skills on the part of the administrator and users, but offer easy ways of storing, accessing and presenting information to meet different purposes.

LEARNING MANAGEMENT SYSTEMS

So far the computerised systems mentioned have been one-dimensional, in that they are generally maintained and managed centrally, even if data is occasionally inputted by other users.

However, this is not the case with newer generations of information systems which integrate many of the functions already discussed and allow interactive, multi-user access. These data systems are commonly known as Learning Management Systems (LMS) and are now widely available and increasingly affordable to all sizes of organisation.

A typical LMS system will include:

- a catalogue of available L&D opportunities, with summary information about each, eg content, delivery mode, provider/facilitator, access details and schedules

- links from L&D opportunities to work roles and objectives – employees will usually only have access to opportunities they are 'eligible' to attend

- self-service processes for learners to register for particular L&D activities; systems show availability of places, updated as registrations are made, line-manager approval is often required before a learner's registration is accepted

- interactive processes for the L&D function to confirm acceptance of a learner to a course or activity and return more detailed information to the learner; at the same time, course lists, and related logistical factors (resource, venue and hospitality factors), are updated

- individual L&D records, listing type and amount of L&D undertaken by an individual, and related outcomes, such as assessments, marks and grades

- links to organisational intranets and websites.

LMS systems increasingly include access to internal systems, such as individual performance and development reviews, and other learning functions, such as on-line learning programmes and learning communities.

If you do not have access to an organisation LMS system, have a look at some examples on the internet. They are becoming increasingly sophisticated, useful and interesting to use and no doubt will be further developed and their features expanded, over the next few years.

Virtual Learning Environments

Another development with many similarities to Learning Management Systems is Virtual Learning Environments (VLEs), also sometimes referred to as Learning Platforms or Managed Learning Environments. VLEs are generally seen to have a greater connection to the educational world than the corporate, but share many functions of an LMS system. Perhaps the main difference is the slightly greater emphasis on learning content and interaction between learner and tutor, rather than on the administrative content and integration with business objectives of an LMS system.

However, the different designs and features of the various systems and the increasing integration of learning content within LMS systems make clear categorisation between the two types of system increasingly difficult. Again, you can find examples of these via an internet search.

e-Portfolios

A further development in information management which has impacted on L&D and particularly on those involved with qualifications is the emergence of e-portfolio assessment systems. Several of these are now commercially available.

E-portfolios provide a facility for qualification candidates to upload work (evidence) to a database which is related to a second database containing the qualification criteria.

Typical steps in the use of an e-portfolio are:

- candidates upload their work to the system, make links from their work to particular qualification criteria on a 'matrix' document and then submit all of this to their assessor
- the assessor confirms, deletes or questions the links and chooses to either 'accept' the unit as complete or return it to the candidate with feedback
- the process continues until a unit or module, and ultimately the full qualification, is complete.

All of this activity is captured and retained within the system and visual references are given throughout the process, indicating stages of achievement. At any point the system can also be accessed by an 'internal verifier' who can check an aspect of assessment and confirm, or question any assessment decisions. Most systems also allow other levels of access – perhaps for line managers or external verifiers.

Moodle

Finally in this section, it is worth mentioning Moodle – a free software package which can be used in academic or commercial settings. It is extensively used in the UK by the Open University, and combines many of the features of other platforms. For more details see www.moodle.org.

QUALITY OF INFORMATION

Whatever system is used, the quality of information produced by the system is entirely related to the quality of information entered into the system. A wrongly placed decimal point or wrongly entered assessment result can crucially affect ongoing decision-making of all kinds. (A famous, though non-L&D, example must be the case of the iron content of spinach. It now seems that our long held belief in the ultra-high iron content of this vegetable – and the related twentieth century culture of 'Popeye', the comic book spinach-eating hero – is founded on a simple data recording mistake, a wrongly placed decimal point, indicating 10 times more iron in spinach than is actually the case!)

Currency of data is equally important and many systems might require formal update schedules to ensure that data is valid. Also spelling and formatting can be crucial to search criteria, and, if not done correctly, could cause records to be missed from wider searches and therefore not represented within summary reports – or located by other users.

Fortunately, modern systems seek to minimise opportunities for error, either by setting ranges for data entry and informing the user if an entry is 'out of range' or by generally reducing human involvement through the automatic transfer of data between relational systems. However, inaccurate input remains a problem and some form of system check, however simple, should be built into any record keeping process.

USING SURVEYS

A really useful way of collecting L&D related information is to conduct a survey. The advent of online survey sites has made it very easy, and inexpensive, to collect and analyse all sorts of information.

We can, for example, use online surveys to collect information about the learning needs of a group, to assess the level of knowledge or skill prior to undertaking an L&D activity, or to evaluate the learning gained.

TEN TIPS FOR DESIGNING AN ONLINE SURVEY

1. Give your survey an appropriate title and write a short introduction explaining the purpose, how it works, and how the results will be used.

2. Keep it brief, and think about your respondents – always ask yourself 'will this make sense to the people competing it?'

3. Start with interesting questions that will encourage your respondents to want to complete the whole survey.

4. Develop questions that are suitable for your purpose, but avoid asking 'leading' questions.

5. Use simple language that everyone will understand, and make sure that your language is 'neutral', rather than biased towards certain views.

6. Ask your questions one at a time, and follow a logical order.

7. Avoid questions with double negatives.

8. Closed questions are usually easier to answer and easier for you to analyse.

9. Scaled responses should be balanced: for example 'excellent – good – average – below average – poor' is more balanced than 'excellent – very good – above average – average – not very good'.

However, if you think there will be a tendency to opt for an 'easy' middle rating then just use four or six different ratings.

10. Always think in advance about how you are going to analyse and present the answers, as this will have an impact on how you design them.

Here is an extract from a survey about staff satisfaction with L&D provision:

Figure 3.4 Staff satisfaction with learning and development provision

1. There are sufficient opportunities for me to develop new skills.

☐ Strongly Disagree

☐ Somewhat Disagree

☐ Neutral

☐ Somewhat Agree

☐ Strongly Agree

☐ Not Applicable

2. Overall, how satisfied are you with the training and development you have received in the last year?

☐ Dissatisfied

☐ Somewhat dissatisfied

☐ Neutral

☐ Satisfied

☐ Very Satisfied

☐ Not Applicable

3. The training that I receive is useful and easy to apply to my job.

☐ Strongly Disagree

☐ Somewhat Disagree

☐ Neutral

☐ Somewhat Agree

☐ Strongly Agree

☐ Not Applicable

CASE STUDY 3.1

CHORLEY BOROUGH COUNCIL

Rik Sterken, HR and OD Consultant at Chorley Council has been using an online survey tool to help to collect, collate and make use of end-of-course evaluation data.

He says that the $200 per year licence provides good value for money as it would have cost much more to develop a suitable in-house system.

Rik re-designed the end-of-course 'evaluation sheet' to make sure that it contains information relevant to the performance targets of the L&D function – for example, the sheets ask questions such as:

- What are you going to start/stop/ continue doing as a result of the training?

- What help will you need from your manager/colleagues/L&D department?

- How relevant was the training event to your role?

The paper forms are still collected manually at the end of an event (Rik has found this is quicker than having to chase delegates afterwards). Once collected the data is transferred onto the online survey.

A link to the survey can then be sent to:

- all the delegates to remind them of the value that everyone got from the event

- the trainer who ran the event, so they can make use of the feedback

- line managers to encourage them to have post-event conversations with their staff.

Rik also uses the statistical information as part of his quest for ongoing improvement. He has just, for example, increased the target of responses in the 'very relevant' and 'relevant' categories of Management Development programmes to 91 per cent.

INFORMATION MANAGEMENT AND LEGAL REQUIREMENTS

Computerised information systems have made the collection, storage and use of vast amounts of data much easier but, have also added to the need for controls and constraints on information usage.

The main legal constraints come from the Data Protection Act of 1998. The Act provides protection for individuals, in relation to the information stored about them by organisations, and affords them appropriate access to such information.

There is a wealth of up-to-date information about the requirements of the data Protection Act and related codes of practice on the Information Commissioner website (http://www.informationcommissioner.gov.uk) and on the CIPD website (http://www.cipd.co.uk).

In brief, all UK organisations which 'process personal data' are required to notify the Information Commissioners Office (ICO) and comply with the Data Protection Act, unless they meet special exemption conditions. Whilst the Act recognises the need for organisations to keep information, it requires them to do this in a responsible and fair manner and not excessively. The main requirements of the Act are summarised in eight clear principles:

1. Personal data shall be processed fairly and lawfully and, in particular, shall not be processed unless: (a) at least one of the conditions in Schedule 2 is met;

and (b), in the case of sensitive personal data, at least one of the conditions in schedule 3 is also met. (More information about the schedules and 'conditions for processing' is available on the ICO website.)

2. Personal data shall be obtained only for one or more specified and lawful purposes, and shall not be further processed in any manner incompatible with that purpose or those purposes.

3. Personal data shall be adequate, relevant and not excessive in relation to the purpose or purposes for which they are processed.

4. Personal data shall be accurate and, where necessary, kept up-to-date.

5. Personal data processed for any purpose or purposes shall not be kept for longer than is necessary for that purpose or those purposes.

6. Personal data shall be processed in accordance with the rights of data subjects under this Act.

7. Appropriate technical and organisational measures shall be taken against unauthorised or unlawful processing of personal data and against accidental loss or destruction of, or damage to, personal data.

8. Personal data shall not be transferred to a country or territory outside the European Economic Area unless that country or territory ensures an adequate level of protection for the rights and freedoms of data subjects in relation to the processing of personal data.

For more detail on each of the eight principles, you can refer to the Information Commissioners website, as listed above, where a number of good practice guides are available. The Commission also provides free paper-based guides and resources – also available through the website.

In addition to the Data Protection Act, public authorities must also comply with the Freedom of Information Acts (there is one for England, Wales and Northern Ireland (2000) and one for Scotland (2002)) requiring them to make certain types of information available to the public. Further information about the Freedom of Information Acts is also available on the Commissioner's website.

PRESENTING INFORMATION

Information about L&D can be presented in many different ways, to suit a number of needs. In this section we will consider using information for publicity and influencing purposes, as well as responding to specific requests.

Publicity information

This is the sort of information that might be published by the L&D function on a regular basis in order to promote learning activities, publicise the work of the team, or provide contact details. It is likely to be provided within staff bulletins, notice boards, intranets, brochures, promotional e-mails and directories.

Material used to promote learning activities needs to be honest and inspirational – making recipients aware of what is available and also making them want to 'buy' what is on offer.

Here are some useful things to include in promotional material to enhance the 'appeal' to your audience:

Table 3.2 **Promotional material**

Key points	Explanation	Example
Who it is for	Make it clear who the event is aimed at	The course is ideal for all staff who deal with telephone calls from the public
Why you should attend	The overall aim or purpose of the event	To learn how to handle difficult calls more effectively and avoid complaints from customers
What you will gain	The planned outcomes of the event	How to build rapport with customers, how to say 'no' effectively, how to manage conversations, how to avoid arguments, how to handle abusive behaviour
What to expect	An overview of what will happen and the methodology of how the event is delivered	A brief timetable of the event. 'This half-day workshop is highly interactive, with a mixture of case studies and practical examples, together with a wealth of tips and techniques for you to use'
What happens next	Practical information about the event	Location, dates and times, costs, booking forms etc

Promotional material works best when it appeals to the different senses of your audience, and so you could make use of some theory about how people process information (VAK) to help you do this.

Ref to ELP 8 – NLP VAK

For example, you could seek to engage the **visual** senses with pictures and colour, the **auditory** senses with quotes and describing what has been said about the event, and the **kinaesthetic** senses with descriptions of what will be happening at the event and how it will make learners feel.

REFLECTIVE ACTIVITY

Take a look at some of the fliers and brochures that you receive from training providers (or look for some online).

How do they compare with the publicity that is given to the internal courses of your organisation?

What can you learn from them?

Using information to be influential

Another main use of information can be to influence policy or action elsewhere in the organisation.

For example:

- using staff turnover data to influence the need for a different type of induction process
- using feedback from the evaluation process to convince line managers to do more pre- and post-course coaching
- using return on investment data to convince budget holders to allocate more funding to training events.

When we want to influence others, it is important to consider what will be the strongest 'convincers' for the person or people we are addressing. If, for example, we know that saving money is important to someone, then we will need to include a well thought through budget plan or forecast. If increased performance is their motivator, then we might use examples of this being achieved elsewhere.

A useful format for making an influential proposal is PROEP – Proposal, Reason, Objections, Explanation, Proposal.

PROPOSAL
Make a clear and straightforward statement of your request – *'I propose that we introduce a mentoring scheme for newly appointed managers.'*

REASON
Give clear 'headline' reasons to back up your proposal – *'A mentoring scheme will integrate managers more quickly into their new role, save money, and increase efficiency.'*

OBJECTIONS
Acknowledge the objections or concerns that your proposal might create – *'I know you will have concerns about the cost and resources that will be needed."*

EXPLANATION
The bulk of your proposal now concentrates on the background, evidence and information that will support your request and overcome the concerns that you have anticipated – *'I'll tell you about some of the problems new managers currently face and the effects these problems have on cost and efficiency. I'll tell you about how mentoring has worked in another part of our organisation, and I'll give detailed plans and costs for my proposal, including anticipated cost savings and productivity gains.'*

PROPOSE
Re-state your proposal, this time with more detailed information about how it would work – *'The proposed scheme would include ... start on ... cost...' etc.*

Responding to requests for information

Typical requests for L&D information could include:

- a manager or individual wanting advice or recommendations on how to meet specific learning needs

- a project manager wanting to know about employee 'readiness' for a new business initiative
- a potential learner wanting to know about availability of courses, activities and programmes
- a learner wanting more in-depth details about specific learning activities and objectives
- particular stakeholders wanting progress on 'live' training initiatives or outcomes of completed ones
- a client or finance function wanting information about L&D costs
- a line manager (or the individual themselves) wanting information about an individuals training, achievement or eligibility for different aspects of work

Because L&D information can be of a sensitive nature, we should always consider some general factors, before responding. Ask yourself:

- Does the enquirer have a right to this information?
- Does providing this information infringe others' rights or contravene any regulations?

And to help you respond in the most appropriate way, establish:

- Why does the enquirer need the information?
- What information do they really want, this may need clarifying?
- When do they need the information for?
- Do they need the information in a particular format?

Having clarified what the information need is, you have a number of options for responding (see Table 3.3).

Table 3.3 **Options when responding to information requests**

Options	Example
Verbal and informal	One-to-one discussion or informal meeting
Verbal and formal	A formal presentation or formal meeting
Written and informal	An e-mail or written note
Written and formal	A report or project charter
Visual	Graphs, charts or images (probably within one of the other approaches listed above)

Responding verbally

TIPS FOR RESPONDING VERBALLY TO A REQUEST FOR INFORMATION

1. Listen to the request – not always as easy as it sounds in a busy office!

2. Do not make assumptions.

3. Ask questions to clarify.

4. Be patient if the enquirer is unsure of exact requirements.

5. Summarise the request back to the recipient – and check your understanding is correct.

6. Avoid using jargon and acronyms in your response.

7. If you cannot answer the request yourself, arrange to find out the information and get back to them or for someone else to respond.

8. Give time-scales for a response and ensure the enquirer is clear about the action you are going to take.

9. If sending on information, ensure you have correct contact details including phone number in case further checking is needed.

Responding in writing

If you are to provide information in a formal written report, then there are established formats that you can follow – making your own adjustments to suit your particular purpose. A typical traditional report format is shown in the box below:

REPORT TITLE

Contents	Page No
1. Executive summary	1
2. Background	3
3. Methodology	5

4. Main findings
   – XXX
   – XXX
   – XXX
	7

5. Conclusions and recommendations	14

6. Appendices
   1. xxx
   2. xxx
	18

Making your information more understandable and appealing

Whether presenting verbally or providing written information it is always helpful to support your content with visual images, which will help the audience to access and absorb the information being presented. Visual images might include graphs, charts, logos and pictures.

Many standard data programmes, particularly spreadsheets, will convert data to graphic forms, like the bar or column graph and pie chart examples below. In these examples, the various formats show statistics relating to the number of training days attended by staff from different areas.

The first example, Table 3.4, shows the data in a tabular layout – good for accuracy, but not so visually appealing.

Table 3.4 **Table for accuracy**

	Quarter one	Quarter two	Quarter three	Quarter four
Sales team	30	40	40	60
Operations	40	60	70	80
Finance Dept	20	20	30	30

The second example, giving the information in the form of a bar chart, helps the viewer to compare the information by making it more visual.

Figure 3.5 Bar chart for easier comparisons

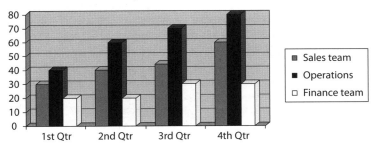

The same information is shown in the third example as a line graph. This type of diagram is good for showing growth or decline over a particular period.

Figure 3.6 Line graph for change

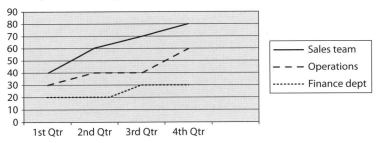

The final example is a pie chart. This example shows the relative proportion of training days taken by each team.

Figure 3.7 Pie chart for proportions

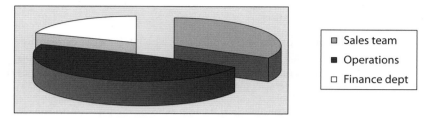

The options for producing images within different software programmes are now vast. Next time you are presenting word processed information, or data of some kind, why not take a few minutes to explore the art, picture or chart functions available to you – and see if you can enhance the information you are providing.

WHAT NEXT

RECORDING, ANALYSING AND USING INFORMATION

1. Consider the information systems used in your department or organisation – and evaluate how fit for purpose they are.

2. Survey users of L&D about how effectively information is provided to them – use one of the online survey sites to do this.

3. Take one aspect of information in an organisation and improve how it is managed.

4. Take one example of written information and improve how it is presented.

5. Research LMS systems, identifying a system that would best meet your (or a particular) organisation's needs and context.

6. Have a look at the case study below, and, following on from item 5 in the list, consider:

   – If you do not have an LMS system already in your organisation: what benefits do you think you (the L&D function) would gain from having one? What would the organisation as a whole gain?

   – If you already work in an organisation with an LMS system: how effective is it? What would you like to add to it?

LEARNING MANAGEMENT SYSTEM

Stephanie is the L&D manager for a Housing Association which runs residential retirement homes across the Midlands and the South West.

When she took over the role there was a semi-computerised system for booking and organising training that had grown organically over a number of years. It soon became clear to Stephanie that the system was not robust enough for the needs of the organisation.

In a previous HR role Stephanie had introduced an integrated HR information system and knew the benefits that a similar system could bring to an L&D function.

Stephanie says:

> I set about gathering information to put a business case to our Management Team to purchase a Learning Management System. My business case included a review of the existing system and a risk analysis of the problems that it could be causing us.
>
> I worked out how much time was currently spent on the manual

collection of learning need data, and the problems being caused as a result of poor record keeping and lack of consistency, and used this information to recommend the purchase of a system.

> The argument that clinched the approval was the need to show the Audit Commission an improvement in how we developed our staff and how we make sure we are safeguarding our vulnerable tenants.

Stephanie reports that 18 months after introducing the system they have seen great improvements, including:

- a 60 per cent increase in recorded staff learning hours

- training of an additional seven staff in safeguarding (these staff had not been identified as needing the training under the previous system)

- on-line training plans in place for all staff, with all but a few being, regularly accessed and updated by staff members.

SUMMARY

This chapter has explored:

The need to maintain effective records

- We have an operational need to keep accurate and up-to-date records of staff and the learning activities that they undertake.

- There is a legal need to keep certain essential records.

Different types of L&D information and how these can be used within organisations

- L&D information can help to define and record learning needs, capture data about L&D activities, and help to assess the value of the activities carried out.

Different systems for recording, analysing and using L&D information

- Stand alone systems can be effective in smaller organisations.
- Many larger organisations are using fully computerised Learning Management Systems.

The legal constraints affecting the use of information in organisations

- The Data Protection Act is the key piece of legislation which governs the correct collection, storage and use of data held about people within an organisation.

Presentation of information

- Think about the needs of the person for whom you are presenting the information, and make it interesting for them.
- Text can be made more interesting by the addition of graphs, charts and images.

EXPLORE FURTHER

BOOKS:

MCGILLIGAN, N. (2009) *Data protection pocket guide: essential facts at your fingertips.* 2nd edn. London: BSI British Standards Institute.

KAVANAGH, M. and THITE, M. (2009) *Human resource information systems: basics, applications and future directions.* London: Sage.

WEBSITES:

Range of booklets, tools and resources relating to data protection from the information commissioner's office:

www.ico.gov.uk/tools_and_resources/document_library.aspx

CIPD factsheet on data protection:

www.cipd.co.uk/subjects/emplaw/dataprot/dataprotec.htm

On-line survey providers (free for basic level usage):

www.freeonlinesurveys.com

www.surveymonkey.com

www.smart-survey.co.uk

CHAPTER 4

Undertaking a Learning Needs Analysis

INTRODUCTION

In this chapter we shall look at why it is important for organisations to analyse learning needs and the benefits that come from this. We will also explore different types and levels of learning need, some of the main reasons why they arise and a wide range of methods for identifying them. Finally, we move on to think about solutions – the factors that affect the choice of learning activity and several different ways of fulfilling a learning need.

LEARNING OUTCOMES

When you have read this chapter, you should be able to:

• describe the reasons for analysing learning needs

• explain different types of learning needs and why they arise

• discuss a range of methods for identifying learning needs

• identify factors affecting the recommendation of a learning solution

• describe the features of a range of different learning activities

• make appropriate recommendations to meet specific learning needs.

THE RATIONALE FOR LEARNING NEEDS ANALYSIS

Few, if any, organisations have unlimited training budgets. Time spent clarifying learning needs and priorities helps ensure limited resources are used to maximum effect.

Different organisations take a whole range of approaches to analysing their learning needs, as in the continuum in Figure 4.1.

Figure 4.1 Learning needs analysis

Reactive	Set planned	Proactive
>>>—————	>>>—————	>>>

Organisations that are completely reactive about their analysis will do nothing until something goes wrong or stops being effective, at which point, of course, it may be too late. They will always be following the pack when it comes to learning and development.

From the middle of the continuum are organisations that do some learning needs analysis, maybe via an appraisal system, but tend not to look too deeply or stray beyond checking that basic training requirements are being met. These organisations provide similar planned programmes of learning year after year, generally ensuring that staff have the main skills and knowledge required and that regulatory requirements are covered.

At the proactive end of the scale are the organisations that really see the benefits of analysing and acting upon their learning needs as they arise. Needs are monitored as the business evolves and new challenges emerge. As well as 'maintenance needs', ie learning that is required to maintain current capabilities, thought is also given to emerging and future requirements. L&D professionals and managers in these organisations use a range of activities to research and analyse learning needs and draw a number of benefits from doing this.

The potential benefits include:

- a well-trained and responsive workforce, who have the knowledge, skills and confidence to carry out their roles, even as those roles evolve and change
- greater employee satisfaction with the organisation as they feel their development needs are being addressed – a factor in higher employee retention rates
- greater customer and stakeholder satisfaction as changing needs and expectations are anticipated and catered for
- increased competitive advantage and a reputation for being 'ahead of the game', through anticipating and preparing for change
- better targeting of the L&D budget on learning activities that are most relevant and likely to have the greatest impact.

> "I have learned over the years that a business area's learning needs are never quite met by a particular project, and that needs keep evolving, even between LNA and design/delivery. So you never really follow a perfect process of analysis, design, delivery, – or achieve the perfect solution. If we accept that development is a journey, each project or initiative is just a step along the way, never an end in itself."
>
> Jill MacLean, Head of Learning (Group), Standard Life Assurance Limited

UNDERSTANDING LEARNING NEEDS

In the simplest terms, a learning need usually exists where there is a gap between current capability and desired or required capability.

In this context, we are using the term 'capability' to refer to a combination of knowledge, skills and behaviours (Table 4.1).

Table 4.1 **Capability**

Knowledge	What someone needs to know, eg facts, processes, causes and effects, technical knowledge
Skills	What someone needs to be able to do, eg operate specific equipment, apply a first-aid dressing or listen actively
Behaviours[a]	How someone needs to do things, personal and inter-personal approaches taken, eg being pro-active or being considerate of others feelings

[a]A gap between current behaviours and desired or required behaviours may not always represent a learning need. There are several reasons why someone may not behave in a desired way – for example interpersonal issues or lack of motivation. However, such a gap could signify a learning need and so behaviours have been included here for completeness.

Maintenance needs or future learning needs?

Learning needs can be about maintaining current capability or about looking ahead at the learning needed to meet future changes and developments.

Learning needs which focus on current capabilities are often referred to as **'maintenance learning needs'**; for example:

- at an organisational level, ensuring that there are sufficient staff with the skill sets required to fulfil the organisation's key purpose
- at an individual or team level, maintaining skills and keeping knowledge up to date, in order to remain competent in a job role.

Learning needs which are about developing readiness for future changes can be referred to as **'future learning needs'** or **'development learning needs'**; for example:

- at an organisational level, preparing for the introduction of a new product or service
- at an individual level, preparing for a significant change to job role or to take on an additional responsibility.

Or not learning needs at all?

It is important to remember that performance problems do not always signify a learning need. We have already mentioned that behaviours may not always be linked to a learning need – and this holds for other factors too. If teams consistently fail to meet required outcomes, there may be a recruitment need (not enough people to do the job) or a system problem (insufficient or inappropriate equipment, cumbersome procedures) or an interpersonal issue (conflict within the team or between team member and manager). Before acting on an apparent learning need, we need to be very clear that learning is indeed the correct solution.

LEARNING NEED OR SYSTEM NEED?

An equipment hire company commissioned software training for staff whose job involved booking out hired equipment in a computerised control system. The system required staff to enter an item code, relating to the item of equipment being booked out. Frequent mistakes in inputting these codes meant that the system rarely gave an accurate picture of stock in and out – hence the decision to commission the training.

The staff attended the training and performed competently. The long complex item codes could be located and copied fairly easily in a training environment, where staff sat at desks and were not under time or other work pressures. However the training had no impact on the level of mistakes in the workplace, and even angered some staff who felt their valid complaints about the unwieldy system were being ignored.

In the workplace, item codes had often faded or been rubbed off equipment which meant staff had to refer to item lists, where it was easy to misread a code or inadvertently select the one above or below the code required. When the system was eventually adapted, so that items could be located by simply using the name of the item as a 'keyword', the level of mistakes immediately fell to almost zero.

DIFFERENT LEVELS OF LEARNING NEED AND HOW THEY ARISE

Many organisations operate on an objective-led structure, where the organisation's vision, mission and goals lead into strategic plans. These plans then feed through into the activities and objectives of teams and ultimately into the job descriptions and targets of each individual. This is represented in Figure 4.2.

Figure 4.2 An objective-led structure

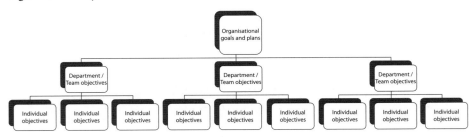

Learning needs can exist at any of these levels. For example, learning needs at an **organisational level** may exist as a result of:

- the need to maintain a sufficiently skilled workforce to achieve organisational purpose
- succession planning
- regulation and compliance requirements
- changes in organisational strategy
- development of new products and services

- mergers and acquisitions
- downsizing and rightsizing of the business operations
- changes in the workforce demographics or working patterns
- changing trends in customer needs
- availability of technology and technological developments
- changes in the organisation's operating environment
- changes in legislation and government policy.

At the next level, there will be team learning needs, which apply to a whole team, department, function or local area. The team could be a project team, as well as a work team.

Team (department or function) learning needs may exist as a result of:

- the need to develop and maintain the skills and knowledge required to fulfil team objectives
- a need to improve team effectiveness or work results
- team re-organisation or changes to team make-up
- new products or services affecting the team
- new technology or changes to specific team work practices
- factors external to the organisation which affect one area of the business more than others.

And at an **individual level**, individual learning needs may exist as a result of:

- induction for new starters
- the need to develop and maintain the skills required to fulfil job requirements
- individual compliance requirements, such as licences or certificates
- individual performance issues and challenges
- promotion or temporary additional responsibilities
- changes or potential changes to job role
- continuous professional development
- qualification requirements
- aspirations and career planning.

Learning needs can also be common to a group of individuals who are not necessarily a team, for example: all managers, all customer service representatives, everyone who accesses a particular IT system, everyone affected by changed legislation, everyone who is to be involved with a new product or service.

Group learning needs are likely to exist for many of the same reasons as individual learning needs, particularly:

- induction

- the development of basic skills and knowledge to fulfil role requirements
- refresher or update training
- changes or additions to job role
- internal changes affecting the identified group, such as new IT systems, new products or services
- external changes affecting the group, such as new legislation.

As you can see in the lists above, learning needs may arise as a result of internal factors such as the development of a new product, or external factors such as changed legislation.

REFLECTIVE ACTIVITY

What have been your main learning needs over the last year or so? What caused them to arise?

Were they about maintaining existing abilities or developing new ones?

Did they just apply to you or to your whole team or organisation?

CASE STUDY 4.2

RIDINGS COMPUTERS: AN EXERCISE IN IDENTIFYING LEARNING NEEDS

Ridings Computers was established eight years ago by Sam Ridings. The company sells, installs, maintains and repairs computers and is the approved local supplier for BBB computers. Ridings also stocks and sells a limited supply of computer consumables, mainly cartridges, paper and storage media.

The sales team, Sam and his colleague, Jovian, are rarely in the office, preferring to get out and see existing and potential clients. Ridings also sell products via their website but Sam is aware that the site is not as effective as it could be – especially for an IT company. Sam has delegated responsibility for developing the website to Jovian and Susanna, who recently joined Ridings as a trainee, which seemed an ideal scenario as Susanna has basic web development skills and Jovian knows everything about Ridings' sales procedures. However, neither of the two have shown much enthusiasm and the developments have still to happen.

System installation and maintenance is looked after by Jenna, Tony and TK. All three are IT graduates and very capable, especially Jenna, who is the most experienced. They get on well together, and with Susanna who seems keen to learn, but get frustrated with the sales team who have a tendency to promise unrealistic deadlines – and in Jovian's case, sometimes sell incompatible equipment. They also get irritated by having to deal with an increasing number of stationery and consumables orders, when they are trying to focus on complex installations or maintenance work.

Along with Sam, Jovian, Susanna, Jenna, Paul and TK, Ridings also employs Hanna, who is responsible for general administration and Chris, who is part-time and looks after the accounts. Hanna knows her admin job 'inside-out' and is looking for more challenge. She would like to interact with customers more, maybe getting involved with the consumables side of the business, but is concerned that she lacks the technical knowledge for this. She has discussed this with Chris, who thought it was a great idea and that he could also help out. This worried Hanna a little, as there is a general rule in the organisation to 'keep Chris away from customers', as his unintentionally brusque manner has spoilt a few good customer relationships in the past.

Chris makes up for this by doing a great job looking after the company's finances. He has set up excellent accounting and control systems which provide the information everyone needs within minutes. To keep things this way though, Chris refuses to let anyone else learn how to use the system – which causes problems on the days he is not in the office.

On the whole, the company is doing well. Sam has recently had some concerns that BBB Computers are losing their edge in the market-place and has begun negotiating a new dealership with MM Computers – an emerging and increasingly well thought of brand. Also, thanks to the excellent work of Jenna, Paul and TK, Ridings has a great reputation for supporting customers and there are some big contracts on the horizon. What's more, since the local stationery superstore re-located a few months ago, the consumables side of the business has really started to take off and could be a real development area for the business.

What learning needs – organisational, team group or individual – seem to exist within Ridings Computers?

LEARNING NEEDS ANALYSIS – IN PRACTICE

Learning needs analysis is a means of monitoring an organisation's (or individual's) capability, in terms of having the required skills, knowledge and behaviours, to fulfil its objectives.

The main objectives of a learning needs analysis are therefore to:

- determine current capability
- determine desired or required capability
- identify any gaps between the two
- identify how these gaps might best be filled.

In practice this might mean determining and comparing any of the capabilities and gaps shown in Table 4.2.

Table 4.2 **Learning needs analysis**

Current position	Gaps	Required position
Actual capability to meet work objectives	<------>	Capability required to meet all work objectives
Capabilities required to meet current demands	<------>	Capabilities required to meet new and emerging demands

Methods to determine or analyse current capabilities include: observation, discussion, manager feedback, customer feedback, questionnaires, testing, examining work results, examining performance or financial data and competitor benchmarking. Several of these methods are explored in more detail below.

Establishing the required position or the required capability may involve some of the same methods mentioned above and additional methods, such as: observing or interviewing staff who are particularly experienced or effective in the role or activity, or interviewing line managers re their expectations.

You may also find that required capabilities are already specified in:

- job descriptions
- role, procedure or task specifications
- internal or external standards of competence
- industry or external quality standards
- models of excellent performance
- CIPD's HR profession map.

REFLECTIVE ACTIVITY 2

How do you know what knowledge, skills and behaviours are required of you at work?

What information could you use to measure yourself against in order to identify any current or future learning needs?

METHODS FOR IDENTIFYING AND ANALYSING LEARNING NEEDS

"An L&D professional should never be afraid to ask their client or manager for an opportunity to spend time with, or even work in, an area of the business before getting involved with their training. Expanding awareness of roles, tasks, and challenges is the best way of understanding learning requirements."

Heather Nielson-Cox, Neilson-Cox Training Ltd

The CIPD Learning and Development Survey (2009) reports that L&D specialists still take primary responsibility for determining learning needs – although the involvement of line managers continues to increase. Below are some of the methods they are using.

Method 1: Interviews and discussions: The most important factor in identifying learning needs is to communicate with the people or individual involved. They are likely to understand the issues more than anyone.

Discussions relating to team or business area learning needs are likely to be held between a manager or representative from the area and an L&D professional, and will focus on:

- reasons for learning needs
- required capabilities
- current capabilities
- perceived gaps
- preferences re how gaps are filled
- logistics and constraints such as timing or resource issues.

Where the analysis is in relation to an individual, the discussion might be between the individual and their line manager or the individual and an L&D practitioner.

The content of an individual learning needs discussion will be similar to that listed above, but because it is about an individual, there are other factors to consider. For example, an individual learner may feel nervous about the discussion or defensive about admitting to learning needs, and extra thought should be given clarifying the purpose of the discussion and putting the learner at ease.

USEFUL STAGES IN A LEARNING NEEDS INTERVIEW:

- Put the job-holder at ease.
- Explain the purpose of the meeting.
- Ask the job holder about their current role (or aspirations). What is important about the role? What is its key purpose?
- Ask what knowledge, skills and behaviours are needed in order for the job to be carried out well. At this stage, the job holder is not assessing their own skills, but describing the skills of people who do the job well. A good question here is 'if I wanted to be good at your job, what would I need to know or do?'
- Ask about the knowledge, skills and behaviours the job holder actually has, possibly reviewing any evidence of this with them.
- Discuss and identify where there are gaps and check with the job holder how filling that gap would improve their performance.
- Discuss possible ways in which the performance gaps could be overcome.
- Agree and record.

Method 2: Examining documentation

There is likely to be a range of information already available in organisations to inform learning needs analysis. For example:

Key performance indicators: many organisations plan and measure their achievement in important areas through key performance indicators (KPIs). KPIs will tell an organisation how it is doing in the areas it considers most vital to success, eg sales, costs, production times, customer feedback, etc. Looking at actual performance against targets can give an indication of a learning need, especially where there has been an under-performance – although there may, of course, be other factors to blame for this.

Performance management records: most organisations have some system of tracking individual performance, such as appraisal or staff development records. Reviewing this documentation, or summaries of it, can highlight:

- specific individual or team learning needs
- general training needs which seem to apply across the organisation or across a particular role or group
- systems or procedures that may be causing problems
- management behaviours or approaches which could be improved
- emerging trends and work developments which indicate future learning needs.

Customer feedback: information from customers and service users can be an excellent source of information about possible learning needs. Comments, complaints and even compliments can all give an indicator of specific areas where there may be a gap in some aspect of capability.

External information: industry and sector publications will highlight emerging trends which may form the basis of future learning needs. Information about oncoming changes to legislation and work practices, provided by professional bodies such as CIPD, will also help organisations identify future learning needs, in good time.

THE FIVE WHYS

When looking for answers, it can be tempting to take information at 'face-value' rather than digging deeper to get to the root cause of an issue. When looking for learning needs it is also essential to distinguish whether the problem is caused by a learning gap or by something else. One of the simplest ways of uncovering root cause is to keep asking the question 'why?'

With this technique, you identify an issue and then ask yourself, or the people most likely to know, 'why is this (A) happening?'

When that question is answered, (say the answer is B) the question 'so why is this (B) happening' is asked.

When an answer is given (say the answer is C), the question is again repeated 'so why is (C) happening?' and so on.

The same line of questioning is repeated until the issue has been taken apart and examined at the most basic level. Five is not necessarily a magic number. The key is to keep asking 'Why?' until the most basic cause has been uncovered.

Method 3: Using an analysis model: SWOT

SWOT analysis is a useful way of starting a learning needs analysis and of engaging people in the process. It can be used in relation to a whole organisation, a work team, project team, group or individual. In Chapter 2 we used the SWOT model as a means of developing understanding of the organisation, and as SWOT leads us to explore both current performance and potential future performance it can also be a useful indicator of learning needs.

SWOT stands for: **S**trengths, **W**eaknesses, **O**pportunities, **T**hreats.

In an organisational context, strengths and weaknesses are usually 'internal factors', things that are happening within the organisation:

- Strengths are the things that an organisation is good at and which it may be able to build upon, to help it to achieve its goals.

- Weaknesses are the things that can let the organisation down and may get in the way of success, if they are not somehow addressed or compensated for.

Opportunities and threats are usually 'external factors', things in the wider world that may impact on the organisation:

- Opportunities are those things that an organisation could take advantage of if they prepare ahead.

- Threats are factors which could have an adverse effect on the business, and may require some avoidant action or damage limitation.

It is useful to get as many views and contributions to the SWOT as possible to bring out lots of ideas. An organisational SWOT will be more accurate and informative if different people within, and possibly external to, the organisation are involved. A team SWOT analysis will be most useful and meaningful if all team members are involved and able to contribute.

In Chapter 2 we looked at a SWOT for an organisation, the example below reflects a team based SWOT analysis, in this case, for a new customer relations team.

Strengths	Weaknesses
Team get on well	Team admin resource not yet recruited – will be external recruit
All qualified in technical aspect of role	
High technical expertise	Team newly formed – still some uncertainty around specific roles
Lots of contacts in the organisation	
Good at building relationships across the organisation	Not much experience in dealing with difficult or complex customer issues
Established procedures, based on good customer service practice	Remote working limits team communication and 'bonding'
Opportunities	**Threats**
New team, new start	High-performance targets to be met
New IT system could lead to new and better ways of communicating across team	New system could prove difficult to operate

Chance to develop new skills in customer relations	Lack of customer relations skills could lead to wrong decisions or wrong advice (could be legal issues to tackle)
Team and individual roles could expand and develop if successful	Lack of communication could mean essential details are not passed on
Good customer records available for follow-up contact	Customers might feel hassled
New loyalty products available to offer customers	Technical skills could become outdated
Chance to contribute in a very obvious way to the organisation	Risk of team not being successful and being discontinued

This analysis suggests potential learning needs for everyone in general customer care and relations skills, related legal issues and the operation of the new IT systems. There may also be a need for the team manager to undertake some training in managing a remote team and for all the team to consider how they can best facilitate good team communications. The team manager may also consider undertaking some team development activities with the whole team, and thought needs to be given to the induction of the new admin person. Finally, to ensure team members remain technically competent, there is a need for ongoing CPD or refresher activities in relation to each team member's technical areas.

Method 4: Individual assessment, observation and testing

A more precise way of identifying learning needs is to undertake direct assessment activities – such as observation or testing.

Observation is particularly useful for practical skills such as interviewing a client or repairing a heating system. Typically, an observation would be done against specific standards or requirements, such as, internal or external performance standards, quality standards or specific qualification criteria.

Tests can take various forms from simple knowledge tests, through to formal, in-depth occupational tests. They may focus on technical knowledge, basic skills – literacy, language and numeracy – or practical work skills. There are also a wide range of psychometric tests available which test behaviours and personality styles.

It is crucial that tests and assessments are operated within clear and fair guidelines and that methods used are valid for the type of assessment being undertaken. For example it would usually be inappropriate to ask someone to write an essay in order to demonstrate their basic plumbing skills! A much better way would be to observe them actually using these skills in the workplace.

Some formal tests and assessments require that the people operating them are trained or licensed as assessors – and, as a minimum, assessors should be competent in what they are assessing and have a good understanding of the criteria they are assessing against. Before operating a formal test or assessment it is important to check guidelines and requirements with the test provider.

There are many pre-designed tests and assessments available commercially and from educational or professional bodies. The CIPD, for example, provides a range of practical assessment tasks for HR and L&D professionals, and some other references are provided at the end of this chapter.

If we can assess or test knowledge and skills before learning, it will enable us to better measure the impact of learning activities later on. The same tests or assessments can be repeated after learning has taken place, giving a measure of how knowledge and skills have improved.

Method 5: Developing a skills matrix

Developing a skills matrix can be a really useful way of exploring learning needs within a team.

With this technique, you begin by listing all of the separate skill areas or activities involved in the team's work. This could come from job descriptions, team objectives, or by getting team members to analyse the skills or activities involved in their roles.

Each team member's abilities, based on direct assessment, qualifications or self-rating, are then marked against each of the activities on the matrix. The resulting pattern gives a very visual indication of where there may be gaps.

For example, Figure 4.3 is a skills matrix for a catering team within a large leisure centre.

Figure 4.3 Skills matrix example 1

Team	Food hygiene	Ordering & stock	Receive delivery	Menu	Cold food prep	Hot food prep	Bakery	Service	Cash till	Wash up	Super-vise	Assess
AJ	✓	✓	✓	✓	✓	✓	✓	✓	✓	✓	✓	
BM	✓	✓	✓	✓	✓	✓		✓	✓	✓	✓	✓
CJ	✓	✓	✓	✓	✓	✓		✓	✓	✓		
DG	✓		✓		✓	✓	✓	✓		✓		
EL	✓				✓					✓		
FR	✓				✓			✓				
GA	✓				✓							

In this version, the matrix just shows who is deemed competent or not competent within each activity. A more sophisticated version might give more information about the level of competence of each team member, say on a scale of 0–3, where

0 = no training or experience, 1 = trained but no experience, 2 = trained and some experience, 3 = fully competent.

Knowing which team members are fully competent also helps identify who could coach or role-model the skills for the other team members.

Of course, not all of the gaps in the 'boxes' need to be filled. It may only be necessary for some team members to have some of the skills. Again, the matrix can be adapted to reflect this, as in Figure 4.4.

Figure 4.4 Skills matrix example 2

Team	Food hygiene	Ordering & stock	Receive delivery	Menu	Cold food prep	Hot food prep	Bakery	Service	Cash till	Wash up	Super -vise	Assess
AJ	3	3	3	3	3	3	3	3	3	3	3	1
BM	3	3	3	3	3	3		3	3	3	2	3
CJ	3	1	2	2	3	3		3	1	3		
DG	3	0	2		3	2	3	3	0	2		
EL	3				3	2		0		2		
FR	3				2	1		1		1		
GA	3				1	1				1		

Here, the shaded boxes reflect where the skill area is a requirement of a team member's job, and the rating indicates the level of competence reached by that team member.

Skills matrices can be adapted to fit different contexts and requirements. As a bonus, users report they can also be motivational, as team members like to see themselves well represented in the visual matrix.

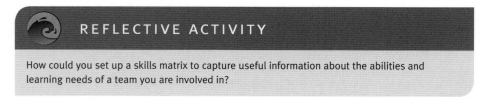

REFLECTIVE ACTIVITY

How could you set up a skills matrix to capture useful information about the abilities and learning needs of a team you are involved in?

Method 6: Focus groups

Focus groups are useful to identify the learning needs of a particular work role or of groups within the organisation. In this context, a focus group would bring together representatives of the role or groups being analysed to explore their potential learning needs.

CASE STUDY 4.3

INTRODUCING A NEW FINANCIAL PRODUCT

When a national bank launches a new product – such as a different type of investment account – this is likely to create learning needs for a wide range of people across the organisation. For example, a new product could affect the work of call centre staff, branch staff, customer relations staff, back office/processing teams, marketing and merchandising teams, and general managers.

To ensure everyone's learning needs are recognised and appropriately addressed, the central training team holds focus groups for one or two representatives from each affected area (ideally 10 to 12 people). The group then explores the training implications of the product launch from everyone's different angle. The kind of issues discussed include:

- How will the new product impact on different areas?

- How will the new product impact on how areas work together?

- How will this change current ways of working?

- What will different areas need to know about the product?

- What other learning needs might the launch generate for different areas? (eg in relation to new systems involved or new customer groups)?

- How many people are affected in each area?

- What are the best ways of up-skilling different areas?

- How will this fit with other training initiatives in the area?

- What logistical issues might get in the way of training?

Having collected this information the central team has a full picture of requirements to help them design an appropriate overall learning solution. A second focus group is likely to be held to review the proposed solution and check that all needs are being fully addressed before the training is implemented.

Method 7: Questionnaires and surveys

Questionnaires can be used to help individuals prepare for a learning needs discussion or as the basis of larger-scale (group)learning needs surveys.

Questionnaires can be designed to capture whatever type of information is required, including quantitative data (data that is easily measured – such as percentage improvements, statistics, definite responses such as 'yes' or 'no' or selections from multiple choice answers – questions 1, 2, 4 and 5 in the questionnaire in Figure 4.5, for example) or qualitative information such as general opinion and personal comments (question 6 in Figure 4.5).

In a learning needs scenario, questionnaires will focus on performance requirements, performance issues, self-assessment of capabilities, views on potential improvements and personal aspirations.

The example in Figure 4.5 was developed by a training centre to start collecting information on their assessor team's learning needs.

Figure 4.5 Questionnaire

Learning needs analysis for assessor team					
Name:		Location:			
1. What assessor qualifications do you hold? None ☐ D32 ☐ D33 ☐ A1 ☐ Other ☐ – please specify:					
2. Please rate your self from 0–4 (0 = no knowledge/competence, 1 = low competence/awareness, 2 = moderate competence/awareness, 3 = high competence/awareness, 4 = confident to train others):					
	0	1	2	3	4
Developing assessment plans					
Assessment of assignment					
Assessment by observation					
Assessment of work evidence					
Assessment by Q&A					
Assessment by professional discussion					
Assessment of candidate reports					
Assessment of witness testimony					
Assessment of prior learning					
Special assessment needs					
Giving feedback					
Identifying development needs					
Interim assessment & records					
Summative assessment & records					
The electronic portfolio system					
IV role & working with the IV					
How the centre works with the awarding body					
Preparing for the EV visit					
Appeals and complaints procedures					
Assessor occupational competence requirements					
Assessor cpd requirements					
3. Any other areas where you feel further training or support would benefit you in your assessor role?					
4. Please specify your preferred learning method: Workshop ☐ Reading material ☐ On-line ☐ 1:1 IV Support ☐ Mix/no preference ☐					
5. Please specify your availability/preferred timing? ½ day ☐ lunchtime ☐ full day ☐ evening ☐ specific day/time ☐ – please specify:					
6. Any other information about your learning needs and preferences in relation to your assessor role?					

These same questions could be covered in interviews or focus groups, but questionnaires allow respondents more time to reflect on the questions as well as providing a written record of their responses. Importantly they also allow information to be collected from larger numbers of people.

The questionnaire above could be quickly and easily converted into an on-line survey document. Some very effective systems which are freely available (for basic functions) can be found via an internet search or the references given at the end of the chapter. Most systems allow you to work through pre-set design steps and access 'templates' which make the creation of on-line questionnaires relatively easy. E-mail addresses are added to the system so that all relevant people can be included and the survey is automatically sent to all, with an invitation to respond (other ways for people to access the survey are also available). Respondents then complete the survey on-line, selecting the relevant 'buttons' for multiple-choice questions or providing qualitative comments, as required. As completed surveys are submitted back into the system, results are automatically collated and analysed. As survey 'owner' you can browse through individual responses, to identify particular individual requirements, or access a range of collated and analysed summary information.

Method 8: Performance review and 360° feedback

Performance review or appraisal is one of the most commonly used methods of assessing learning and development needs. As appraisal is generally about reviewing current performance and agreeing objectives for future performance, it is often a timely occasion to also discuss learning needs.

Performance review is often a culmination of a number of assessment activities, including self-reflection, manager observation, feedback from colleagues and customers, and examination of work results. These factors form the basis of a discussion where any gaps in current or future capability can be explored and agreed and consideration given to how gaps can best be filled.

Some organisations separate performance review from development review so that development can be explored 'in the round', rather than just being seen as a response to performance issues.

Most appraisals/performance reviews and development reviews are carried out by line managers, supported by the L&D function.

360° feedback in this context refers to an activity where feedback is collected from people positioned *all around* (hence 360°) the subject – eg the subject's manager, the subject's colleagues and people managed by the subject.

This method of 'assessing' performance through the gathering and analysis of others' opinion has grown in popularity over the last few years, to a point where a number of organisations now specialise in just providing this service. However, the process can be managed internally, with L&D taking a co-ordinating role.

Whether co-ordinated internally or externally, the process involves the collection, analysis and summarising of comments which are then presented back, in a balanced manner, to the individual involved. Findings from 360° feedback can provide useful information to inform a further discussion about learning needs.

RECOMMENDING LEARNING SOLUTIONS

Once learning needs information has been collected and analysed, the next stage is to recommend suitable ways of providing the necessary learning. However, there are a number of important factors to consider before making a recommendation, including:

Priorities

- If budgets are insufficient to fulfil all learning needs, which needs are most important?
- Which needs are most closely linked to business objectives?
- Which learning needs are having most impact on performance?
- What learning will have most impact on long-term success?
- What learning is most urgent?

Organisational policy and culture

- What policies, procedures or guidelines govern access to learning?
- Who are key stakeholders in relation to the learning need and what are their expectations?
- Is there an expected or preferred way of delivering the learning in the organisation (eg e-learning or a particular training supplier)?
- To what extent is adherence to usual practice expected? How much freedom is there to 'try something new'?

Financial factors

- What budget is available?
- Is any funding available from external sources?
- Comparative costs of solutions – for example, would it be better value to commission an in-house training course for several learners or for individuals to attend an external event? Or could one person be trained, who could then coach others?
- What are the 'opportunity costs' – ie business lost during staff downtime?
- Taking opportunity costs into account could mean that more expensive 'quicker' training costs less in real terms, than cheaper training which involves more time away from the workplace.
- What return can be expected from different training options – might one give better return on investment (ROI), even if it involves higher initial outlay?

Ref to ELP 12 – Return on Investment

Timing and time-scales

- How urgent is it to fulfil the need? Can learners wait for an ideal solution to be developed, or is the training needed immediately?

- Does everyone have to be trained at once, or can learning be 'staged'?

- How can learning be arranged to best fit with operational schedules?

Equality of opportunity factors

- Is organisational budget being fairly allocated across different groups and individuals?

- Legislative requirements – eg providing training for some groups and not others on the basis of race, age, gender or to some extent, employment status is likely to be unlawful. Are discriminatory assumptions being made eg 'older people cannot learn new skills'?

- How will timing, location and logistics of training fit with staff's individual situations – working hours, care commitments, ability to travel. What flexibility is there?

- Are there any unfair barriers to accessing learning, eg a need for equipment or particular skills, such as IT skills to access e-learning?

- How will learning accommodate different learning styles, levels and preferences?

Learner factors

- Characteristics and preferences of adult learners, including: being involved in learning decisions and being treated like adults, not children.

- Learning styles and group learning solutions – how can a mix of learning styles and preferences be accommodated?

- Learning styles and individual learning solutions – should learning methods reflect individual learning style and preferences?

> Ref to ELP 7 – Principles of adult learning

> Ref to ELP 3 – Learning styles

Options for learning and development solutions

When we consider the different types of learning needs that can exist, the different combinations of people that can be involved and the many factors that can impact on choice of learning, we can see that there is a need for a range of different learning solutions. Whilst traditional options – often a training course – still have a major role to play in learning and development, there are several other possibilities to consider.

Table 4.3 **Professional course**

Solution	Professional qualification course
Overview	Learners study and/or undergo assessment to gain a professional qualification – such as CIPD
Good for	Developing and accrediting specialist staff
Pros	Shows commitment to professionalism and can aid career progression Shows a commitment to staff (if funded or supported by the organisation) May meet essential legal or professional requirement required for staff to practice – eg legal or accounting qualifications
Cons	Can be expensive and time consuming There may be limited opportunity to put the learning into practice The qualification 'content' and learning may not relate fully to job role

Table 4.4 **Externally run course**

Solution	Externally run training course
Overview	Group-based training event delivered outside the organisation, usually by professionals (experts?) in the subject area
Good for	Developing specific skills or specialist knowledge
Pros	Can select most appropriate provider Should be delivered by experts in the field A chance to get away from the pressures of the workplace and reflect on practice Can provide a forum to meet with, and learn from, staff from other organisations
Cons	May be costly May be difficult to release several staff members at once Likely to be generic rather than tailored to individual or organisational needs Difficult to control/influence quality of training

Table 4.5 **Internally run course**

Solution	Internally run training course
Overview	Group-based training event delivered by and within the organisation ('in-house')
Good for	Skills or knowledge; training specific to the organisation
Pros	Can be tailored to specific needs Subject can be positioned within an organisational context Opportunity for everyone to get 'a common message' Activities and case studies etc likely to relate to real work Timing and logistics can be tailored to organisational arrangements May be more accessible for staff to attend Organisation controls quality of training

Cons	There may not be the right expertise in-house – either in subject or in training skills
	No 'outsider perspective' – internal 'bad habits' may be compounded
	May be difficult to release several staff members at once
	Learners less likely to 'cut off' from work demands to focus on learning

Table 4.6 **On-the-job training**

Solution	**On-the-job training**
Overview	Learning in the workplace through real work activities
Good for	Learning essential job skills
Pros	Very timely – training as it is needed
	Learner learns the 'realities of the job'
	Training done by an expert in the job
	May help engage learner's manager in the training
	No major reduction in work time
Cons	Might lose out on the bigger picture
	No time to reflect on learning or ask questions
	Pressures of workplace might detract from quality of training
	Learner might feel uneasy about admitting weaknesses

Table 4.7 **Shadowing**

Solution	**Job shadowing**
Overview	Watching someone else performing their role
Good for	Widening knowledge of other roles; preparing for new roles
Pros	Gives the bigger picture
	Learner sees what is involved before 'being thrown in at the deep end'
	Chance to learn 'the reality of the job' from experienced person
Cons	Possibility that the person demonstrating the role may not be getting it right
	Can be tedious if done for long periods
	Benefits may not justify time-spend

Table 4.8 **Job swapping**

Solution	**Job swaps**
Overview	Swapping jobs to learn new aspects of a role
Good for	Learning new skills and understanding impact of own work on others' work
Pros	Can keep 'business as usual' going whilst learning takes place
	Helps towards multi-skilling of a team
Cons	Needs at least two people who are ready to swap
	May cause temporary disruption in the early stages

Table 4.9 **Projects**

Solution	Projects
Overview	Learning new skills by taking part in a project
Good for	New skills or knowledge; personal career development
Pros	Project gets done as well as individuals getting development Learner can immerse themselves in the project
Cons	May have to provide job cover whilst project is taking place Learner may feel over-stretched if they have to continue with their own work as well

Table 4.10 **Coaching**

Solution	Coaching
Overview	Having one-to-one learning/coaching sessions
Good for	Developing skills. Improving behaviours. Developing confidence
Pros	Tailored to individual needs Develops learner responsibility for own development
Cons	Coach needs to have good coaching skills Coach style may clash with learner style

See Chapter 8 for more details on coaching in the workplace

Table 4.11 **Mentoring**

Solution	Mentoring
Overview	Getting support from an independent source
Good for	Building confidence; improving behaviours
Pros	Attention focused on individual needs Can cover a wide range of areas
Cons	Line manager role may be unclear and could alienate them Dependent on availability of mentors.

See Chapter 9 for more details on mentoring in the workplace

Table 4.12 **Peer learning**

Solution	Action learning set/peer learning
Overview	Groups meet together to support each other through work projects and share learning and ideas
Good for	Getting new ideas, different perspectives
Pros	Learn from others' experiences Saves time in learning Outlet for discussing and resolving workplace frustrations Encourages ownership of learning and action

Cons	Dependant on others wanting the same format
	Takes time away from the workplace
	Can be difficult to sustain a group – requires discipline and commitment

Table 4.13 **Self-study**

Solution	E-learning, reading, workbooks (self-study)
Overview	Learner manages own learning through pre-prepared modules
Good for	Acquiring knowledge
Pros	Flexible in terms of access – as and when required
	Inexpensive if used for large number of learners
	Learner can work at own pace
Cons	Knowledge may not be retained without some application
	Learners miss stimulation of learning with others
	Requires self-discipline to sustain
	May require extra equipment or IT skills to access

Presenting a recommendation for learning

Finally, having collected and analysed learning need information and identified potential solutions, you will need to present your conclusions back to key stakeholders.

A formally written Learning Needs Analysis report or recommendation should include:

- an introduction and reasons for the learning needs analysis
- a summary of the methods used and information collected
- an overview of existing capabilities
- details of required capabilities
- needs identified and prioritised
- recommendations for learning.

WHAT NEXT

LEARNING NEEDS ANALYSIS

1. Look into your own organisation's methods for conducting a learning needs analysis. How is it carried out in your organisation and who by? How quickly does the organisation recognise and respond to learning needs? Is there room for improvement in this approach? What improvements would you recommend?

2. Log on to an on-line survey site and have a go at developing a questionnaire you could use to survey learning needs for a particular group of people.

3. Find someone who would benefit from clarifying their learning needs and undertake a learning needs interview with them.

4. Consider the various learning solutions discussed above:

   – which ones have you experienced?
   – which work best for your personal learning preference?
   – which ones work best for each of Honey and Mumford's four learning styles?

5. Finally, have a look at the case study below and consider:

   – how would you help Andrea to identify her learning needs?
   – if help was not available, how could Andrea identify her own learning needs?
   – having uncovered the needs, what solutions do you think might help?

CASE STUDY 4.4

AN INDIVIDUAL LEARNING NEEDS ANALYSIS: ANDREA

Andrea works for a large Metropolitan Council. When she joined the council 21 years ago she was an administrator in the Pensions Team, which was then part of the HR function. In 1996 the administration of the pension fund was transferred to a newly-formed body which took over the pensions administration for several councils in the region.

At the time of that transfer, many of Andrea's colleagues moved to other jobs– either in the new pensions body (based in a town 40 miles away), or elsewhere within the Council. Andrea, however, remained in the HR team as a Pension Liaison Officer; giving advice to staff who were members of the scheme and helping to maintain good communications between the Council and the Pensions Body.

A review of roles within the Council has now shown that Andrea's role is no longer necessary, it can be absorbed within other HR roles. As there has also been a recent reduction in other HR staff numbers it seems likely that Andrea will need to seek redeployment within the next six months.

There may be similarly graded posts available in other part of the Council; in areas such as debt recovery and neighbourhood initiatives on anti-social behaviour.

Andrea has expressed a concern that she has 'only ever done one job', and has requested help to identify and address learning needs which will help her to prepare for the changes ahead.

SUMMARY

This chapter has explored:

The reasons for analysing learning needs

- There are many potential benefits of undertaking regular learning needs analysis, including: a well-trained workforce, greater employee satisfaction with the organisation, greater customer and stakeholder satisfaction, increased competitive advantage and better targeting of the L&D budget on learning activities.

Different types of learning needs and why they arise

- Learning needs arise for many different reasons and at different levels – organisational, team, group and individual.

- Organisational learning needs may occur because of internal or external changes, and the need to maintain an appropriately skilled workforce.

- Team learning needs may occur because of a need to maintain or improve team performance, or because of changes to the team's structure or work practices.

- Individual learning needs arise because of new responsibilities, changes to job role, changes to work practice, individual aspirations, CPD requirements and career planning.

Methods for identifying learning needs

- Methods for identifying learning needs include: interviews and discussions, examining documentation, using analysis models, assessment observation and testing, developing skills matrices, focus groups, questionnaires, surveys and performance reviews.

Factors affecting the recommendation of a learning solution

- We should consider the needs and preferences of the learners as well as the needs of the organisation.

- We should ensure that learning activities do not unnecessarily exclude certain learner groups or individual learners.

- Decisions may be affected by organisational culture and past experience as well as practical factors such as costs, timing and availability.

- We should consider costs in terms of 'staff down-time' as well as the costs of the learning activity.

Features of different learning activities

- Different types of learning activities include: courses, job-based training, coaching, mentoring and self-directed learning.

- Each activity has different advantages and disadvantages.

- We should choose activities which are the best fit for the learner, the organisation and the particular context of the learning need.

EXPLORE FURTHER

BOOKS:

Boydell, T. and Leary, M. (1996) *Identifying training needs*. London: CIPD.

WEBSITES:

CIPD factsheet on Identifying Learning Needs:

www.cipd.co.uk/subjects/lrnanddev/trainingneeds/idtlneeds.htm

Free (or partially free) on-line access to learning needs analysis tools:

www.businessballs.com

www.businesslink.gov.uk (select employment and skills)

On-line survey providers (free for basic level usage):

www.freeonlinesurveys.com

www.surveymonkey.com

www.smart-survey.co.uk

Range of free (or partially free) information, advice and assessment tools relating to health, safety and well-being at work:

www.hse.gov.uk

www.iosh.co.uk/information_and_resources.aspx

www.cipd.co.uk/subjects/health/general

CIPD data protection factsheet:

www.cipd.co.uk/subjects/emplaw/dataprot/dataprotec.htm

CHAPTER 5

Designing Learning and Development Activities

INTRODUCTION

This chapter begins with a consideration of why good training design is important and some clarification of design activities. We continue with an in-depth exploration of the factors which affect design and a look at some of the principles and theories which inform practice in this area. Along the way we consider good practice in setting objectives, determining and sequencing learning content and selecting learning methods. Finally we consider the benefits and challenges of a range of learning activities and training approaches for learning programmes and sessions.

LEARNING OUTCOMES

When you have read this chapter you should be able to:

- explain what good training design means and why it is important
- discuss key factors which impact on the design of learning
- explain how to determine objectives and sequence learning content
- describe some examples of key thinking and learning theory which can inform the selection of learning methods
- describe a range of learning methods and training approaches and the relative benefits and challenges of each
- prepare written session notes which include summary information, timings, content and information about resources to be used.

THE IMPORTANCE OF GOOD TRAINING DESIGN

In a previous chapter we explored the benefits of formally identifying learning needs. Being clear about key learning needs, requirements and priorities means resources can be focused on areas of development that will have the most impact on individual and organisational performance.

However, just knowing what we want or need to achieve is not enough. To ensure learning needs are met effectively and in the available timescales we need a carefully planned route to achievement.

> "People do not wander around and then find themselves at the top of Mount Everest."
>
> Zig Ziglar

Good training design is about carefully planning the most effective, most appropriate and most engaging route to achieving desired learning and development.

Understanding training design

The terms 'designing training' and 'designing learning and development activities' encompass a range of different design tasks.

For example, a trainer may be involved in the design of a particular learning activity or material, perhaps a case study or a self-learning resource, to be used as a stand-alone activity or within a wider training session or programme.

Equally a trainer may be involved in designing a learning session which may be delivered separately or within a bigger programme. Designing a learning session is about bringing together a range of training approaches and learner activities to meet a specific area of learning need. This is often for a group of learners, but could also be for an individual.

Finally a trainer may be involved in designing a training or learning programme of learning, combining a range of different learning sessions and activities in a bigger learning experience. For example a learning programme for retail staff, aimed at developing new selling skills, might consist of:

Introductory – group session	⇨	Application in workplace – using 'guide cards'	⇨	Observation assessment in workplace	⇨	1:1 review session with coach	⇨	Further application in workplace	⇨	Review – group session

Whatever the context, good training design combines an understanding of some key training theory and principle with a strong practical understanding of learner and organisation needs and the factors that affect how needs can be met.

Typical stages in designing learning and development activities are:

Clarify requirements and factors which affect design
⇩
Convert requirements to aims and learning outcomes
⇩
Determine and sequence learning content
⇩

Select methods to meet learning needs
⇩
Designing learning materials
⇩
Select assessment activities
⇩
Select evaluation activities
⇩
Produce a plan for the training session or programme
⇩
Agree plan with stakeholders

TRAINING DESIGN – IN PRACTICE

FACTORS AFFECTING THE DESIGN OF LEARNING ACTIVITIES

Clarifying requirements

The first stage in training design is to be absolutely clear about what the design is seeking to achieve.

If there has been a thorough learning needs analysis then much of this information will be available, but there will still be a need to fully clarify requirements.

Perhaps the most crucial area of information, in relation to the success of the training, is to clarify who are the key stakeholders and what exactly are their requirements and expectations. Time spent on this stage is likely to pay off several times over, in terms of best allocation of resources and clarity of criteria for review and later evaluation of the training.

Key stakeholders might be: the learner(s), a team manager, a function or product manager, a project manager, the chief executive – whoever is the main owner of the need. Some stakeholders will have a very clear idea of their requirements whilst others may need some assistance to analyse their own requirements more deeply.

Ask questions such as:

- What do you expect learners (yourself) to be able to do differently as a result of this training?
- What specific outcome/result/situation are you wanting to be brought about by this training?
- What would the best outcome of this training be (or look like) for you?

Having gained this information, it is good practice to confirm it in writing – either within an overall training agreement or an e-mail detailing discussions and agreeing requirements.

Organisational factors

As well as stakeholder requirements, there are other wider organisation concerns to be considered in training design. Some of these are listed below.

ORGANISATIONAL FACTORS WHICH CAN IMPACT ON LEARNING DESIGN

- What are key current business priorities and how does the training relate to and fit in with these?
- What resources – space, equipment, existing learning materials, are available?
- How is the learning to be funded? Is there a specific budget?
- What time-scales are involved? Time available for design? Timings for delivery?
- What is the training culture of the organisation? Is there a strong learning culture (a learning organisation), a general resistance to training, or somewhere in-between?
- What are the organisations preferred training approaches – traditional classroom style, external provision, on-job training, self-managed development?
- How open and adaptive is the organisation to new training methods and systems?
- How important is external accreditation to the organisation? Does this learning initiative link to any external accreditation or qualification processes?
- How do internal or external employment regulations impact on the learning – eg working hours, flexible work, training entitlement?
- Do other legal and organisational requirements impact on the training – eg health and safety, equality legislation, data protection or copyright legislation?
- Who else in the organisation may be affected by this initiative?
- What else is happening in the organisation that might affect or align with this area of learning?
- Has anything similar been done before in the organisation and are there lessons to be learned from this?

Individual factors

At an individual level, consideration needs to be given not only to learning needs, but also to factors which may affect how needs should be met.

Malcolm Knowles, in his 'Theory of Andragogy' discusses how adult learners need to feel responsible for their own decisions and directions, and the negative impact of imposing learning on adults, in the way it might be done more typically for children.

Ref to ELP 7 – Principles of adult learning

The more involvement we can give learners in determining the nature and format of their learning, and the more ownership they feel, then the greater their engagement in the learning is likely to be.

INDIVIDUAL FACTORS THAT AFFECT LEARNING DESIGN

- What does the learner particularly want to achieve from the learning? What are the priorities?
- What is learner's preferred ways of learning and their learning style?
- What is learner's previous experience of learning (positive and negative)? Their self-perception as a learner? Any concerns or barriers to overcome? Learners' likes and dislikes about learning?

- What level of related knowledge and skills which might affect access to learning (eg literacy, IT skills, language skills, numeracy) does the learner have?
- What support is available to the learner beyond the specific learning activity?
- What are learners' personal circumstances (and how might this impact on their learning time, funding, other responsibilities and priorities)?

Obviously the depth to which individual factors can be explored and individual needs accommodated depends on circumstances and the number of learners involved. When working with groups of learners, the prior information collected will be more general but equally important.

GROUP-BASED FACTORS THAT AFFECT LEARNING DESIGN

- Who is the target group – profile and numbers?
- What is their starting point in relation to the learning topic?
- Are certain training methods already in use or preferred by the team/group?
- What constraints are there in relation to time, access, working hours and release for training arrangements?

CONFIRMING REQUIREMENTS

As suggested earlier, once essential information is collected about the required learning activity, it is good practice to capture this information in a summary document – such as a training project plan or training agreement – and seek confirmation from key stakeholders. Smaller initiatives or less formal contexts may be equally served by an e-mail detailing discussions and agreeing requirements.

This documentation and the agreement process itself will not just assist design and evaluation but will also help engage stakeholders in the ongoing training activities.

A training agreement might look like:

TITLE OF TRAINING 'PROJECT'

General requirements/aims/objectives:
What is required of the training – including learning needs and preferences for how learning is delivered?

Scope:
Numbers and profiles of people to be trained and any different levels of training for different groups.

Deliverables:
Outline agreements about what is required of L&D and what can actually be provided in relation to requirements. Say, 'a two-day in-house training programme plus materials to aid transfer of learning to the workplace'.

Resources:
Available people, space, equipment, funding, expertise – especially where it is being made available by stakeholders.

Time scales:
When the training has to be complete. Likely duration of training.

> **Risks:**
> Anything likely to throw the training 'off track' – eg if it is dependant on the availability of a new system or there is a particularly busy work period coming up – and what has been agreed for these circumstances.

AIMS, OBJECTIVES AND LEARNING OUTCOMES

Having thoroughly clarified requirements of the learning activity, the next stage is to convert requirements into specific aims and objectives. As this is a subject with a range of differing approaches, let's begin by considering some definitions and differences.

Aims: aims tend to be fairly general statements, broad ranging and possibly combining a number of intentions into a 'bigger' statement. For example:

- The course aims to develop the skills and knowledge required to operate Cashtime Accounting software.

Aims can be long term or indefinite and, for all the reasons mentioned above, are generally quite difficult to measure. They are, nonetheless, important as they give an overall perspective to the proposed activity.

Objectives: objectives are often considered to be a 'sub-division' of aims – a means of breaking down an aim into measurable chunks. Objectives are more precise and specific than aims and are intended to be measurable. For example:

- List the Cashtime System data input commands.
- State the categories of information held within sales ledger.
- Create an invoice template.

There are a number of guiding principles to assist our specification of objectives:

1. As far back as the 1960s Robert Mager proposed that objectives should be positioned as outcomes and be composed of three elements:

   - a behaviour: what should be done
   - a condition: the context or conditions in which it should be done
   - a standard: the standard to which the outcome should be performed.

   For example:

   - trainees will be able to undertake an outbound sales call, in a real work situation, to the standard set out in XCo's 'Quality Calls' checklist.

While this approach holds true as good practice in devising objectives, it is not always necessary to explicitly state each of the three parts – for example, we often make the assumption that the condition or context is 'in the workplace' or, maybe, that the standard required is 'correctly'. Providing the meaning of any unstated parts of the objective are obvious, this flexibility allows us to write more simple and concise objectives. For example, the following objective may be sufficient when used *within XCo's*: trainees will be able to undertake an outbound sales call.

2. Another popular guiding principle relating to objective setting is SMART. Although more closely linked to the setting of performance objectives, and opinion is divided on whether SMART can always be applied to learning objectives, SMART provides a useful reminder that objectives should seek to be concise and measurable.

Table 5.1 **SMART**

Specific	Objectives should be clearly and simply defined, usually, with a single focus.
Measurable	Objectives should be written in a way that will make it possible to assess/observe/measure whether or not the objective has been met.
Achievable	Objectives should be achievable within the context they are set. Are they supported by the relevant skills, equipment and access? Alternate words sometimes used here are 'agreed' or 'appropriate'.
Relevant	Objectives should be relevant to the context they are set in and aligned to surrounding contexts, eg team or organisational plans. Alternate words used here are 'realistic' (although this is very similar to 'achievable').
Timebound	Objectives should have a related time period, partly to increase motivation to complete, but also to aid accurate measurability against the objective.

Note: Some updated models of SMART are extended to SMARTER, where E represents Exciting or Ethical, and R represents Recorded, Rewarded or Re-visited.

One slight problem with setting objectives is that, because they are so useful, they have a range of different applications – for example, we often have performance objectives at work, as trainers we have objectives for our training activity, and this book has chapter objectives – and the wording of objectives can vary slightly depending on how they are being used.

In a learning context, objectives are most useful when they are written from the point of view of the learner, not the trainer. They should also focus on outcomes, ie what learners will be able to do as a result of the learning, rather than inputs, ie what they will spend time doing during the training.

Trainer (and inputs) point of view:

● to teach learners how to apply a dressing to an open wound

● to provide an opportunity to practice applying dressings.

Learner (and outcomes) point of view:

● learners will be able to select appropriate dressings for different wounds

● learners will be able to apply the dressings in a safe and correct manner.

To help ensure objectives are always positioned from the learner point of view and always focus on outcomes, it can be helpful to think of 'learning outcomes', rather than 'objectives'.

Learning outcomes would then always be written with the starting sentence:

> As a result of the learning, learners will … (or learners will be able to):
> - select appropriate dressings for different wounds
> - apply the dressings in a safe and correct manner.

A final aspect of setting objectives or learning outcomes to consider is the choice of verb used, as this will impact considerably on how measurable or assessable objectives are – probably the most important factor about objectives. On the other hand, the desire to keep things wholly measurable can lead to an overuse of lower level outcomes, such as 'state', 'demonstrate' or 'describe' and trainers need to think more creatively about this.

There are many verbs to choose from, for example:

> write   identify   contrast   describe
> classify   recognise   select   compare
> state   discuss   connect   repair   open
> manipulate   replace   operate   assemble   solve
> define   construct   measure   align   critique
> name   adjust   develop   create   list   accept   listen
> receive   perceive   design   decide   influence
> appreciate   judge   rationalise   justify
> associate   derive   determine

If it proves essential to use more general terms, for example 'understand' or 'be aware of' then it may be appropriate to consider, and somewhere provide more information about, how that learning outcome will be assessed. This is the approach taken by awarding bodies when specifying the learning requirements for many new qualifications – including the CIPD's foundation and intermediate qualifications. The qualifications are specified in terms of learning outcomes, but each learning outcome has extra information in the form of 'assessment criteria' to qualify how it should be assessed. Examples of these qualification specifications are available in CIPD materials and via approved CIPD centres.

In most learning situations, however, it is sufficient to capture the intended learning in a number of simple and clearly written learning outcomes.

REFLECTIVE ACTIVITY

Considering the information about objectives above, which of the following do you consider to be effective objectives (or learning outcomes) for a learning activity – and why/why not?

Can you improve any that are not effective?

1. Learners will improve their communication skills.

2. Learners will understand the challenges faced by lone-workers.

3. Learners will be able to justify the selection of different food groups within a lunchtime menu for five- to seven-year-olds.

4. Learners will be able to record their daily behaviours in a time log.

5. To build confidence in making loan recovery calls.

6. Learners will have a go at replacing a heat exchanger.

7. During the training, learners will select and apply appropriate dressings for a range of surface wounds.

8. Key points of the data protection act and how they impact on our work.

9. Learners will be able to compare the advantages and disadvantages of two different home-care approaches.

10. To demonstrate the stages in soufflé preparation and cooking.

DETERMINING AND SEQUENCING LEARNING CONTENT

General learning content will be determined by previous needs analysis or by a particular stimulus for the training, such as a product launch. However, there may be further analysis required, perhaps of a specific task, process, product or topic, in order to identify learning content in more detail.

Task, job or process analysis is usually undertaken through observation, examination of documentation, or discussion with experts. General topic analysis can be undertaken by starting at the highest level (topic or job title) and asking:

● What does someone need to know/do to understand/be capable in this area?

Then for each answer to the above question, ask again:

● What does someone need to know/do to understand/be capable in this area?

And so on.

This kind of analysis is similar to the 'five whys' technique described in the previous chapter and is sometimes referred to as 'pyramid analysis', because of the resulting shape of information. It is best done on a big piece of flip-chart paper or on 'post-its' which can be moved around until the final content and sub-division is complete. Ideally the activity should be done by or with someone who knows the job, activity or subject very well. An example analysis of time management is illustrated in Figure 5.1.

Ultimately the range and depth of the subject covered will always depend on the requirements identified in the learning needs analysis, the level of prior learning and the time available to deliver the training. If in doubt, refer back to the learners/stakeholders and agree the best balance of material with them.

Sequencing learning requires us to consider how learners will be best able to 'take-in' the learning topic. For example, it may be necessary for learners to have grasped one concept before they can think productively about another. It can be helpful for us to think about learning as 'blocks', which build on top of each other until the desired level and scope of learning has been covered. To be most accessible, learning content should be delivered in a logical flow, allowing learners to build up through simple to more complex areas of learning:

Simple → Complex → Increasing complexity

Figure 5.1 General Topic Analysis

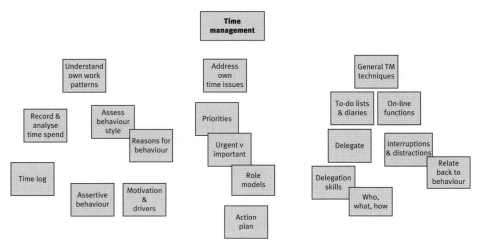

However, there may be other logical approaches to sequencing, perhaps:

- following the natural sequence of a task, process or activity
- following any related timelines, eg activities on each day of the working week or seasonal considerations for outdoor work
- natural groupings, eg age groups or categories of products
- the structure and sequence of a related qualification.

SELECTING METHODS TO MEET LEARNING NEEDS

Related theory and principles

There are a number of useful theories, models and principles which can help us select learning methods. Some of these and how they impact on the design of learning activities are discussed below and, for readers who would like to explore the theories in more detail, followed up in the Essential learning pages. You may also find two other ELPs of interest here: Multiple intelligences and Left brain–right brain.

Ref to ELP 5 – Multiple intelligences

Ref to ELP 6 – Left brain, right brain

The Learning Cycle

The Learning Cycle (David Kolb) gives us an overall framework for learning design. The cycle has four stages: experiencing, reflecting, thinking/having new ideas, and experimenting, all of which are essential for effective learning. To help learners to 'move around the full learning cycle', we should design training activities which include all of the following: activities/experiences (or these may be brought forward from learners' experiences), opportunities to reflect

Ref to ELP 2 – Learning cycle

on experiences, new thinking and ideas to inform how things could be done differently, and safe opportunities to experiment with new ideas.

Learning styles

Peter Honey and Alan Mumford built on Kolb's work to identify four different learning styles or preferences – activists, reflectors, theorists and pragmatists. This work helps us recognise that individuals learn in different ways and therefore that we, as trainers, need to include different learning approaches and activities in our training design. There is also an inherent danger in training design that the designer will naturally select methods that appeal to them. Honey and Mumford's work reminds us of the need to step outside our own preferences and consider an individual learner's style when working with individuals, or include a mix of approaches when designing for groups of learners.

Ref to ELP 3 – Learning styles

4MAT

In her 4MAT model Bernice McCarthy discusses four styles of learner, characterised by the questions that they will typically need answering in their learning. 'Why' learners need to have strong personal reasons for wanting to learn, 'what' learners like to know background and theories, 'how' learners need to know how things work and 'what if' learners like to find things out

Ref to ELP 4 – 4MAT

CASE STUDY 5.1

USING DIFFERENT TRAINING METHODS TO ENGAGE LEARNERS

John Rodwell describes how part of a session about 'using questions' was re-designed to make it more useful and engaging for all the learners.

The original session had already been designed to be 'participative'. As well as providing some general information – the trainer also posed questions to the learners about:

- the names of the various types of question and their definitions

- examples of each type of question

- the extent to which they should be used in training.

The trainer wrote learners' answers on the flip-chart as they were given.

Whilst this activity engaged some learners, it certainly didn't engage all. Learners often struggled to get the answers the trainer

was looking for, and overall the session was something of a slog for both the group and the trainer – even though it was generally a 'participative' session. John decided to re-design this part of the session.

Looking back at the main objectives – which were about participants being able to identify the various types of questions and use them appropriately in their work – John decided to convert the Question and Answer (Q&A) session into an activity.

For the activity, he developed sets of cards detailing:

- the name of each type of question (leading, multiple, probing, hypothetical, testing, rhetorical, etc)

- a definition of each type

- an example of each type.

As well as the 'question cards', circular

'traffic light' cards were also developed – to be used to indicate if the type of question should be used:

- green: frequently

- amber: rarely, with caution, or in particular circumstances

- red: avoided altogether.

The groups' task was to stick the cards up on flipcharts, making a big chart which explained the different types of questions, relevant examples, and how they should be used.

John comments:

> With this change of approach the delivered session had a much greater 'buzz' about it. There was far more discussion and animation in the way the task was carried out. Cards were put into one place, discussed, and moved to another place. There was movement, there was noise, there was the physical holding and touching of the card materials, there was colour, and there was learning.

> The difference in the atmosphere generated by the old Q&A approach, and the new card-sort activity based approach was amazing. The new approach wasn't rocket science just a different way of meeting the objectives of the session – but it dramatically increased learner involvement and engagement in the learning.

Adapted from: Rodwell, J. *Activity based training design* (2007) Gower. Used with permission.

for themselves. McCarthy's model helps us see that different learners will have different motivations for learning and that, as with learning styles, we need to try and accommodate these differences when designing learning.

Domains of learning

Another area of work, primarily attributed to Benjamin Bloom, is Domains of Learning. In this model or 'taxonomy', the term used by Bloom, learning is divided into three main domains or categories:

- cognitive: about knowledge and facts and understanding

- psychomotor: about physical dexterity, practical skills and doing

- affective: about attitude and beliefs and the basis of some of our behaviours.

For learning to be effective, learning methods should be appropriate to the type of learning required. For example, appropriate methods to develop knowledge might include reading, listening to presentations, or questioning experts. Physical skills, however, will be more effectively developed through the use of demonstration, supported practice or coaching. Finally if we want to influence peoples' opinions or beliefs, then training methods may need to include discussion, real examples, or coaching which challenges their current thinking.

AFFECTIVE LEARNING METHODS

When a large public organisation wanted to introduce a new staff performance review system, the training team knew it would not be enough for people to just understand how to use the system. The previous system had been unpopular and the team knew that for the new system to be implemented effectively, they would have to convince staff of its merits.

The session they developed to introduce the new system therefore included:

- factual information about how the system worked.

plus:

- a comparison with the previous system showing the need for the change and how unpopular aspects of the previous system had been addressed
- opportunities for staff to discuss the new system and air their doubts and concerns.

Although the discussion sessions made the delivery of the training more demanding and challenging for the training teams, approaching the subject at a cognitive level only (ie how the system worked) would not have met the required need.

In reality, most work-related learning will involve more than one domain or type of learning, and therefore a mix of approaches will be required within most learning programmes.

MUD

Similar guidance to Bloom's comes from Sylvia Downs, who also categorises learning into three different areas: Memory, Understanding and Doing (MUD). 'Memory' is about learning hard facts, eg procedures and aspects of technical knowledge, 'understanding' is about understanding reasons, concepts and abstract ideas, and 'doing' is about developing skills. As with Bloom's work, MUD reminds us to think carefully about the purpose of our training and find methods that can really address our purpose.

Different methods and approaches

Learning sessions

Here, we have defined a learning session as a learning activity with a single main focus, involving a trainer (tutor, facilitator, coach) and a group of learners, or, possibly, an individual learner. A learning session may be an element of a bigger programme of learning.

The days when a training session consisted of a trainer giving out information to learners for the whole session, possibly with the information also on slides, are hopefully long gone (and technically this would have been a presentation rather than training.) Designing a learning session is now a fascinating and creative activity involving the selection and combination of a range of different approaches. Several options for consideration are detailed below in Table 5.2.

"The change in emphasis from classroom trainer to learning facilitator that has taken place over the past 10–15 years has proved incredibly valuable, both for us as trainers and for our learners. As trainers, it has encouraged us to develop new skills and imaginative approaches to the design of learning opportunities. For our learners it has encouraged a real shift in approach, from passive recipients of whatever the trainer decided they needed to know, to active partners in the learning process."

Jane Church, Learning Facilitator, Novus Professional Development Ltd

Table 5.2 **Designing a learning session**

	Reasons for selecting	**Challenges**
Tutor input (presentation, PowerPoint)	• is an effective and quick way of passing on information • allows for learners to hear a 'common message' • provides an opportunity for learners to check own knowledge against input, ask questions and clarify • provides initial learning/information for use within further activities • takes pressure and attention off learners when they might be feeling most uncertain, eg at the beginning of a session and allows time to 'settle in'	• can be boring if it goes on too long • little learner involvement • does not encourage learner ownership of learning • dependent on quality of presentation skills
Demonstration	• quick way of passing on information • crucial first step in skills development • allows learners to see activity 'done properly'	• demonstrator might pass on bad habits • task might be over-simplified to make demonstration possible • in-course demonstration may not reflect actual pressures of workplace
Group discussion	• provides an opportunity for learners 'agendas' to be aired • hearing others views can help challenge learners limiting beliefs or resistance to change • can be learner-led and engage learners in the topic – providing the subject has meaning for them	• learners might not participate • discussion may be dominated by a few • discussion may stray into areas where the trainer lacks knowledge or feels uncomfortable • discussion may stray away from learning focus • requires good facilitation skills
Videos/actors	• adds variety to the input of information • makes learning more interesting • use of actors allows complete customisation of presented scenarios	• can be expensive • videos soon become out of date

	Reasons for selecting	Challenges
Expert speakers	• adds variety to the input of information • learners tend to respect info from 'experts' • expert will be able to talk about and answer questions about the real situation • experts can enthuse listeners if passionate about their subject and proficient speakers	• dependent on availability of speakers • could be a speaker bias to information • expert could be technically brilliant – but poor speaker
Learner activities: ice breakers and games – not directly related to learning topic	• can help put learners at ease and act as 'a warm up' • can introduce a fun, light-hearted atmosphere to the learning • high energy activities – can lift group energy levels • can leave learners in a relaxed state for learning to take place	• need to be used with care • should be appropriate to age group, type of learning, organisational culture • can embarrass learners if inappropriate • can be considered childish or irrelevant by learners unless carefully selected
Learner activities: written exercises, case studies, real work examples	• allows learners to work together in an in-depth way and learn from each other • can help 'settle' learners into deeper level of learning and concentration • opportunity to apply knowledge and skills • begins transition of knowledge to workplace activity • can provide assessment opportunities	• activities need to be well constructed to be valid and have credibility • may be dependant on access to real work examples from workplace • confidentiality and data protection issues may have to be addressed • can be 'low energy' activities
Learner activities: brainstorming, preparing and delivering presentations, knowledge tests and quizzes	• allows learners to work together and share knowledge • moderate energy activities – can lift energy levels, whilst still focussing on learning topic • can be a useful activity to end a session – end on a high • opportunity for learners to check knowledge and fill gaps • provides assessment opportunities	• tend to be about knowledge retention rather than application • brainstorming can be stilted if wrongly focused on getting the 'right answer' rather than on bringing out creative thinking and ideas • can create competition and division

	Reasons for selecting	**Challenges**
Learner activities: role play and skills practice	• allows learners to work together and share knowledge • moderate energy activities – can lift energy levels, whilst still focussing on learning topic • opportunity to act out procedures and skills in safe environment • begins transition of knowledge and skills to real work activities	• can be considered artificial and not representative of real work • response from learners is usually more positive if asked to do 'skills practice' rather than 'role play'
Learner activities: individual analysis, self-reflection and action-planning	• helps to identify needs • reviews where learning is, in relation to desired goals • informs further learning • can be motivational • action planning helps in the transfer of learning to the workplace • action planning provides a vehicle for later evaluation	• learners can find concentration for self-assessment difficult within or just after a high energy group session • learners may feel uncomfortable about self reflection or analysis • learners may 'skew' analysis results to make them more favourable

Learning programmes

The options for designing programmes are slightly different. If we think of a learning programme as something bigger than a session – a structured series of different learning events, activities or sessions – then options for inclusion in a programme might be:

• group training sessions

• on-job training or practice

• coaching

• mentoring

• action learning/peer learning

• workbooks/books/guides

• e-learning.

(For a reminder of the advantages and disadvantages of these options you might want to return to Chapter 4, pp 92–95.)

In putting together a programme, it is important to consider:

• the overall timing of the programme

- the timing of any gaps between different programme elements
- the variety and blend of activities and flow from one activity to another
- the availability of learners in relation to the availability of resources, such as space or equipment
- any logistical issues around people moving from one activity to another.

Blended and flexible learning

Whilst group training sessions remain one of the most popular ways of delivering learning and have much to offer learners – there are disadvantages. Managers can be reluctant to release staff for a whole or even half-day of training and flexible working hours and busy schedules make it difficult to get groups together. Some flexible approaches to help meet these issues include:

Blended learning

Blended learning usually refers to a combination of group session and online (or paper based) self-learning activity.

> For example: a one-day course on handling customer complaints could be converted to:
>
> - pre-course reading covering the organisational policy on complaint handling
> - an on-line learning module about the theory of positive behaviour, with a built-in test to confirm learning
> - a video podcast of a simulated complaint interview being handled badly and then handled well
> - a two-hour group session in which learners put the theory into practice with role play sessions and feedback
> - action plans developed by learners and submitted on-line.
>
> The timing of each event here would be flexible and different for each learner (except for the group session), to fit in with individual work demands.

Teach and coach

A method that combines a short group input session with one-to-one coaching sessions.

> For example: instead of a one-day course for team leaders on managing attendance, the topic could be covered by:
>
> - a 90-minute group session covering the organisational policy and the process of return-to-work interviews
> - follow-up 45-minute coaching sessions with each team leader about how they can apply the learning with their own team.

Lunch and learn

Lunch and learn involves combining the provision of a light meal with a presentation by an expert speaker or trainer, followed by informal discussion about the topic. This can be an effective way of combining group learning with the opportunity to network, and can bring together people from across an organisation who might not normally learn together. Because of the informality it may be best used for optional training, or for encouraging people who are uncomfortable in a 'classroom' setting. Breakfast learning sessions can also be effective.

Bite-sized training

It is possible to break almost any subject down into bite sized chunks – anything from 10 minutes to an hour. Key aspects of the sales process, for example, could be broken into 30 minute chunks and delivered as a series of short sessions, minimising the disruption to work. Bite sized sessions like this often fit well into environments where time is particularly 'precious' – retail, contact centres and healthcare for example. Even the shortest of sessions can still follow best practice for learning, with an activity, reflection, practical input and planning.

Team meetings and briefings

Including an element of learning and development into a team meeting can add value to a time slot, where people have already been brought together. Short, timely and interactive training sessions on key aspects, such as health and safety or other statutory training, can be added, without significantly extending the duration of the meeting. The big benefit of training in this way is that it makes use of an existing medium (the meeting) and can bring a potentially dull or routine subject to life by finding new and short ways of delivering it.

Training cascades

Cascading training is a way of getting practical learning out to a large number of people in a short space of time. A training session on a new staff appraisal scheme, for example, could be designed by the central training team and then sent out to a nominated trainer in each business area. That trainer would then train line managers in how to deliver the session, and they in turn would cascade the training to each of their teams.

CASE STUDY 5.2

DEVELOPMENT FOR RETAIL STAFF WITHIN A NATIONAL CHARITY

A national charity with a large number of stores in the UK had a requirement to develop staff in aspects of customer service. This presented a number of challenges – retail outlets were widely spread across the UK, several of the store teams were unpaid volunteers, and a number of store workers possessed learning difficulties, needing training to be tailored to their individual needs.

Following a learning needs analysis, a meeting was held with a small group of store managers and deputies to consider different training approaches. Lots of learning interventions were considered and rejected. For example, e-learning was considered impractical as not every store had access to a computer for training purposes and it was also considered too impersonal for the charity's culture.

Formal classroom style training was also discounted as delivery would have to be done by the management teams, many of whom felt uncomfortable and unskilled in formal trainer skills, and it would have involved too many staff hours off the sales floor.

The agreed solution was:

1. Development of a kit of training tools for store management teams, with a suite of options they could use to meet their specific store's learning needs. The kit consisted of:

   - scripts and handouts to run a 15-minute group session (during team huddles)

   - practical mini exercises to be delivered at quiet footfall times on the shop floor

   - coaching cards to help the store management follow up the information delivered in the mini training sessions.

2. A pilot programme in six stores of different size and flexibility to test and refine the materials.

3. A train-the-trainer event for managers co-delivered by the training consultant who had designed the training and the store managers involved in the pilot programme, who were able to share their personal stories of practical implementation and answer questions pragmatically and honestly.

The training has now been implemented and in a relatively short period of time a customer service culture has been created, where managers are clear on their training and coaching responsibilities and able to use the tools available to them as required. Teams are enthused by the training and are hungry for more – and are now investigating how to tackle other service issues.

Steven Cartwright, Retail Training Consultant, With a V Ltd.

DESIGNING LEARNING MATERIALS

In the tables above, we have already considered the uses and challenges of a number of learning materials. In terms of designing materials, here are some tips from the experts:

POWERPOINT SLIDES

General rules:

- an easy-to-read font and big letters (never less than 22 point – ideally bigger)
- bullets rather than sentences
- no more than around six words per bullet and six bullets per slide
- pictures and images rather than all bullets (or a good mix)
- don't use too many slides (never more than 10 in one session – ideally less).

  "PowerPoint is an excellent tool – as long as it is used as a visual aid and not a crutch (ie something to remind the trainer what to read out)! Slides should support what you are saying, whilst you remain the main focus. Using colour, images and effects make slides more interesting, and helps learners remember the key learning points. Personally, I prefer to use images instead of bullet point lists. Consider the two slides below – they both say the same things but one is much more visually interesting and pleasant for the audience.

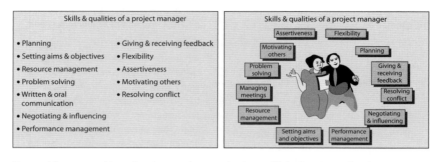

You could even consider using your spoken words alone with just a strong visual to support your message, and virtually no words on the screen at all! This allows the audience to listen to what the presenter is saying but still have the visual link to help recall the message later."

John Rodwell, Training Consultant and Author

HANDOUTS/WRITTEN MATERIALS

General rules:

- Consider whether handouts are really needed – maybe the information is already available within work systems.

- Make handouts appropriate (level and content) for the potential reader and as clear and concise as they can be without missing out anything essential.

- Ensure language does not discriminate or offend – check for indirect discrimination (eg shorthand, acronyms or language that only certain learners will understand).

- Include diagrams, charts, illustrations, if relevant.

- Use colours or coloured paper to make hand outs more interesting (pale yellow paper with black print is often deemed the easiest to read).

- Use different-coloured paper to classify handouts into different topic areas.

- Print copies of slides as handouts, using the 'Notes' facility so that learners can add their own thoughts.

- Provide handouts electronically, maybe after the event, so that learners can easily store them for future reference.

CASE STUDIES AND ACTIVITIES

General rules:

- Make case studies and activities as real and related to the learners' work roles or situation as possible.

- Have a look at case studies in text books, such as this one, to get some ideas.

- If taken from real work – be careful about data protection and confidentiality issues.

- If developing your own case studies – think carefully about how your examples may be received, be careful to avoid stereotyping or offending. Get someone else to read through case studies before you use them – both for accuracy and sensitivity purposes.

"When asked to deliver a Health and Safety course for a group of women's refuge organisations, I felt that the standard course they had requested would not be the most relevant solution for them. As the course was linked to a qualification, I did not have much room to adapt the content and so I decided to use case studies as a means of making the material relate more closely to them. I spent time with a representative of one of the organisations to increase my awareness of health and safety issues in a refuge context, and then researched a number of court cases relating to refuges which could be used as the basis of case studies.

Although the case studies took some time to develop, they really made the training. What was potentially a dry subject was brought to life by the discussion around each case study – with different refuge representatives sharing how they had addressed the issues concerned and everyone sharing good practice. The case studies helped generate lots of ideas and new thinking as well as engaging everyone in the subject matter. The feedback from the learners was excellent, and more courses have now been requested. For me, the course turned out to be one of the most fulfilling and enjoyable I have ever designed or delivered."

Gordon Linford, Risk Manager, D E Ford Insurance Brokers

SELECTING METHODS FOR ASSESSMENT

Assessment can be divided into initial assessment (testing suitability for learning), formative assessment (assessment of how learners are progressing in their learning) and summative assessment (judgements about learning achievement, usually at the end of a period of learning).

Formative assessment is useful to both the trainer and the learner as it helps inform any adjustments that need to be made during the learning process. Summative assessment gives us an explicit outcome of learning – which helps inform the action taken by both learner and trainer after the learning. Importantly both types of assessment should provide an opportunity for a learner to be given objective and motivational feedback about their performance.

Most learner activities within a learning session can also form the basis of formative and/or summative assessment – case studies, quizzes, presentations, performance in discussions and activities – all reflect how well a learner is progressing towards learning objectives. Similarly in a wider programme, the basis of assessment might be performance in projects or work activities (reflected in work results or manager feedback) or results from e-learning modules.

Our selection of assessment activities for a learning event will depend on the context and nature of the learning. For example, learning undertaken as part of a qualification course is likely to require formal assessment activities, such as tests, assignments or observations against standards, undertaken in specific conditions and fully recorded.

Assessment undertaken to check learning and inform future action may involve similar activities but be less formally undertaken – for example, a self-assessed knowledge test or an observation by a co-learner rather than a licensed assessor.

Some of the most valid assessment of learning is likely to be undertaken some time after the learning event and focus on how well a learner has applied their new skills and knowledge to their work role.

When you are designing learning it is important to think about the type of assessment that is required, the timing of assessment, and the most appropriate assessment methods and embed these into the learning design.

SELECTING METHODS FOR EVALUATION

Finally any session design is incomplete without consideration of how it will be evaluated. If this thinking is left until after the session vital opportunities to evaluate will be missed. Consideration should include what to evaluate, how to evaluate and when to evaluate. All of these factors are well covered in Chapter 7: Evaluating Learning and Development Activities.

PRESENTING PROGRAMME PLANS AND SESSION DESIGNS

When all factors have been considered and learning activity has been designed, the information can be presented in a number of formats. The main guiding principle is that a programme plan or session design should be 'written up' in a way that another trainer, with the same technical expertise as you, could follow.

A good format to follow for session notes is provided in Figures 5.2 and 5.3. An example 'high level' programme is provided in Figure 5.4.

Figure 5.2 Session notes: front cover

Delivering induction for new team members (1-day session for team leaders)		
Session aim To equip delegates with the knowledge and skills to deliver induction at local sites		
Learning outcomes By the end of the workshop, delegates will be able to: • describe the six areas of new staff induction • explain the support information required for each area • complete an induction checklist and induction record • explain the purpose of weekly review meetings for inductees • demonstrate active listening and effective questioning within a review scenario.		
Links: Part of overall induction programme for new starters.		

Sessions:	Mins:	Resources:
Welcome & introductions	30	• Projector, flip chart, paper & pens
The induction experience	30	• Session outlines (sent in advance)
The six areas of induction	120	• Blank induction checklists
The 'paperwork'	30	• Induction records – blank and
Successful reviews	90	completed examples
Summary review & evaluation	30	• Active listening exercise materials
		• Organisation info

Planned evaluation:	Reaction sheet (level 1). Observation of delivering induction within 12 month period (level 2, 3).

Figure 5.3 Session notes: first of several session note pages

Timing	Activity	Content	Resources/Notes
10 mins	Tutor input	**Introductions, welcomes & admin** **Welcome** delegates to the session & introduce self. Ask delegates to introduce selves. **Housekeeping** – fire exits, toilets, mobiles, breaks, additional needs etc. **Admin** – check register completed and everyone has session outline, is aware of timings etc. **Overview** of the session – explain what is included in the session. (PowerPoint 1) Share the **aim and learning outcomes** for the session. Anything learners want to add?	Flip chart with welcome message Session outline PP - 1
20 mins	Pairs activity	**Delegate introduction presentations**	
30 mins	Individual activity	**Session 1: The induction experience** Ask each delegate to reflect on their own experiences of starting new job(s) in the past, and the induction (or lack of) they received. Ideally, each delegate to think of a positive and a negative example of this.	Flip chart
	Group discussion	Take feedback from each person, creating 2 lists on flip chart – 'factors that made induction good' and 'factors that made induction bad'. For any negative experiences ask "what could have improved the experience" and, if not already listed, add these improvement ideas to the 'good factors' list.	
	Small groups	**Distribute written scenario** – ask delegates to identify the 'good and the bad' aspects.	
120	Six Groups activity	**Session 2: The six areas of induction** Introduce the 6 areas – and allocate an area to each group. Groups to research and create an outline of essential content for their area.	Access to intranet policies & procedures file organisation literature

Figure 5.4 An example (high level) learning programme plan

When	Where	People	Activity	Resources	Notes
			New starters induction – programme overview		
April 5th	Head office	Regional managers	Training day - 'Delivering Induction'	See session plan	Delivered by L&D
May to July	Own settings	Managers & new staff	- Managers to undertake staff inductions on site - On-line support provided by L&D - Weekly 1:1 reviews to monitor progress	- checklists - records - review forms	– all forms on intranet
July 12th	Head office	New staff	- Starters attend 'Staff development & performance framework' workshop - and, 'Induction to VQ'	See session notes	Delivered by L&D
July - Dec	Own settings	Managers, new staff & assessors	- New staff work towards trainee performance targets, supported by line manager - 6-8 weekly visit from L&D/assessor to review progress towards performance targets and VQ	Development files	Files awaiting AB approval
Dec 15th	Own settings	Managers, new staff & assessors	Final assessments to be completed – all records to central team		

WHAT NEXT

DESIGNING LEARNING ACTIVITIES

Here are some things that you could consider doing to help you increase your working knowledge of designing learning activities:

1. Have a look at some of the different learning activities that take place within your organisation:

    – What range of activities are there?
    – Which ones seem to be used the most?
    – Which ones are missing or underused?

2. Take a look at a learning need within your organisation (you could pick something fairly generic such as 'customer care'):

    – What learning activities could be used to increase the capability of staff to improve in this area?
    – What would be involved in designing each of them?
    – What would be the advantages and disadvantages of the activities or methods that you are considering?

3. Look at the aim and objectives of some of the training events run within your organisation (or look at external training events on the Internet):

    – Is the overall aim stated?
    – How do they use objectives or learning outcomes?
    – How clear and measurable are the objectives or learning outcomes?
    – How could you re-write any of these to make them clearer?

4. Pick a training module or other learning activity that you have been involved in as a learner:

    – Reflect on the activities that were involved; was there something for each of the learning styles?
    – Reflect on the running order of the event; is there evidence that it followed Kolb's Experiential Learning Cycle?
    – How might you have designed it differently?

5. Consider the case study below – and the related questions at the end of the case study.

CASE STUDY 5.3

EXTENDING HOME-WORKING

A medium-sized organisation has business objectives to increase flexibility of working arrangements and reduce the use of office space costs. In connection with this, the training team has been asked to support the organisation's plans to:

● significantly increase the number of home-workers (specific targets have been set)

● introduce 'hot-desking'.

Home-working had been piloted some years previously, resulting in 14 staff already being 'home-workers'. Originally these people had been managed by one line manager, but had gradually been deployed across the organisation and moved to working under different managers, who had not necessarily been trained in the relevant procedures and practices. Overtime, this had resulted in inconsistency – a mix of some very good and some 'not so good' practice in the way the 'home-workers' were managed.

The training team identified that, along with updating the home-working procedures, they needed to address three main areas of learning need:

1. For Managers (approximately 20):
   - how home-working should be implemented
   - the supporting documentation
   - how to select people for home-working
   - how to manage home-workers (this could be quite a 'culture change' for some managers who had reservations about how levels and quality of work could be ensured 'from a distance').

2. For Staff, before selection (up to 150):
   - what is involved in home-working
   - how to decide if home-working is for them or not
   - how to apply for home-working.

3. For Staff, after selection (up to 50):

   - more detailed information about what is involved in home-working
   - their responsibilities as home-workers
   - procedures and supporting documentation
   - strategies, tips and techniques for managing themselves as home-workers.

Questions:

1. How would you approach designing a learning solution to meet these needs?

2. What overall programme might you suggest?

3. Take any one of the three areas of need above and design an outline training session or workshop (content areas, sequencing, methods, activities, etc) that would address the requirement.

SUMMARY

This chapter has explored:

What good training design means and why it is important

- The term 'designing training' can relate to designing training programmes, designing the sessions that make up training programmes or designing specific learning activities.

- Typical stages in designing learning include: clarifying requirements, determining objectives or learning outcomes, determining and sequencing learning content, selecting methods to meet learning needs and selecting assessment and evaluation activities.

- A training session should be written up as a detailed session plan and agreed with key stakeholders.

Key factors which impact on the design of learning

- Organisational factors, which impact on learning design include: business priorities, availability of resources and organisational culture and values.

- Legislative requirements such as health and safety, entitlement to training, equal opportunities, data protection and copyright may also impact on training design and we should be aware of the requirements.

- We should also consider how any new training initiatives will fit with existing provision.

- Individual factors that affect learning design include: learners' previous experience of learning, learning preferences, prior knowledge and personal circumstances.

How to determine objectives and sequence learning content

- Classic guidance (Mager) regarding objectives, is that they should contain: a behaviour, a condition and a standard.

- Learning objectives should be written from the point of view of the learner, and be stated in terms of what the learner should be able to achieve as a result of the learning.

- A simple way to ensure that you always position objectives in this way is to think of them as learning outcomes – and start the listing by saying… 'As a result of this session … learners will be able to…'

Examples of key thinking and learning theory

- There is much excellent learning theory available to guide our design of learning activities.

- Examples of this include: the Learning Cycle (Kolb), Learning styles (Honey and Mumford), Domains of Learning (Bloom), MUD (Sylvia Downs) and 4MAT (Bernice McCarthy).

A range of learning methods and training approaches

- There are a wide range of learning methods and approaches to choose from.

- These include trainer led activities such as giving a presentation or demonstration or group activities such as discussion, watching a video or watching actors demonstrate a scenario.

- Learner activities include case studies, written exercises, quizzes, brain-storming, knowledge tests, presentations.

- Individual activities include self-assessment, self-analysis exercises and reflection.

- We can also blend different learning activities with e-learning or make use of 'bite-size' learning approaches.

Preparing written session notes

- Session notes should include: timings, learning content, information about resources to be used.

- They should be written clearly and logically.

- There are some straightforward examples of session note formats we can follow.

EXPLORE FURTHER

BOOKS:

Mager, R.F. (1998) *Preparing instructional objectives: a critical tool in the development of effective instruction,* 3rd edn, London: Atlantic Books.

Downs, S. (1995) *Learning at work: effective strategies for making learning happen,* London: Kogan Page.

Anderson, L.W, Krathwohl D.R. *et al* (2001) *A taxonomy for learning, teaching and assessing: a revision of Bloom's* Taxonomy of Educational Objectives, 1st rev edn, USA: Allyn and Bacon.

Hackett, P. (2003) *Training practice,* London: CIPD.

WEBSITES:

Range of information and guidance relating to learning and training design:

www.cipd.co.uk/subjects/lrnanddev/designdelivery

www.cipd.co.uk/subjects/lrnanddev/selfdev

www.cipd.co.uk/subjects/lrnanddev/elearning/elearnprog.htm

www.cipd.co.uk/subjects/lrnanddev/designdelivery/creatmthds.htm

Free (or partially free) on-line access to learning activities:

www.mindtools.com

www.trainingzone.co.uk

www.brainboxx.co.uk

Advice across a wide range of legislative requirements (select area of legislation required from 'a–z of resources'):

www.cipd.co.uk/onlineinfodocuments/atozresources.htm

CHAPTER 6

Delivering Learning and Development Activities

INTRODUCTION

The chapter begins with a look at why the effective delivery of learning is so important and what we actually mean by 'good quality training delivery'. We then move on to explore different aspects of delivering learning – planning for delivery, the skills of effective delivery and ways in which we can help manage group dynamics. Throughout these sections we also consider some of the barriers learners may face in accessing and participating in learning and how we can address these within our training delivery.

LEARNING OUTCOMES

When you have read this chapter you should be able to:

- explain why effective training/learning delivery is important
- describe key features of 'good quality training delivery'
- discuss a range of potential barriers to learning
- describe aspects of planning and preparation for learning that will help overcome individual barriers to learning
- identify the skills required to deliver learning effectively and explain aspects of good practice for each
- describe techniques for managing group dynamics.

THE IMPORTANCE OF GOOD QUALITY TRAINING DELIVERY

Despite the growth in distance learning, self-study and on-line options, face-to-face learning remains the most popular way of delivering learning and development.

> "In-house development programmes are still seen as the most effective L&TD practice."
> CIPD Learning and Talent Development Survey 2010

Face-to-face training is popular with organisations and sponsors of L&D, because it is a tried and tested method – and it is often the way in which people in organisations expect to be trained. Well-designed and delivered training sessions can appeal to all four learning style preferences, while delivering a common and consistent message to several people at once.

Training sessions and programmes also have lots of advantages for learners: time away from the workplace, a chance to develop themselves and learn new skills, and an opportunity to spend time with and learn from others with the same goals.

Along with all the advantages though, there are costs – face-to-face training can be expensive. It takes people away from their workplace, it costs money in terms of venue and travel costs, and it costs money to prepare and deliver.

All of these cost factors make it even more important that learning is delivered skilfully and effectively and that it accurately meets learning requirements.

> "Training is a big investment and not one to be made lightly … but as a manager there is nothing better than seeing staff who have previously struggled with aspects of their job flourish after they have had the benefit of appropriate and good quality training."
>
> Janet Medcalf, Manager

WHAT IS 'GOOD QUALITY TRAINING DELIVERY'?

Have you ever attended a training event where the content was not what you had expected or did not relate to your learning objectives? Or one where the content was generally good but somehow the trainer just could not bring it to life for you? What about a session where the group did not work together well or was dominated by one or two of the more extrovert delegates?

When learners describe their 'best training experiences', the descriptions usually include three aspects:

1. The content was just right to meet learning needs and objectives.

2. It was delivered effectively by a skilled and competent trainer.

3. The learner group 'bonded' or worked well together, sharing ideas and learning from each other.

A fourth aspect sometimes mentioned is where the learning provides something very new to the learner or one of those 'light-bulb moments' when something suddenly 'falls into place' or the solution to a long-held problem comes to mind.

As trainers, we can provide all of these aspects by carefully planning our training to meet learning needs and using our training skills to deliver activities effectively and manage the group dynamics.

However, learning is not all about the trainer and, however well we play our part in providing good quality opportunities, the responsibility for learning is not all ours. Adult learning is dependent on adults choosing to access and participate in learning and undertake the activities required to meet their learning needs.

Sometimes things get in the way of people accessing and participating in learning – maybe personal internal issues or just factors about how the learning is promoted or delivered.

Ref to ELP 7 – Principles of adult learning

These 'barriers to learning' can take many forms; for example:

- Learning opportunities may be promoted or described in a way that unnecessarily excludes learners or is not attractive to them.
- Learners may not see the relevance of the learning to them.
- Learning may be provided at a time or place that is inaccessible for some.
- Learning might be delivered in a physical environment that limits learners desire or ability to participate – noisy, poorly laid out, too hot, too cold, too chaotic.
- Learning may be delivered in a style that does not appeal to the learner.
- Learners may have negative prior experiences of learning, which make them uneasy about participating.
- Learners may lack, or believe they lack, some of the essential skills needed to access particular learning.
- Learners might be uncomfortable about working with a group of people they do not know.
- Learners may be dominated by others within a group and unable to get their voice heard or needs met.

Ref to ELP 3 – Learning styles

This brings another dimension to 'good quality training delivery' – the need to avoid, minimise or overcome barriers to individual learning and provide a positive environment in which learners can thrive.

In summary then, good quality learning delivery requires us to:

- plan training that will meet learner's needs
- use our skills to deliver it effectively
- manage the dynamics of the learning group.

At the same time, we should always seek to overcome barriers and create an environment in which learners have the very best chance of accessing the learning they need.

REFLECTIVE ACTIVITY

What are your best experiences of being a learner?

What made them so positive for you?

How could you use this awareness in your training delivery?

EFFECTIVE TRAINING DELIVERY – IN PRACTICE

PLANNING THE SESSION

Before we embark on any training activity we need to be sure about what we are seeking to achieve and how we intend to get there. This involves being clear about learning needs (see Chapter 4: Undertaking a Learning Needs Analysis) and designing learning to meet identified needs (see Chapter 5: Designing learning and development activities).

A good training plan will include an appropriate combination of the following:

- learning objectives or outcomes
- 'opening activities' – welcomes and introductions
- a good mix of training activities and approaches which encompasses different learning styles and includes:
  - activities to assist learning – eg presentations, demonstrations, case studies, group activities, skills practice, discussions
  - activities to gauge learning – eg learner reviews, case studies, role plays, tests, quizzes
  - activities to assist transfer of learning to the workplace – eg learner activities reflecting real work, use of learning materials and guides, individual action planning
- 'closing activities' to conclude learning – eg question and answer sessions, learning reviews, action-planning
- evaluation activity – eg final group review of the programme, individual completion of 'reactionnaires'.

COMMUNICATING WITH LEARNERS BEFORE THE EVENT

Overcoming barriers and creating the best environment for learning starts long before the actual session or learning programme. Here are some of the steps we can take before the training sessions.

Promotion of the learning

Potential learners need accurate information in order to make choices and decisions about learning. For learners to be motivated to attend sessions and see the relevance of the learning to their needs, we need to ensure that:

- the opportunity is accurately described (on leaflets, internal intranet, notices)
- we make the training sound appealing without 'overselling' it or setting unrealistic expectations
- learners know what they might achieve, what new knowledge, skills or behaviours they could acquire as a result of attending
- line managers know how the event will meet staff's learning needs and what value (return on investment) they will get for the time and money involved in releasing staff for training.

Practical Information for learners – 'Joining instructions'

For many learning sessions and programmes the main communication with learners will be through 'joining instructions'. The main purpose of these is to convey practical information about the learning event(s), so that learners are clear about where they need to be when and what is required of them when they get there.

Learners are unlikely to feel comfortable in a learning situation if they are worried about logistical, personal or domestic factors – and often need information well in advance of learning so that they can ensure any necessary arrangements are made. It is worth noting that one of the most common negative comments on evaluation sheets is 'the joining instructions' – either because they arrived too late, causing stress in making personal or travel arrangements, or because they provided inaccurate information.

Areas to include in joining instructions are:
- the full address of the venue and instructions on how to find it
- full timings
- what refreshments will be available
- any special information or arrangements for individual circumstances, eg access or dietary requirements
- the dress code if there is one
- any preparation work or anything that delegates should bring with them
- contact details in case learners have any questions
- some organisations also include a delegate list.

The way the instructions are written can also subtly set the tone of the event – a formal style, if you want to emphasise the business-like approach of the training, or a more friendly tone, if you want to reassure learners.

Where appropriate, the joining instructions can also be used creatively to intrigue or engage learners in the training event – maybe using an 'invitation' style or a format that reflects learning content (a 'to do' list for a time management session, perhaps).

Pre-course work

If there is to be any pre-course work or preparation, learners will need plenty of notice and very clear instructions about what is required. Pre-course work does not have to be paper based, it could for example involve: completing an on-line survey or questionnaire, viewing a podcast or taking part in an on-line meeting, or getting an observation or feedback from a third party – providing of course, that we know learners have the skills and opportunities to complete these things and we are not inadvertently creating more barriers for them.

Pre-course activities can provide extremely useful information to use later on in the session. Remember the learning cycle and how learners need to have experiences to reflect on, followed by opportunities to gain new ideas and then to experiment with these. Pre-course work can help learners have or bring forward relevant experiences that they can build on in the training session.

Ref to ELP 2 – Experiential learning cycle

ESTABLISHING THE PHYSICAL ENVIRONMENT FOR LEARNING

Sometimes we put so much time and effort into planning the content of a training event that we forget about the physical environment for learning. Yet the physical environment can be a major factor in the success of any session. Imagine the frustration of sitting through a presentation you cannot really hear or a demonstration you cannot see very well or the discomfort of being crammed into a small room with lots of other people where you are unable to move about or claim your personal space.

Some learning environment factors to consider are accessibility and safety, room layout and learner comfort.

Accessibility and safety

If learners are to take up learning, then we need to ensure that the physical environment in which it is provided is accessible to them. Barriers can be created by the location of a building or particular design of a room and we need to address these, particularly where learners have special equipment needs or are wheelchairs users. Careful consideration of learners and their access needs is an essential stage in the organisation of any learning activity.

Along with ensuring that everyone can access the training area, we must ensure that our learners and the areas they attend are safe. A trainer should always undertake a risk assessment of the learning environment – and make sure that any risks have been addressed before the session (see references at the end of this chapter for more information about risk assessments). As well as following procedures for any specialist equipment being used, we must also consider potential training-room hazards, such as:

- fire exits made less accessible by room layout
- unsafe positioning of learning equipment, flip-chart stands or screens
- trailing wires

- too many electrical items plugged into an extension lead.

As the trainer of a session, you have a responsibility to be aware of and inform your learners of key safety information including: location of fire exits, frequency of alarm tests and the assembly point in the event of an evacuation.

Room layout

The layout of a room can have a huge influence on how the occupants of the room behave – and this can be a powerful tool for trainers. Levels of participation, interaction between group members, and individual learning and enjoyment can all be affected by how a room, and particularly seating, is arranged.

"I am dismayed when trainers turn up at the training room five minutes before the event starts having not given any thought to the room layout or assuming that it will have been laid out satisfactorily by someone else. By this time, learners have already arrived and sat down and, even if the trainer recognises that the arrangement is not good, it is too late to move it around. Ironically, the trainer might later complain that groups 'never join in very much', oblivious to how the cramped and poor layout of the room made learners uncomfortable and inhibited group interaction."

Training Practice Assessor

REFLECTIVE ACTIVITY

Consider how some different types of 'room' are arranged, for example: restaurants, cinemas, libraries, schools.

How do these different layouts affect the way people behave?

What can you learn from this for your delivery of training?

As well as choosing a layout that suits the learning activities being delivered – and remember that you can rearrange the room a little during the day – your choice of room layout will also depend on the size of the group and the type of the event. An event which requires individual IT equipment, for example, would be set up differently to an event which was mainly based on group activities and interaction.

You might also consider the use of tables – some people see them as a barrier to interaction, while others believe that learners are more comfortable when they have tables around them to put things on and can comfortably make notes or carry out activities. The key is to give the matter some consideration and select a layout suitable for the size of the group and most conducive to the type of learning activities to be undertaken. If possible, build in some flexibility so you can use the room in different ways during the day.

Some example seating arrangements are shown in the following boxes.

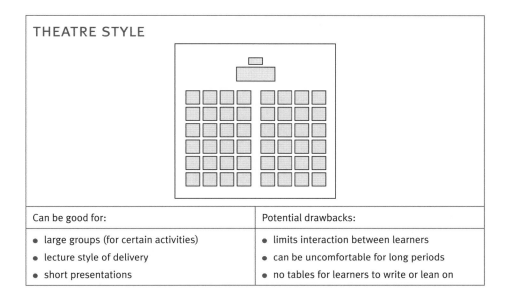

THEATRE STYLE

Can be good for:	Potential drawbacks:
• large groups (for certain activities) • lecture style of delivery • short presentations	• limits interaction between learners • can be uncomfortable for long periods • no tables for learners to write or lean on

SCHOOLROOM STYLE

Can be good for:	Potential drawbacks:
• large groups (for certain activities) • teacher style of delivery • tests or individual working	• limited interaction • may give learners negative feelings of school • trainer has to remain at the front to be seen and heard

HORSESHOE STYLE

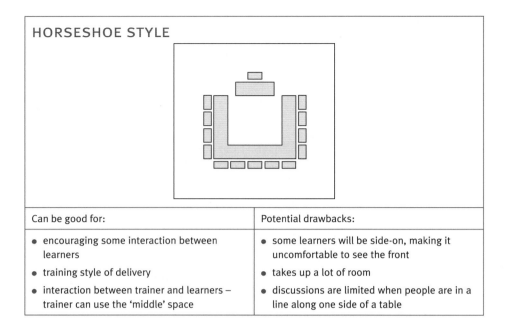

Can be good for:	Potential drawbacks:
• encouraging some interaction between learners	• some learners will be side-on, making it uncomfortable to see the front
• training style of delivery	• takes up a lot of room
• interaction between trainer and learners – trainer can use the 'middle' space	• discussions are limited when people are in a line along one side of a table

BOARDROOM STYLE

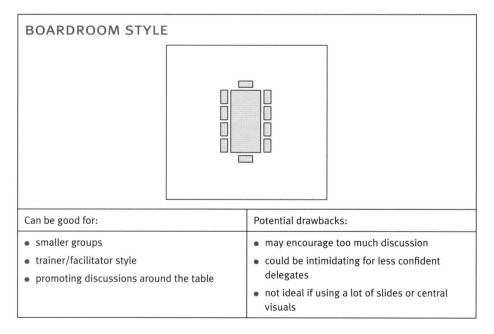

Can be good for:	Potential drawbacks:
• smaller groups	• may encourage too much discussion
• trainer/facilitator style	• could be intimidating for less confident delegates
• promoting discussions around the table	• not ideal if using a lot of slides or central visuals

CABARET STYLE

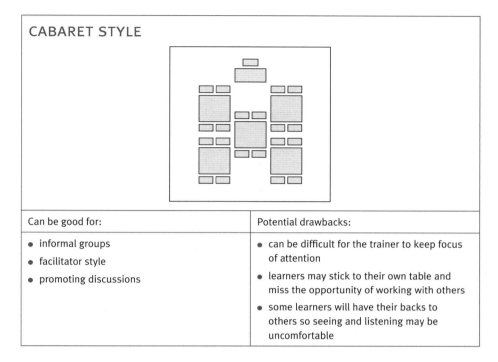

Can be good for:	Potential drawbacks:
• informal groups • facilitator style • promoting discussions	• can be difficult for the trainer to keep focus of attention • learners may stick to their own table and miss the opportunity of working with others • some learners will have their backs to others so seeing and listening may be uncomfortable

As well as seating arrangements, do not forget to consider how training equipment is arranged. If using slides, for example, consider where the screen and projector will be – can the audience see all they need to? Too many training rooms (in the opinion of the authors) put the screen in the prominent central position, while pushing the trainer off to the side of the room, giving the impression that the message on the screen is more important than the contribution and explanation of the trainer. A better arrangement might be for you to be in the middle, with screen at one side and flipchart at the other.

Comfort factors

Heating and ventilation: making sure that the temperature is at a comfortable average to suit most people and that there is sufficient flow of fresh air to keep people energised.

Lighting: if lights are too bright it can cause tiredness and headaches; too dim may lead to eyestrain and lethargy.

Distractions: relevant posters, pictures or interesting quotes on the walls can all help set the tone of an event and add interest for learners. But remember to remove things that are not relevant and which will be distracting. A whiteboard that still has the details from another training session or old flip-chart pages left on the walls indicates that you have not paid much attention to preparing the training room and can devalue your training for the learners.

Refreshments: if your session is running for more than an hour or two, it is appropriate to provide refreshments. Your budget might not allow for lavish entertainment, but, as a minimum, provide water and access to hot drinks or a vending machine. You might also consider healthier alternatives to sweets and biscuits, such as pieces of fruit.

MANAGING AND PRESENTING YOURSELF AS TRAINER

How we conduct ourselves in the training room has a big impact on our credibility with learners. Areas to take account of include:

- Look the part. Make sure that you dress in a way that is congruent with your message and with the expectations of your audience. You might feel more confident in your power suit and gold jewellery, but if your audience are more used to jeans and work boots you might be setting the wrong impression and turning your audience against you, rather than getting them on your side. Equally jeans and casual wear could seriously affect your credibility with some learner groups.

- Body language. Make sure that your body language is one of confidence. Practice your posture and stance and make sure that you are upright and open. Avoid using gestures that cover your mouth or make you look as though you are unsure of yourself.

- Eye contact. We tend to trust people who make appropriate eye contact with us. It is harder to believe someone who seems to be avoiding looking us in the eye!

- Eradicate your worst habits. Are you aware that you have any particular habits or mannerisms that might be a distraction to your audience? Maybe you are a fidget, a swayer, or perhaps you are over-fond of a particular vocal expression 'you know'. Ask for feedback on the effect these habits might have on your audience – and if the impact is a negative one then learn to overcome the habit.

- Train your voice. Learning to use your voice is essential to good delivery. Make sure that you can be heard properly by projecting well and taking care over your pronunciation. Good volume comes from good breathing. Practice the art of diaphragmatic breathing, breathing all the way down to the diaphragm, which will help get the volume without straining your vocal chords.

DIAPHRAGMATIC BREATHING (ALSO KNOWN AS 'BELLY BREATHING')

1. Good breathing should fill your whole lungs with air, right the way down to your diaphragm (in your belly). If your shoulders rise or only your upper chest expands when you breathe in you are only inhaling about one-third of the air that you could be taking.

2. Sit or stand up straight, but feel your shoulders relaxing.

3. Take in a breath, but do not allow your relaxed shoulders to move. Instead, imagine the breath going all the way down into your belly, and notice how your tummy expands slightly.

4. Count to five as you inhale.

5. Hold the breath for the count of two.

6. Exhale slowly to the count of five.

7. Repeat several times.

- Learn to use your space. Pick a point to train from where you can be seen and from where you can see. Make this your 'training spot' and always begin your session standing up and on your 'training spot'. Every time you want to get the attention of the group you simply need to return to your spot. Similarly, when you want to encourage discussion, sit down – putting yourself on the same level as your delegates – and then, when you need to signify that discussion time is over you simply need to stand and return to your 'training spot'.

> Ref to ELP 9 – NLP Anchoring learning

- Be a role model. It is important for the credibility of your message that you are a congruent role model. You must be seen to 'practice what you preach'. You cannot get away with 'do what I say, not what I do'.

DELIVERING LEARNING EFFECTIVELY

BEGINNING LEARNING SESSIONS

Arrivals and welcome

When learners arrive for a learning session they may be experiencing a number of different feelings or emotions. Some may feel confident and positive, while others may be thinking 'I wish I did not have to be here', or 'I am worried about what is going to be expected of me'. Anxiety is a natural response to doing something new or joining a new group of people – and something we can probably all relate to. Happily, there are a number of things we can do to reassure anxious learners.

- It is usually better to let learners come into the learning environment as they arrive (or once the room is set up) so that they can prepare themselves for the activities ahead. Keeping everyone waiting outside the room can build up tension and frustrate those who like to arrive early and settle themselves in.

- Greet people individually when they arrive – think of it as like welcoming guests to a party at your home! Even if you are busy organising things, you can still take a few minutes to welcome them and point out essentials, such as toilets and drink machines. A friendly 'just make yourself comfortable and let me know if you need anything' gives them the freedom to do whatever they need to do to prepare for the learning, knowing you are there if needed. A welcoming message can also be written on the flip-chart for people to see as they come in.

- Unless there is a very good reason to delay, start the session at the agreed time. Not starting on time is likely to irritate learners or make them anxious that the session may over-run the agreed finish time.

Introductions

To begin the training, a good starting point is to introduce yourself to the group. This may be as simple as telling everyone your name, or you may think it appropriate to give a little more information – your background, your experience – to help establish your credentials in the subject area.

The next area of introduction might be to 'the domestics' and the learning session. This is a chance to ensure learners are aware of:

- health and safety requirements – eg fire procedures
- domestic arrangements – eg refreshments, toilets
- the overall aim of the session
- the planned learning outcomes
- timings
- the overall structure of the session.

This introduction can also establish the style of the session: for example the level of formality, the amount of input that will be required by the participants, how and when you will be dealing with their questions, what type of activities will be used, what handouts are going to be available.

Finally it is important to give learners a chance to introduce themselves – except perhaps in a short formal session, such as a presentation, where there is no real need for whole group introductions. Introductions are the first step in getting the group to work together and people will generally feel more at ease if they know who the other people in the room are.

Learner introductions could equally be made before the introduction to the session. We prefer to position them afterwards, partly because this gives learners a little more time to settle in before they are asked to contribute, but also because it can be useful to use some programme information within the learner introductions. For example, as well as introducing themselves, learners could say a little about:

- their own learning objectives and reasons for attending the learning – this will help you to pitch the event at the right level (or to manage expectations about personal objectives that may not be met)
- their existing knowledge or experience of the subject – again useful for getting the level right, or for allowing delegates to reflect on how much they already know, and so build their confidence
- any questions they would like covering during the day – allowing you to add these in to the content if not in already and so meet learning needs more fully.

Learners will need some time to collect their thoughts before giving this information and, rather than asking them to give it one by one, going round the room in 'creeping death' style, it can work better to ask people to volunteer until everyone has been included.

Ice-breakers

An ice-breaker is an activity at the start of an event which helps to lessen formality and breakdown people's reserve, and can help the process of group members getting to know each other a little.

An easy and 'low risk' ice-breaker is to make the learner introductions the basis of the activity. Ask people to form pairs or small groups to introduce themselves to each other and then to feedback a summary of their learning objectives, prior experience, further questions, etc, as a pair or group. As well as covering the introductory information, this gets learners talking to one another and working in smaller groups, where some may feel more comfortable. It also gives everyone a bit of time to move about and 'relax a little' before returning to the whole group session.

Another effective way of using an ice-breaker is to choose an activity which sets the scene for the event or whets the appetite for the learning that is to come. A short activity which draws on the skills that are going to be learned during the event will give the trainer and the learners some reference points which can be drawn upon later. For example, at the start of a training session about 'influencing skills' you could have an ice-breaker in which participants have to persuade a partner to do a simple but random task, such as swap seats or leave the room. The variety of tactics learners employ to do this, both ethical and manipulative, will provide a wealth of examples throughout the event about the skills to use and those to avoid!

Ice-breakers can be very effective in relaxing or energising the group; however, they can also embarrass or alienate group members or reduce the credibility of the training session if used inappropriately – so always use with care!

> "Shortly after we arrived at the event we were each given a card with the name of an animal on it – mine said 'horse' – then, we were asked to walk around the room introducing ourselves to each other by making the noise of the animal on our card! When we found someone making the same noise (there were two of each animal) we had found our 'partner' for the introductory exercise. It may have worked for some people – but most of us just seemed embarrassed."

There are whole books devoted to ice-breakers (references at the end of the chapter) and here are just a few ideas:

- everyone thinks of a saying that represents them or how they feel today
- everyone states the title of their favourite film or book, and why
- people draw a diagram to represent themselves or how they feel (lack of drawing skills is no obstacle and should add a humorous element)
- the group is presented with a list of personal characteristics or facts (eg 'has an unusual hobby', 'can speak another language', 'has appeared on TV or radio') and tries to identify a group member who can fit (or nearly fit) each of the descriptions (these may be known characteristics of learners or just random ideas).

USING DIFFERENT DELIVERY STYLES

Trainers may become used to always delivering material in a similar style. This might be a style that comes naturally to them, or one they have learned over time. The best trainers, however, choose from a range of different styles – basing that choice, not on their personal preference, but on the needs of their learners.

One way to think of this is to imagine a continuum of delivery styles, from the primarily 'tell' style of the lecture, through to the learner-led style of facilitation.

Lecturer/presenter   Trainer   Facilitator

→─────────────────────────────────→──────────────────────────────────→

Lecturer style

This is:

- Primarily a one-way method of delivery in which the presenter imparts information to the learners.
- A 'tutor-led' style which makes the learners passive receivers of learning.
- Good for situations where the audience know little about the subject or where the presenter is recognised as an expert in the field.
- A good style for providing knowledge to the learners, but will do little to enhance their practical skills.

Trainer style

- More of a two-way method of delivery, which employs a number of different tools and techniques.
- The trainer still imparts information to the learners, but also provides opportunities for them to experience and experiment with the topic and make some decisions about how they participate in the session.
- The learners are therefore active receivers of the learning, with some of their learning coming directly from the input of the trainer, and some of it being the result of their participation in the activities and experiences the trainer planned for them.
- This style is ideal to develop both skills and knowledge as it combines a mixture of knowledge input, demonstration and skill practice all in a safe environment that has been created and controlled by the trainer.

Facilitator style

- This focuses on supporting learners to find their own learning and message.
- This creates an environment in which the learners explore a subject for themselves, but gives very little input or direction.
- The facilitator does not need to be an expert in the subject matter – the skill here is of enabling people to learn for themselves.

- This works best where learners already have a knowledge of the subject and some experience or existing skills.

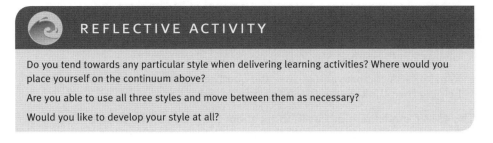

REFLECTIVE ACTIVITY

Do you tend towards any particular style when delivering learning activities? Where would you place yourself on the continuum above?

Are you able to use all three styles and move between them as necessary?

Would you like to develop your style at all?

GIVING PRESENTATIONS

Whether we are delivering a discrete presentation or including some presentation of learning input within a wider training session, there are lots of guidelines, tips and techniques to help.

Winston Churchill is reported to have said that his technique for speech-making (ie a presentation) was:

- Tell them what you are going to tell them.
- Tell them.
- Tell them what you have told them.

This is a good simple structure to consider for any presentation as it helps to keep the speaker on track while reinforcing the message and learning points for the audience/learner.

The first sentence or two of any presentation is probably the most important, as that is when we grab learners' attention and set their expectations of what is to come. Try to find something with high impact – a quote or anecdote, a current film, book or TV reference or even an object or visual – that will hook people in and make them want to hear more, and use this as your opener for presentations and learning inputs.

REFLECTIVE ACTIVITY

The technique of having an impactful first sentence or two can often be seen in books – at the beginning of chapters.

Have a look at a few and see if you can identify some good examples of first sentences that grab attention and pull the readers in. Then consider some of your past or future presentations and see if you can think of a good opening to grab listeners' attention.

Bernice McCarthy's 4MAT model can also help us to structure a presentation. McCarthy says that we should address the following four learner questions in our delivery:

Ref to ELP 4 – 4MAT

- Why? – Give the reasons why your audience should listen. Tune them into 'wii. fm' (what's in it for me?).

- What? – Make sure you give the right amount of background and description about the subject. Present the subject clearly.

- How? – Give practical examples of the skills involved and how and where the subject can be applied. How can learners use it?

- What if? – Anticipate and answer the questions your audience may ask, helping them link the topic to their own worlds.

The 4MAT model reminds us to think about the presentation from the learners' point of view. What do they need to get from it? What will make it more interesting and more useful for them?

Another useful concept to consider when presenting here is 'VAK' – visual, auditory and kinaesthetic learning styles. VAK reminds us that people use different senses for taking in and thinking about information, and therefore have different ways of learning.

Even a formal, one-way presentation can be brought to life more effectively for all listeners by appealing to different senses:

- The auditory sense is engaged through voice, sounds and words – written as well as verbal. Handouts, the words on slides, the notes people make while listening, are all ways in which people with a dominant auditory preference will remember your message.

- The visual sense is engaged through visual images and effects. Colour and pattern are very important – and for visual learners, 'a picture paints a thousand words'. If there is nothing else for visual learners to look at, they will probably look at (examine) you, or look out of the window. Spoken words can also engage the visual sense by providing strong visual descriptions of how things look, or by inviting the audience to imagine or envision how something looks for them.

- The kinaesthetic sense is engaged through activity or emotion. Talking about actions and feelings – describing what people have done or the emotions they have felt, and expressing your own feelings and passion for your subject. Inviting the audience to imagine they are actually doing a particular activity or asking how they would feel if X happened are all ways of engaging people with a kinaesthetic preference.

Learner questions

Because we are used to some presentations having a 'save questions until the end' policy, learners may feel uncomfortable about interrupting a trainer while they are presenting information, unless this has been clarified with them. This can mean opportunities to clarify and resolve learner questions and uncertainties get missed.

Ref to ELP 8 – NLP VAK

It is usually far more beneficial to invite and encourage learners to 'chip in' and ask questions as things go along. This can be made clear at the beginning of some input and reinforced by checking for questions throughout the input. If answering a question at the point it is asked will detract from the overall logic of the presentation, then it is usually enough to thank the questioner for raising the point and reassure them that the question will be answered later on – or, if not done so to their satisfaction, that you will re-visit the point at the end.

GIVING DEMONSTRATIONS

Demonstration is an essential method for helping learners develop new skills, understand processes and even develop new behaviours. Imagine how long it would take to teach someone to drive, for example, or operate a computer if you could not demonstrate the skills and processes to them.

Demonstration can be useful for many topics, from how to use a spreadsheet to how to deal with an angry customer. A good structure to follow when demonstrating is:

1. Demonstrate the whole process first – this gives the 'big picture'.

2. Break down the process into manageable chunks and demonstrate them step by step – this helps people to understand the detail and sequence of the process.

3. Repeat the step-by-step demonstration, this time encouraging questions from the audience – this helps people to make sense of the process in their own way.

4. Demonstrate the whole process again – to pull it all together and embed the understanding.

Depending on the subject being covered, the next useful step would be for learners to try the process for themselves, under supervision from the trainer, and to get feedback on their efforts. An old proverb states 'I hear and I forget. I see and I remember. I do and I understand.' Whatever our learning preferences most of us will need to practise a skill or process in order to fully understand it.

Some very practical points about demonstration:

- Make sure everyone can see and hear.

- Make sure you know how to do it properly yourself (practice first!).

- Have enough materials to complete and be able to repeat the demonstration several times.

- Have a Plan B – if it goes wrong, how else will you provide the learning (perhaps, 'one I prepared earlier'?).

REFLECTIVE ACTIVITY

Think of a process that you know well – something at work, or an everyday day task like peeling an orange. Imagine you need to demonstrate this to a group of people who have never seen it before. How would you break it down?

How would you describe each step?

What questions could you anticipate from your audience and how would you answer them?

MANAGING LEARNER ACTIVITIES

A good training session will involve a range of learner activities – games, discussions, case studies and work based activities, self-analysis exercises, skills practice and role plays.

> "One message rings out loud and clear from all the research that I have undertaken on how people learn. That is, to involve the learners. Get them interested, excited. Intrigue them. Tell them stories and get them to construct their own. Use colourful language – employ humour – bring your message to life. Only by capturing people's imaginations and engaging their emotions will we provide learning that really makes a difference."
>
> Jane Church, Learning Facilitator, Novus Professional Development Ltd

Here are some practical steps to help manage learner activities:

1. If the activity requires the group to divide into smaller 'syndicate groups', decide beforehand whether these should be specific groupings (different job roles, different levels of prior learning, a mix of experience, people who work together, people who do not, etc) or whether random groupings will be best. If it is to be random groups, then either leave learners to self-select or, to avoid the awkwardness sometimes caused by this, have a bag of coloured counters (if you want three groups then you need three colours of counter) or a number of straws cut to different lengths – long, medium and short – which people select from. Then the 'reds' work together, the 'blues' work together, etc.

2. Provide a context for the activity, ie why has the activity been included in the session and how is it helpful to learning?

3. Give clear instructions – these could be verbal, or written, or ideally, both. Make sure that your instructions include the process you want learners to follow, the amount of time they have, and the output that you are expecting at the end.

4. Make sure that you have provided the resources that they will need – space, equipment, copies of the instructions etc.

5. Check in with the groups after a couple of minutes to make sure that they are underway and that they have understood the instructions. Clarify anything that is confusing them.

6. Monitor progress from a distance. Although you need to keep an eye on the groups and check occasionally that all is well, it is usually best to leave them to function if they seem to be progressing satisfactorily. On the whole you should trust the activity, trust the groups and leave them to get on with it.

7. Of course if they do not appear to be progressing you may need to intervene – to clarify goals or processes or perhaps to remind the group of the time constraints. If the group is completely off-track you may need to re-direct them, and if they are struggling offer some hints or advice.

8. After the activity, ask the groups to report back and share their outputs. Thank them for their efforts and praise the results.

9. Debrief the activity, giving any 'official' answers and discussing any differences with or between group responses. Make sure that a correct solution is clearly agreed before moving on.

10. To conclude the activity, ask groups to consider the learning processes of the activity, as opposed to the 'technical answers' referred to at point 9 above. For example, you could ask learners:

- how their group 'functioned'
- what they have learned from the activity
- what they will do differently as a result of the learning.

USING VISUAL AIDS

> "Learn to read your learners, not your slides."
>
> Rosie Renold, Trainer

Whether we are presenting, demonstrating or managing activities, there will often be a need for visual aids – remember VAK (above) – the different ways people have of taking information in. Visual aids can also clarify, reinforce or liven up information being presented in other ways. Let us have a look at three of the most popular visual aids for training (Table 6.1).

Table 6.1 **Visual aids**

Visual aid	Advantages	Tips
Flip-charts	– Great for building up ideas and models as you go along – Learners can contribute and write on them for themselves – Ease and immediacy of use encourages spontaneity and creativity – or both learners and trainers – Can be pre-prepared or instantaneous	– Write legibly and use colours that can be seen (not yellow on white paper) – Check, before the session, that your writing can be seen from the back of the training room – Make small pencil notes on the flips to remind you of your key points or do outline drawings of diagrams in pencil, in advance, to help you produce them accurately in the session – Try the new 'magic' types of whiteboard/flip-chart that stick directly on the wall and are wipe-able and re-useable to increase portability and flexibility of use even further – Use a digital camera to capture the content of your completed flip-charts so that you can distribute them later

PowerPoint Slides	– Easy to prepare – with the appropriate software – Once prepared can be used many times and easily adapted for different sessions – Great for giving structure and consistency across sessions – Can also be printed as handouts	– Keep use of slides to a minimum and avoid 'death by PowerPoint' – Use pictures, images and graphs to bring a subject to life – There is no need to have a slide for every learning point – inter-mingle slides with other visuals – Some projectors are noisy or give off a lot of heat/light – turn them off when not using them – Spend a bit of time using the help menus and tutorials to learn how to use more features, then you can create more interesting and impactful slides when needed – Check back at the PowerPoint tips in the previous chapter
Interactive White Boards (SMART Boards)	– Great for combining video, PowerPoint and written material – Can allow dual use by the trainer and the learners – Allows for structure and flexibility	– Make sure that you know how all the equipment works – Experiment and make best use of all the functions – Do not over-rely on the technology – remember that you are still the trainer – let the Smart Board support your session rather than become the session – If you use interactive boards frequently you might consider some of the commercially available training on how to use them effectively and more fully

USING QUESTIONING AND LISTENING SKILLS

Questioning and listening skills are essential skills for trainers.

So, why are questions so useful?

- To gain or keep attention. Because questions are usually directed at others, people tend to pay attention when they hear a question – even if you are not expecting anyone to answer it.

- Sign-posting what is next to be discussed. We started this section with the question 'So why are questions so useful?' This was an example of a rhetorical question used to get the reader thinking about the subject and sign-post that this was the area we would be covering next.

So, how else can a trainer use questions?

- Questions can help a trainer to check for understanding, either directly or indirectly. The direct way would be to ask, for example, 'Does that make sense?' We do not even need a verbal answer to this type of question – observation of the group's response and body language can reveal enough for us to know whether learning has been effective. Alternatively, we can check for understanding more indirectly, by asking 'How could I use questions to check for understanding?' and then wait to hear if learners know the answers.

- Using probing or exploratory questions can help extend the learning. 'Where else would this be useful?' 'How exactly are you going to make this happen?' 'What do you think would happen if...?' These are all examples of questions that encourage learners to take their learning a stage further or deeper.

- Finally, questions can be a way of responding to other people's questions – either to clarify what is being asked, or to encourage the questioner to find the answer for themselves or to bring others into the discussion. For example, if a learner asks a question, a trainer might reply with:
  - 'Tell me more about what you mean.'
  - 'What do you think the options are?'
  - 'What do you think I'll say to that?'
  - 'How could you find the answer to that?'
  - 'What does everyone else think?'

Listening skills are equally if not more important for trainers, so that we can:

- monitor how learners are taking in the learning

- respond accurately to learners' questions

- value, acknowledge and respond to learner contributions.

Many learners find it difficult to speak up in a large group setting – and will only be encouraged to do so if they feel their contributions are heard and valued. Listening and acknowledging contributions is very important, but can be difficult in a lively multi-way discussion.

To show that we are listening we can:

- give full attention to the speaker – eye contact, nods, etc

- reflect back what has been said to check that we have understood

- take action on what has been said – acknowledge it, respond to it, incorporate it if appropriate

- notice when someone is trying to make a point, but maybe not managing to make themselves heard for whatever reason (often a lack of confidence), and give them an 'in', eg 'What were you going to say there Michael?'

While listening to individuals is important, there is also a responsibility to the wider group and to balance our attention across all group members. Try to avoid getting into a detailed conversation with one learner at the expense of the rest of the group.

Good listening skills help build rapport and empathy with learners, as well as making learners feel validated and more confident about making further contributions.

GIVING FEEDBACK

Giving learners feedback is another crucial step in helping them move around Kolb's Learning Cycle. It is especially useful after delegates have taken part in an activity such as a role play, skill demonstration or case study, as it helps them to reflect on their performance in the activity and provides a better balance of information, ie not just their own perceptions, on which to reflect.

Ref to ELP 2 – Experiential learning cycle

Some key guidelines for giving feedback are:

- Always deliver it in a positive way, and for the benefit of the receiver.
- Concentrate on things that are within the receivers' control.
- Feedback on what went well, as well as what could be done differently – if a learner knows what they did well they can choose to do it again.
- Make feedback as specific as possible – 'That was very good' might make your learner feel good for a few minutes, but it does not really help them to learn from the experience. 'That was very good because you gave a detailed explanation that was pitched just right for your customer' is much more useful.

For example, imagine that on a course for presentation skills, the first learner has just delivered their presentation. A useful format to follow for giving them feedback could be:

1. Ask them how they think it went – and specifically for one thing they think was particularly good and one they think was less good.

2. Tell them something you really liked about their presentation and why you liked it.

3. Tell them something you think they could change or do differently. Again, be clear about what they did and how they could change or improve it. Give reasons – the difference the change could make.

4. Give an overall assessment of their performance.

5. Ask the learner to summarise what they learned from the experience and what they will keep and what they will change next time.

It can be a good idea to get learners to feedback to one another. Not only are the extra comments and suggestions likely to be useful to the recipient, but the practice will also help everyone to develop their feedback skills. If using this approach, it might be a good idea to cover some information on 'good practice in giving and receiving feedback' first and to use observation and listening skills to ensure that feedback is being given supportively.

BOOST FOR FEEDBACK

Balanced: include strengths as well as development points
Observed: base it on what you personally have observed
Objective: check for and avoid any bias or 'personal agenda'
Specific: give specific examples
Timely: give it as soon as possible after the event, when it is most useful – and likely to be most accurate.

For me, the important factor about feedback is the need for balance. Even if someone has not done something very well, there is always something positive to say. For example, in a presentation situation; if the presenter is reading from notes it is not good presenting but it could be fair to praise the attention to detail. If the presenter is 'winging it' and there is little content it is not good presenting but it could be fair to praise the open and friendly style.

Wendy Strohm, Wendy Strohm Associates Ltd

MONITORING LEARNING AND MAKING ADJUSTMENTS

Much of what we have discussed so far in this section has been about providing good quality learning – through presentations, demonstrations and learner activities. This is crucially important, but not enough in itself. We also need to monitor how well the learning is being 'received' by learners and, if necessary, make adjustments to ensure learning objectives are met.

Monitoring individuals within a group

When we are working just with individuals it is fairly straight-forward to monitor and adjust learning – we can ask questions, look at learners' work, discuss progress with them and then make the necessary adjustments. Within group sessions it is more difficult to monitor individual progress and make related adjustments, but it can and should still be done.

One way to approach this is to consider a classic training cycle, with the four stages of: identify needs, design learning, deliver learning and evaluate learning, as in Figure 6.1. (Some also add a fifth stage of 'assessment' between deliver and evaluate.) When we are delivering learning sessions we are, of course, operating in the third stage of the cycle.

Then, while we are delivering learning we can *repeat the cycle for each individual*, as in Figure 6.2.

So, while we are delivering learning for the group we can also think about how the training is impacting on each individual, asking ourselves: how well is the learning working for a particular learner (evaluate)? What needs are not being met or are emerging that require the learning to be adjusted for that individual (identify)? What adjustments need to be made (design)? We can then make the required adjustments (deliver), and the cycle begins again.

Ref to ELP 1 – Training cycle

Figure 6.1 Training cycle

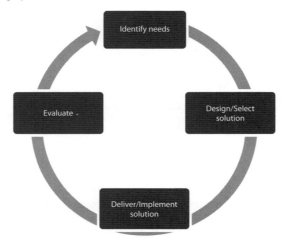

Figure 6.2 Embedded training cycle

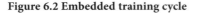
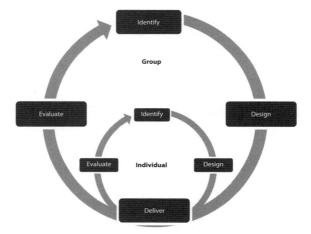

For example, while we are working with a group we may notice that a learner is struggling with a particular learning material and would benefit from working on a different example or case study – and so give them the different material in the next activity. Or we might see that a learner is not getting the best out of the learning because of the particular syndicate group they are working in – maybe the group is too advanced for them or not advanced enough – and so for the next activity we can rearrange the groups to overcome this. Or we might recognise that a learner lacks confidence in relation to the learning and decide to focus on giving more constructive and confirming feedback to help with this. The subtle needs you identify and respond to through making small adjustments are endless, but your efforts to do this will help ensure a more valuable experience for all your learners.

Group reviews

As well as listening to the spontaneous comments made by learners and making our own observations of learner behaviour and performance, we also need to hold regular structured reviews with the group. These are useful for several reasons:

- The trainer gets information to help them manage the ongoing session.
- Learners have an opportunity to reflect on their learning so far and identify how they may want to adjust the session or the way they are contributing.
- The review provides a break, and a chance to refresh thinking, before the next chunk of learning.

A group review might just be a short (few minutes) group discussion, where everyone considers: how they are progressing? Whether they are happy with the learning? Is there anything they want to add or change?

Reviews can also take a more creative form, engaging learners' different senses and helping to reinforce and embed learning. You can use your imagination here – as long as you follow the essential rule of 'keep it appropriate'.

Here are a few examples:

- discussions in groups or pairs
- creating a drawing that represents what has been learned
- colouring in the bars on a graph to represent learning progress
- creating a song, poem or mnemonic that reflects the learning so far
- creating a radio news report about the proceedings of the day
- creating a mime or short performance to demonstrates learning points
- forming a human chain continuum, ordered to represent different levels of individual understanding of the topic, within the group
- finding an object in the room that is a metaphor for what has been learned.

It is usually a good idea to have reviews just before a break – giving you time to make small adjustments before the group returns.

> Always have extra learning activities to hand just in case the group, or some individuals, turn out to be 'extra smart'. Also have parts of the training earmarked as 'non-essential' in case the group are less quick on the up-take.'
>
> Rosie Renold, Trainer

BRINGING LEARNING SESSIONS TO A CLOSE

Assisting the transfer of learning to the workplace

To get the most value from learning you will need to assist learners to transfer their learning back to the workplace. The most effective means of achieving this is through the completion of an action plan.

Useful questions to encourage future action could be:

- What are you going to do differently as a result of this training?
- What specific actions do you need to take?
- Who else do you need to involve?
- When will you do it?
- What could stop you from being successful?
- How could you prevent this?
- How will you know that you have achieved your plan? What results do you expect to see?

All too often the action planning stage of a training event is combined with the first level of evaluation (reaction) – so although delegates do an action plan, they then leave it with the trainer. This might help the trainer to assess how successful their delivery has been ('look at all these action points – haven't I done well') but it limits the transfer of learning into the workplace, and, therefore, restricts the eventual value of the training.

Sufficient time should be allowed at the end of the session for learners to complete their action plan – and the plan should be taken with them when they leave. Learners should, ideally, share their action plans with their line manager after the event, so that managers can monitor and measure the change in knowledge, skill or behaviour.

Evaluation

Part of the delivery process of any learning event is to begin the evaluation process. It is likely that level one (reaction) and level two (learning) can be measured by the trainer 'on the day'.

Ref to ELP 11 – Levels of Evaluation

For help with this, you may want to have a look at the next chapter: Evaluating Learning and Development Activities. The subject is also covered in Chapter 5: Designing Learning and Development Activities.

MANAGING GROUP DYNAMICS

A note about one-to-one training

This chapter has mainly concentrated on the delivery of training to a group, but many of the principles discussed apply equally to one-to-one training.

Ref to ELP 3 – Learning styles

When training one-to-one, it can be quite tempting to tailor sessions to suit a learner's learning style – for example giving lots of background knowledge and theory to the 'theorist'. Although this is very considerate, it is not always the best approach. A good learning experience depends on the learner journeying through all four stages of the cycle, and so a theorist also needs opportunities for activity, reflection and planning.

Ref to ELP 2 – Experiential learning cycle

Working with large groups

On the whole, the techniques that we have covered in this chapter can be 'scaled up' to work with groups of any size. Once groups get particularly large, however (20 or more people), you will need to consider some other issues:

- Being seen and heard. You will need to pay particular attention to the room layout and make sure that everyone can see and hear you. Also remember that delegates might not be able to hear each other – so a comment or question asked by one participant may need to be repeated so that everyone in the room has heard it.

- Timing. Some activities that work well with a smaller group may need to be curtailed with a larger one. Ten people taking one or two minutes each to introduce themselves is fine – 30 taking two minutes each would be tedious and a poor use of time. Similarly, if you are using group activities you will have to weigh up the value of each group reporting back to the whole room against the time that it will take. It can also take longer to get large groups back from breaks or from syndicates, so you will need to build this into your timings.

- Number of trainers. If you are planning to do a lot of syndicate activities, you will find it harder to pay sufficient attention to them all, or to provide an adequate level of feedback. It will also be more difficult to monitor how individuals are faring in the group learning environment. For groups of around 20 or more, it is worth considering a co-trainer, if this is possible within your resources.

Mixing up the group

There are many benefits to moving a group around and mixing it up:

- It can help break up 'cliques' or groups that are not working together well.

- It enables you to arrange learners in groupings that are most conducive to their learning.

- It can help manage involvement levels by, say, mixing (or separating) introverts and extroverts to get a better balance of participation.

- It can give learners the opportunity to meet and work with a different set of colleagues and to learn other points of view.

- Moving about will help energise the group.

Use syndicate work and activities to successfully move a group around without them feeling that they have been manipulated.

Managing involvement

There is no requirement for every learner to participate in learning in the same way. Some people are naturally more inclined to contribute comments than others, and there will be times when some individuals in the group simply do not have anything to say. Remember too that people with a 'reflector' preference are much happier listening to other peoples' views than offering their own.

What you must strive for, however, is equality of *opportunity* to contribute. Some helpful ways of managing over-involvement and under-involvement might be:

HIGH CONTRIBUTORS

- Thank them, but say that you would like to hear from someone else.
- Check your body language and rapport – are you encouraging them with your eye contact and reactions?
- Give them another role – observer, flip-chart writer etc.
- Consider mixing the groups so that they cannot dominate so easily.
- Monitor the effect they are having on the rest of the group – is it OK for them to dominate?
- Consider having a quiet word with them in a break. Thank them for their contribution but request that they let others have a say too.

LOW CONTRIBUTORS

- Some people just find it difficult to speak up in a group but have plenty to say – and need to be 'invited in' or given a space to speak up. You can give this by asking some direct questions of individuals or asking questions of learners in turn, going around the room. To avoid this approach embarrassing anyone, make a point of saying beforehand that it is fine to say 'pass' if people do not have, or do not want, to contribute an answer.
- Say that you would like to hear from some people who haven't said much yet – but avoid putting them on the spot in a way that can cause embarrassment.
- Give them a particular role – spokesperson, syndicate 'group leader'.
- Put people into small discussion groups. A shy person may be more likely to put themselves forward in a less dominating group.
- Monitor the engagement – if someone is really engaged and attentive, but simply not speaking much, that is usually OK.
- Take the opportunity to have a quiet word in a break and check that they are 'OK' with the style and level.

Managing energy

As a trainer you can use your 'birds eye' position at the front of the room to monitor the group's energy levels. You may sense that levels are low when you start seeing tired body language, yawns or general disengagement.

When energy levels are beginning to flag there are a number of things you can do, including:

- Consider how you are presenting the material – are you sounding tired, quiet or talking at too slow a pace? Try mixing up the speed and volume of your speech a little to stimulate a stronger group response.
- Assess whether the level of input is causing the problem – too detailed or too simple, and then change the level.
- Get people moving – maybe as an adaptation to an exercise, eg instead of groups preparing a response to feedback verbally, get them to come up and write their 'answers' on the flip-chart or to feedback via a short presentation.

- Ask the group to write something down – changing their body posture will also change the energy levels.

- Ask a question – questions tend to make people more attentive.

- Add some humour into your delivery – laughter is one of the best energisers.

- Suggest a quick comfort break.

Learner choice

While it is important for trainers to monitor and manage the group dynamic and help ensure the best learning climate for everyone, there is no need for a trainer to control everything. Giving learners choice and ownership over how they learn is an important pre-requisite for adult learning.

For example:

- Leave people to choose where they sit on arrival. Learners may choose a particular spot because they can see or hear better from there or feel more at ease if they are sitting next to someone they know. You can always mix people up later, during learning activities and syndicate work.

- On a longer event (all day or more) you might invite the group to determine some 'ground rules' about how they want to work together. These might include practical items like time keeping and finish times as well as behaviours, such as agreeing to listen to each other, being open to ideas, no-one to dominate, etc. If the whole group has determined the 'rules' they are more likely to follow them later on.

- If the group has produced flip-charts or other outputs, put these on display around the room – they are a constant reminder of the learning that is happening, and they 'belong' to the group.

- Wherever possible, let the group decide – not just temperature control, lighting levels, etc, but also the order of some activities or how they are undertaken – or maybe occasionally, you could offer learners a choice from alternative activities. The more learners can make decisions about their own learning and feel involved in the process, the more likely they are to value the learning and put it into practise after the event (and complete their learning cycles).

WHAT NEXT

DELIVERY

Some things you could do to expand and develop your learning from this chapter are:

1. Review how well you fulfil your H&S responsibilities as a trainer? Could you improve your performance in this area? Take some action towards this, such as: reading up on H&S requirements for trainers or talking to H&S representatives in your organisation and develop a risk assessment form you can use before each of your training courses (if you do not already have one).

2. Sit in on a training course delivered by one of your trainer colleagues and give them feedback on their style. Pick something that you particularly liked and something that you think they could improve on.

3. Ask a colleague to observe you delivering an L&D activity and ask them for the same area of feedback as at 2 above.

4. Use your network to get an invite to sit in on some training delivery in another organisation. What are the similarities and differences with the delivery that you do? What can you learn from them?

5. Join some on-line trainer networks and see what other trainers are doing and the sort of questions that they ask of each other.

6. Have a look at the scenarios exercise below.

SCENARIO ACTIVITY

Below are five scenarios an L&D professional/trainer could face. Have a look at the scenarios – and imagine that they have happened to you. Then consider the following questions:

1. What, if anything, could you have done to avoid the situation happening?

2. How would you manage the situation when it happened?

Scenario 1

You are delivering a one-day programme on 'Communication Skills'. During the introductions, one delegate mentions that he is attending the day because his manager is 'always complaining about my spelling' and he is hoping that today might help him improve this. Spelling is definitely not covered in your planned session, nor was it mentioned in any of the session information.

Scenario 2

Two delegates arrive at an event together and sit next to each other. The first session is a mixture of input from you and contributions from the group. The pair keep whispering to each other throughout this session. In the next activity, you ask people to work in pairs with someone they have not met before. The two delegates announce that they will work together and ignore any attempts from other delegates to pair up with them.

Scenario 3

You arrive at a venue some distance from your work-base where you are due to deliver a half-day training session. On arrival you discover there has been a mix-up with the booking, and that there is no screen, projector or laptop available for you to use. All you have with you is the USB stick containing your slides. You had planned to organise the whole session around the slides and some of them show diagrams of processes that are quite complex and essential to the delegates' learning.

Scenario 4

It becomes apparent from the introductory sessions that the delegates in your learner group have very different levels of prior knowledge. You had been led to believe that everyone had some basic knowledge, but no more than that. In fact, a few of the delegates seem to have a high level of knowledge and experience, while others are completely new to the subject.

Scenario 5

You are co-ordinating a management development programme which includes managers getting feedback from their teams. When you pass the feedback on to one manager, you mention that one of her team thinks she is 'rather poor at giving her staff constructive feedback on their work'. The manager does not take this very well – and you later find out she has interviewed every team member and 'interrogated them' in an attempt to find out who made the comment, and will no doubt see them 'punished' for it. Feelings within the team are not good.

SUMMARY

This chapter has explored:

Why effective training/learning delivery is important

- Development programmes are still considered to be the most effective learning and talent development practice according to the CIPD 2010 survey.

- However, face-to-face training is expensive and therefore it must be done well and effectively.

Key features of 'good quality training delivery'

- Good-quality training delivery includes high quality learning content that is targeted to meet learning needs.

- It is delivered effectively by skilled and competent trainers.

- The learning environment and group dynamics are managed to ensure maximum learning can take place.

A range of potential barriers to learning

- Barriers to learning could be created in the way learning opportunities are described or how they are delivered.

- Individual barriers may also be created as a result of negative prior learning experiences or negative self-perceptions.

- Learning materials may also provide barriers to learning if they confuse, offend, or exclude.

Aspects of planning and preparation to help overcome barriers

- Good planning for learning includes communicating with learners before the event, providing clear joining instructions and instructions regarding any pre-work, establishing the right environment for learning and preparing ourselves to undertake training.

- If we consider causal factors, and take action before learning, we can minimise the potential barriers faced by learners.

The skills required to deliver learning effectively

- Delivering learning effectively requires trainers to be competent in many skills.
- These include being able to open and close learning sessions effectively, use different trainer styles, give presentations and demonstrations, use visual aids, use questioning, listening and feedback skills, monitor individual learning and make adjustments and manage group dynamics.

Techniques for managing group dynamics

- We can manage group dynamics by how we organise the group and how we encourage or discourage learner involvement.
- We can also use our voice, movements and style of training to influence the energy levels within a group.
- While it is important to manage the group effectively, it is also important to allow learners as much choice as possible within their learning.

BOOKS:

Tizzard, P. and Evans, A. (2003) *The ice-breakers pocketbook*. Alresford: Management Pocketbooks.

Townsend, J. (2003) *The trainer's pocketbook*. 10th edn. Alresford: Management Pocketbooks.

Truelove, S. (2006) *Training in practice*. London: CIPD.

WEBSITES:

Range of on-line information and guidance relating to learning and training delivery:

www.cipd.co.uk/subjects/lrnanddev

Free (or partially free) on-line access to learning activities:

www.businessballs.com

www.mindtools.com

www.trainingzone.co.uk

Commercially available learning materials, activities, resources (there are many others available via internet search):

www.trainerslibrary.com

www.fenman.co.uk/traineractive/index.php

www.keyfax.net

www.mlruk.com

www.gowertraining.co.uk

www.magicwhiteboard.co.uk

Range of free (or partially free) information, advice and assessment tools relating to health, safety and wellbeing at work:

www.hse.gov.uk

www.iosh.co.uk/information_and_resources.aspx

www.cipd.co.uk/subjects/health/general

EXPLORE FURTHER

CHAPTER 7

Evaluating Learning and Development Activities

INTRODUCTION

In this chapter we will consider the importance of undertaking evaluation and the benefits to be gained from this. We will then explore the full meaning of evaluation and how it has been defined by some key thinkers in this area. The main part of the chapter presents a staged process to undertaking evaluation, exploring different methods, different sources of information and some guidelines for collecting and analysing information. Finally we examine the options for presenting evaluation findings and the factors to consider when presenting these to different stakeholder groups.

LEARNING OUTCOMES

When you have read this chapter you should be able to:

● explain and promote the value of evaluation activity

● define and explain evaluation and related terms

● explain some key theories and thinking on evaluation

● describe different evaluation methods

● describe and discuss key factors to be considered in the collection and analysis of information

● describe and discuss key factors to be considered when reporting evaluation findings and making recommendations.

MAKING A CASE FOR EVALUATION

> "My former manager told me that 'we did not have time to do evaluation', unsurprisingly we spent a lot of time crisis managing."

In the CIPD 2009 Learning and Development Survey, 24 per cent of the L&D professionals surveyed selected '*monitoring and evaluating training*' as one of their main activities. In many ways this is a good 'score', and it is an increase on the year before, but we firmly agree with the 60 per cent of the overall survey respondents who anticipate a greater emphasis on evaluation in the future.

Without real evaluation, the same products can be delivered over and over again, whether or not they are effective. If organisations have allowed this to happen in the past, they are unlikely to do so in the future, as L&D, quite rightly, is increasingly required to be accountable for its offerings.

Perhaps evaluation has not always had the best image – considered by some to be a vague and time-consuming process – but, with our growing understanding of the purposes and benefits of evaluation and with technological developments making evaluation activities easier and more engaging, this is need no longer be the case.

Evaluation skills are essential to our profession. If we are to deliver training we are proud of and know that we are making a significant contribution to our organisations, we have to be skilled in evaluating and improving the learning activities we provide. In return we can expect:

- continuously improved learning activities for our learners
- increased learner and line manager engagement in learning
- a clearer understanding of our organisations and how we can support the achievement of organisational objectives
- greater confidence (ours and others') in our training delivery
- greater respect from our colleagues in the business
- an evidence base to demonstrate our contribution to the business.

"Part of my work involves assessing learning processes within organisations – and so often the weakest link is evaluation. Some organisations see the importance of it, but rely on one method only and never revisit whether this is effective or not. Others might spend time and resources on carrying out evaluation but then do nothing with it, or do the evaluation, the analysis and even act on it, but then never promote the action they have taken. Then there is the rare group who regularly consider whether their evaluation methods are producing constructive feedback, target key areas to be evaluated, use a variety of different methods – paper-based, electronic and face-to-face – and not only analyse the results but use them to inform continuous improvement and then promote what has been done as a result. Where evaluation is given the importance it deserves and is one of the key business processes – IT REALLY WORKS!!"

Sue Harding, Harding Associates

UNDERSTANDING EVALUATION

So, what do we actually mean by the term 'evaluation'? According to the dictionaries:

> Evaluate … to ascertain or set the amount or value of; to judge or assess the worth of.
>
> *Collins Concise Dictionary*

> Evaluation … the act or result of judging the worth or value of something.
>
> *Roget's II: The New Thesaurus*, 3rd edn

In a training context, evaluation is about measuring and analysing various aspects of L&D provision, with a view to determining the effectiveness and value of the provision and informing decisions about how it can be improved.

The last four chapters have focused on the stages of the training cycle. Evaluation is the final stage of the training cycle and so completes it. However, the nature of a cycle is that one flows into the next, hence much evaluation activity overlaps with learning needs analysis, taking us into the next cycle. While evaluation essentially looks back at training that has already taken place and learning needs analysis looks forwards at learning that is required, some of the same activities will inform both processes.

Ref to ELP 1– Training cycle

It is important that we see evaluation as part of a cycle – something to be done on an ongoing basis as an integral part of continuous improvement. If we view evaluation in this way we make it easier to manage and less off-putting than the idea of big 'one-off', and probably more costly, evaluation initiatives.

"The organisations that really understand evaluation have few forms but do have:

- line managers that are actively involved in the development of their people
- people who are involved in their own development and are very clear what any learning and development activity should achieve for them and their organisation
- a learning and development function that constantly seeks information from managers and individuals as part of a much wider approach to evaluation and uses the information to bring about continuous improvement."

Jane Elliott-Poxon, Elliott Partnership

SOME RELATED TERMS AND PROCESSES

There are several similar terms and processes which are associated with evaluation but which have slightly different meanings. Some of the most widely used of these are explained in Table 7.1.

Table 7.1 **Evaluation**

Process	Definition	Links to evaluation
Validation	Validation – meaning to establish the truth of, confirm or corroborate – is about establishing whether learning activity achieved its stated objectives. Did the training do what it said it would do?	Evaluation (usually) includes validation, but may also include other factors or purposes, such as whether training activity was good value for money – or whether resources were used effectively. For example, a learning programme may achieve all its learning objectives and be deemed very successful. However, the programme may be expensive and the costs may not be worth paying for the level of organisational benefits gained from the programme.
Assessment	In a training context, generally applied to individual progress and achievement. The measuring, by a range of methods, of how well someone can perform an activity or demonstrate knowledge, usually against some pre-set criteria.	Assessment is frequently used to establish levels of individual learning and ability. It might be undertaken prior to, during or after (various duration) a learning activity to establish any impact of learning and/or to establish further learning requirements.
Testing	Very similar to assessment but often used to describe an assessment activity which is specifically set within a very controlled environment – such as an exam or observed practical activity.	Similar to assessment above. The format of testing will vary depending on what is being tested – for example, knowledge may require written or verbal tests, while skills may be best tested through observation.
Monitoring and review	A collection of activities to gauge learner progress towards goals.	Information collected for, and from, monitoring and review activities will often be useful to evaluation processes.
Return on investment (ROI)	A measure of the financial impact of training/learning activities on an organisation	Assessing ROI is about accurately calculating the financial impact of the training. ROI is usually considered to be the highest level of evaluation (and if it can be done absolutely remains the subject of debate). Our understanding of this practice has been enhanced by the work of Jack Philips.

Ref to ELP 12 – ROI

| Return on expectation (ROE) | Whereas ROI explores quantitative factors and specifically financial return, ROE is more concerned with stakeholder satisfaction and whether learning activities have met the expectations of key stakeholder groups (learners, managers or customers)? | Stakeholder satisfaction with learning initiatives should be a part of any evaluation. CIPD has championed this approach and captured its importance in the term 'ROE'. An ROE approach to evaluation begins with an understanding of stakeholder expectations and then seeks to measure the extent to which these have been met. In assessing the contribution of learning to an organisation equal consideration is given to intangible, long term benefits as to more tangible and quantifiable outcomes. |

EVALUATION – IN PRACTICE

PLANNING TO EVALUATE

Evaluation need not be a cumbersome nor costly process. Here is a 10-stage plan to approaching evaluation in a logical and efficient way.

1. Identify what learning activity is being evaluated (the 'scope' of the evaluation).
2. Determine the purpose(s) of the evaluation – what are you trying to establish and why (your 'evaluation objectives').
3. Work out the information you need for each purpose/objective and the source of that information.
4. Select appropriate methods and timing to obtain the information you need.
5. You now have your evaluation plan – and should embed this in your training design, you may also need to agree your plan with managers.
6. Design any required evaluation 'tools'– questionnaire, survey form, test, observation sheet.
7. Collect information as per your plan.
8. Analyse information in relation to each of your objectives.
9. Draw conclusions and consider improvement actions.
10. Present your findings and recommendations to relevant partners and stakeholders.

Now, let us consider each stage.

IDENTIFYING WHAT IS TO BE EVALUATED

Where evaluation is in relation to a single session, it might be relatively straightforward to state what you are evaluating. However, bigger or blended programmes may be more complex.

For example, a 'Team leader development programme' might include an initial self-analysis exercise, a one-to-one meeting with line manager, a number of workshops and some optional e-learning modules. If you want to evaluate the programme fully then you will need to include all these aspects in your evaluation. On another occasion, however, you might just want to focus your evaluation on the e-learning modules or the self-analysis exercise.

Clarifying the scope of your evaluation is important as it sets the boundaries for the evaluation activity to be undertaken and provides a clear context when presenting your findings and recommendations.

The purpose(s) of evaluation

There are many different reasons for undertaking evaluation and before we start any evaluation activity we should be clear about why we are doing it and what our specific purposes are.

One way of clarifying this is to consider the different parties who may have an interest in a learning initiative and what their particular interest might be. In any evaluation there will usually be learner, trainer and organisational interests to consider and possibly those of other internal and external partners. For example:

- Learners need to be sure that the learning activities they are giving their time and effort to are effective and are providing an appropriate vehicle for their development.

- The L&D team might be particularly interested in how well immediate programme objectives have been met and how learners respond to the particular training methods and approach used by the trainer.

- The finance function might be particularly interested in the costs and financial impact of the training.

- Managers will be concerned with if, and how, training has impacted on learners' performance in the workplace.

- Awarding, accrediting and regulatory bodies may have an interest in the type of training and learning support provided, as well as aspects of learner achievement.

In fact, evaluation can answer many questions.

REFLECTIVE ACTIVITY

Thinking about a learning programme you have delivered or been involved in, consider the list of evaluation outcomes below and who each outcome would benefit or be useful for: the learners, the trainer, the organisation involved or any external partners, such as regulatory or awarding bodies (AB).

Table 7.2 **Evaluation outcomes**

	Potential purposes (and benefits) of evaluation	Useful to:			
		Learner	Trainer	Organisation	AB
1	Establish whether learning objectives have been met				
2	Establish whether selected learning methods were effective				
3	Establish whether learners enjoyed the learning				
4	Receive feedback on trainer performance				
5	Establish the costs of L&D				
6	Establish 'value for money' of L&D activities				
7	Establish whether learning has been transferred to the workplace				
8	Demonstrate a recognition of the value of learner opinion by asking for their views				
9	Increase learner engagement in learning activities by asking them to reflect and give feedback				
10	Enable learners to influence future learning provision				
11	Measure how much/how well different stakeholder interests have been met				
12	Generate information required for finance department or funding partners				
13	Generate information to 'prove' and promote the value (or not) of L&D to the organisation				
14	Identify gaps in the current provision of L&D				
15	Get new ideas on how L&D could be improved or extended				
16	Establish how L&D is contributing to the achievement of a particular business objective				
17	Help learners to consolidate, recognise and be more aware of learning achieved				

18	Help learners to establish next steps in their learning				
19	Increase engagement of managers and other stakeholders in L&D provision				
20	Establish comparative costs of different L&D options				
21	Establish learner achievement of qualification units or modules and factors that are having an impact on this				
22	Identify gaps in the skill areas of people in the organisation				

Validation or evaluation?

We can also think about the purpose of evaluation in terms of whether we are purely validating learning or whether we are also considering other factors within a wider evaluation of learning. Our main concern if we are validating learning is whether learning objectives have been achieved. Our concerns in evaluating learning are likely to include validation issues but may also include other factors; for example, was the training cost-effective or how has the training benefitted the organisation?

Key thinking on the purpose of evaluation

Our understanding of the purpose of evaluation has been extended by the work of various contributors to this area, including Mark Easterby-Smith and Donald Kirkpatrick.

A useful way of viewing evaluation is that of Mark Easterby-Smith, who describes four main underpinning purposes of evaluation – proving, controlling, improving and learning:

Proving: demonstrating that training has worked and that it has had the desired impact on learners.

Controlling: checking and ensuring that learning is being delivered in the way it is required to be (that trainers are following any required procedures and fulfilling any requirements).

Improving: exploring and identifying how the learning programme can be adapted and improved.

Learning: using evaluation activities (such as self-reflection) to aid and reinforce individual learning.

Considering these 'definitions' may help you clarify what you want to achieve in your evaluation.

Another major piece of work which has had a big impact on our thinking about evaluation and our evaluation practice is Donald Kirkpatrick's model of evaluation levels.

Kirkpatrick describes four levels of evaluation:

Ref to ELP 11 –
Levels of
evaluation

Level 1: reaction

At level 1, evaluation is primarily about how well the training or learning initiative is received by the learners. Did learners enjoy it? Did they find it useful? Did they perceive it to be of value?

Level 2: learning

At level 2, we are seeking to establish whether learners did actually learn as a result of the training. It is quite possible that learners could have enjoyed the training activities while learning very little. Level 2 evaluation is concerned with testing and establishing whether learning has actually taken place.

Level 3: behaviour

Even though learning may have taken place, there is no guarantee that new learning will be applied and result in changed behaviour (performance). Level 3 evaluation is concerned with identifying the impact of training on learner behaviour, ie do learners do something extra, better, quicker, differently as a result of their learning?

Level 4: results

Level 4 evaluation considers the impact of any individual behaviour change on the organisation. Has changed behaviour had an impact on organisational results such as targets, production figures and sales figures? In other words, has the training initiative had a positive impact on organisational performance?

Kirkpatrick's work is not without its challengers, primarily because of the simplicity of the model, but it continues to help many trainers understand and relate to evaluation and has given us a framework in which to carry out our evaluation activities.

It is unlikely that any evaluation initiative would have just one purpose – we are usually seeking to establish a number of things – and most evaluation will involve a combination of several of the purposes discussed above. For example, we might decide to carry out an evaluation to:

- identify the extent to which learning has met its stated objectives
- establish the impact of training on learner's work performance
- establish learners reaction to the training and methods used.

A more complex evaluation might also seek to:

- establish the costs of the learning in relation to the benefits achieved.

Before moving on from 'purposes', we should re-emphasise that evaluation is rarely an exact science, particularly when we are seeking to establish the impact of training on individual or organisational performance. Separating out the impact of training from the impact of all kinds of other factors such as the economic climate, organisational culture or personal behaviour and motivation issues is, at best, difficult. However, providing we are aware of the constraints and limitations of evaluation there is a vast amount of essential information to be gained.

IDENTIFYING INFORMATION NEEDED FOR EVALUATION

Once we have identified the key purposes of our evaluation, we can more accurately identify the types of information we need. For example:

Example 1: if the purpose of evaluation is to identify the extent to which a programme has met its objectives, then we will need to collect information relating to each of these objectives. Depending on the particular learning objectives, this could include information about:

- levels of learning before the programme
- levels of learning after the programme
- work performance before the programme
- work performance after the programme.

In this example, the main sources of information might be pre- and post-learning tests, self-assessments, manager assessments and work results.

This clearly takes us back to the need for us to begin evaluation activity before a programme starts and for us to set very clear learning objectives for our learning programmes.

Example 2: if the purpose of an evaluation is to establish the effectiveness of the training methods used and learners' response to these, then we may also seek information about:

- the trainer's reflections on how well the methods worked, the level of participation generated, any constraints or problems encountered and the ease with which the methods led to the desired result
- the learners' feedback on how accessible methods were, how helpful and engaging they were and any problems or limitations caused by the particular methods
- we could also involve an independent observer to give objective feedback on the learning process.

Example 3: a more complex evaluation, seeking to determine whether training was 'worthwhile' through undertaking a cost-benefit analysis, would need information about:

- Costs:
  - trainer-team costs (including LNA and design, as well as delivery)

- learner 'down-time' costs
- materials and equipment costs
- venue and any travel costs.
- Benefits:
  - positive impacts on performance (eg work results, behaviours)
  - positive impacts on the organisation (eg business results, reputation)
  - information about costs saved by the programme (eg production or service delivery issues)
  - information about potential losses or problems avoided by the programme (eg health and safety or compliance issues).

Sources of information

We have already identified that key sources of information for evaluation and the type of information they can provide are:

- learners: their opinions, feedback and experience of the learning, their results in knowledge or skills tests, their demonstration of changed behaviours
- trainers: what they observed, tested, recorded and experienced during the event
- line managers: the differences in knowledge, skills and attitudes they have observed in team members.

We could also add:

- customers and service users: feedback on service delivery, complaints, compliments, defections to other providers
- staff (other than directly involved learners): feedback on colleagues, feedback on L&D processes, perceptions of the organisation, employee satisfaction, staff turnover
- other stakeholder groups: monitoring of service level agreements, measured improvements in partner working, measured improvements in reputation
- external partners: qualification results, awarding or inspection body feedback, compliance issues
- key business information: business/KPI results, production records, wastage rates, achievement of targets
- key financial information: cost savings, increased profits, costs of training.

SELECTING EVALUATION METHODS

We have mentioned some methods of evaluating learning activity above – and here is a summary of some of the main ones.

End of programme 'reactionnaires'

Often known as 'happy sheets', these are primarily useful for collecting learners' general comments and measuring their initial thoughts and feelings about the learning event: do learners consider their needs to have been met, was the training well run, was the venue suitable, etc. Reactionnaires are useful and provide a good opportunity for learners to give their immediate feedback, but they are rarely sufficient to evaluate how *effective* learning activities have been.

Pre- and post-testing

To show an improvement in learning, tests should be done before or at the beginning of learning, as well as at the end of learning activity. The test could also be repeated sometime after the event to assess how much of the knowledge has been retained and can be recalled.

Tests should be appropriate for the learning outcomes being assessed.

Tests for knowledge: you might, for example, have a learning outcome that participants on a training course would be able to 'list at least ten benefits to customers of buying our product X'. This learning outcome could be tested by written questions within a formal test or e-learning module, or by verbal questions within a training session.

More complex areas of knowledge and understanding: this could perhaps be about why customers behave in a certain way or how learners would respond to particular work situations can be assessed by case studies, discussions and scenario exercises, as well as real work performance.

Skills and behaviours: a key method for assessing changes in skills and behaviours is observation. During the training event, you could observe and measure skills demonstrated by learners in a role play – for example, handling a customer complaint. The same skills could be formally observed and recorded in the workplace by learners' line managers, after the training.

Learner self-assessment

In this method the trainee assesses their own level of skill or confidence, against a list of pre-set criteria, both before and after a learning event. Because this method is dependent on personal perception, however, it is possible that a learner's 'score' could actually decrease after training, as learners become more aware of 'what they do not know' or realise that they are not as skilled as they thought they were.

Line manager assessment

A useful evaluation method can be for line managers to assess team members against a list of pre-set criteria or competences before and after a learning event. (Here the assessment is about line managers' perceptions of team members' ability, based on their everyday observations and examination of work outputs – rather than a formal recorded observation as described above.)

If the assessment form is designed to include rating scales, then improvements in performance can be more easily quantified – providing useful evaluation information. This method can also help managers to see the impact (or not) of training for themselves and can help engage them in team members' development.

The assessment form could be completed directly by the line manager or by an L&D representative in an interview with the line manager.

Pre- and post-training review between line manager and learner

This is primarily a discussion between the two, where the reasons for undertaking learning are agreed (pre-training) and then the outcomes of learning, and how these can be transferred to the workplace, are reviewed (post-training). This is usually recorded and can provide useful information for evaluation.

Performance review information/manager interviews

Ongoing performance reviews between line manager and team member will reflect the impact of learning on performance. We may be able to access performance review information, or summaries of it, directly for evaluation purposes. Equally we might be able to interview a small sample of managers about trends in performance, which tell us about the impact of particular learning initiatives.

Learner action plans and records

Towards the end of the learning programme, participants complete a plan of how they will transfer their learning to the workplace. Learners then log their progress against their plan, identifying any problems or barriers along the way. This information can be collected for evaluation purposes, either in writing or via surveys or at a later training event.

Surveys

There are some excellent on-line survey facilities available to assist the collection of evaluation information (see references at the end of this chapter). Professional-looking questionnaires can be designed with relative ease, using the templates provided, and sent to large numbers of participants and/or other stakeholders – eg line managers, customers, service users. Because on-line surveys are easy to use, participant response rates can be increased. An added bonus is that information can be analysed within the same system and presented in a number of formats. Surveys can be carried out before and after the training and are particularly useful if large numbers of learners are to be contacted.

Focus or review groups

For large learning programmes it can be appropriate to establish a programme review group – who will meet to review the progress of the programme, identify any issues or emerging problems and make suggestions for improvements.

Typical representation within a review group would be: at least one learner, one trainer and one line manager, plus maybe some external representation if appropriate (an external provider, external verifier or other stakeholder representative). Depending on the scale and duration of the programme the group might meet just once or several times.

Desk research

Remember that much of the information that is useful to evaluation is already available in the organisation – performance review information, customer comments, production and service statistics, financial and operational information, sales figures, etc. These can usually be accessed directly without having to take other people away from business activities in order to be involved in your evaluation.

SOME LIGHT-HEARTED APPROACHES TO EVALUATION

You may encourage participation in evaluation by employing some quick, easy and engaging methods. While these will not be particularly scientific or give vast amounts of information, they can certainly generate useful feedback. For example you could:

1. Set up two flip-chart stands or designate areas of wall, and label them something similar to: 'I liked X because Y' and 'I did not like X because Y'. 'X' will equal an activity undertaken within the training. Give out sticky post-it notes and ask learners to complete and add at least one sentence to each wall.

2. Give out post it notes that are shaped as 'hearts' and some as 'squares'. Ask learners to complete heart shaped post-its for positive feedback and square shapes for 'suggestions for improvement' and stick them all on a flip-chart or area of wall.

3. Have three buckets in the room – ideally a red, a green and a yellow one (traffic lights). Give each learner a ping pong ball or small suitable item and ask them to put the ball in the green bucket if a session has met their objectives, in the yellow bucket if their objectives have only been partly met, and in the red bucket if their objectives have hardly been met at all. You could ask learners to do this after each main session, ideally as they leave the room for breaks so that you can do a quick summary. Hopefully – there will be more items in the green bucket by the end of the day!

4. Ask learners to describe to the group what they will tell their family about the learning event, when they get home that evening and what they will tell their manager about it when they return to work the next day.

5. Instead of issuing individual 'reactionnaires' draw one big 'reactionnaire' on a flip-chart or whiteboard and ask the group to work together to complete a joint group evaluation. You might want to combine this with some individual verbal questions as well.

Timing of evaluation

Along with determining best evaluation methods, you will also need to give some thought to the timing of evaluation activity and what is best done:

- prior to learning?
- at the beginning of the learning?
- during the learning?

- at the end of the learning?
- immediately after the learning?
- three months after, six months after, longer?

Again this emphasises the need for evaluation to be an ongoing process and not something to be left until the end of a learning programme.

Decisions about the timing of specific evaluation activities will depend on the purpose of your evaluation and the type of information you are collecting.

For example, if you want to assess whether training has impacted on performance, it would make sense to leave this assessment until some time after the training. Showing an impact on performance one week after training may not be too impressive. However, proving an impact on performance six months after training suggests that the training has had long-lasting impact and that changes in performance are becoming entrenched.

EVALUATION APPROACH

A large commercial organisation states on its L&D website:

> We evaluate every course we provide by:
>
> - sending a survey to learners three months after the course, checking how the learning has made a difference to their performance at work
>
> - sending a survey to learners' line managers six months after the course for their views on how the course has impacted on the learner's performance
>
> - checking service information for any improvements 12 months after the course'.

What do you think about this as an organisational approach to evaluation? Can you identify some strengths and weaknesses in this approach?

DESIGNING EVALUATION TOOLS

There may be times in your evaluation activity when you need to design a specific tool, maybe a questionnaire or observation form in order to collect the required information.

Some simple rules to follow are:

- Begin by asking yourself what is the specific purpose of the evaluation instrument? Identify the most appropriate type of instrument for the purpose – eg a questionnaire to use at the end of the session, a survey you can send out, a checklist to use for telephone interviews, an assessment form for use by learners or their managers.

- Ask yourself what you want to find out or measure and consider the questions you need to ask. For example do you need to generate qualitative data or quantitative data or a mixture of both?

QUANTITATIVE INFORMATION	QUALITATIVE INFORMATION
Quantitative information is 'hard' data – eg statistics, definitions and measurable responses to questions.	Qualitative information is 'soft' data – eg opinion, personal narrative and general comments.
Quantitative data is usually easy to measure and compare.	Qualitative data can be difficult to measure or compare.
Examples of quantitative data might be: attendance figures for a learning event, scores obtained in learning tests or outcomes of learning expressed on a rating scale.	Examples of qualitative information might be: a learner's general comments about a learning programme and their suggestions for how it can be improved.

- Consider whether you want to use multiple-choice or closed questions to 'force' a response and provide more measurable data. If you are using rating scales, it can be best to provide an even number of ratings – to avoid people always selecting the middle score.

- Make sure your method is user-friendly. Put yourself in the shoes of the trainer, manager or learner it is aimed at – and check that your questions and instructions make sense. Is it easy and logical to follow? Will it be quick and simple to complete?

- Consider 'piloting' the instrument or questionnaire first – to check that your questions are understood as you intend them to be, that the instrument will generate the type of information you require, and that the information will be provided in a way that makes it easy to analyse.

REFLECTIVE ACTIVITY

We have provided some (extracts of) evaluation questionnaires, in Figures 7.1 and 7.2, that have proved useful within certain learning activities.

Have a look at these and consider how they compare with the ones you use.

What do you consider to be the strengths and weaknesses of these examples?

Figure 7.1 Example 1

Programme evaluation – learner questionnaire				

Learning programme: (Pre-stated) **Dates attended:** **Trainer name:**	**Learning Outcomes:** (Pre-stated)			

1.	**Please rate each item below by ticking the appropriate column.**	Poor	Average	Good	Excellent
a	The joining instructions				
b	The timings of the learning event				
c	The venue & facilities				
d	Your level of skills & knowledge **before** the training				
e	The relevance of the learning outcomes to you				
f	The usefulness of inputs and guidance provided by the trainer				
g	The usefulness of the learning activities undertaken				
h	The usefulness of learning materials provided – handouts, etc				
i	The helpfulness of the trainer to your individual needs?				
j	Your level of skills & knowledge **after** the training				
k	The level of confidence you feel about putting your skills and knowledge into practice, back at work.				
l	Your overall satisfaction with the training				

2. Please comment on any items where you scored 'poor' or 'average'. Or any general comments you wish to make.

Candidate name (optional):

Figure 7.2 Example 2

The aim of this training is to ensure you are have the knowledge and skills required to conduct effective telephone interviews and that you feel confident to do this. For each of the areas below please indicate how confident you feel in your abilities – and indicate any areas where you need further information, support or practice.	
Topic areas	**Comment re further needs**
1. Using the system Not at all 1 2 3 4 5 6 7 8 9 10 Fully	
2. Following the opening procedures Not at all 1 2 3 4 5 6 7 8 9 10 Fully	
3. Effective use of questioning to establish client needs? Not at all 1 2 3 4 5 6 7 8 9 10 Fully	
4. Current range of customer options available (headlines) Not at all 1 2 3 4 5 6 7 8 9 10 Fully	
5. Option 1 – Full features and conditions Not at all 1 2 3 4 5 6 7 8 9 10 Fully	
6. Option 2 – Full features and conditions Not at all 1 2 3 4 5 6 7 8 9 10 Fully	
7. Option 3 – Full features and conditions Not at all 1 2 3 4 5 6 7 8 9 10 Fully	
8. Circumstances in which options can be varied Not at all 1 2 3 4 5 6 7 8 9 10 Fully	

COLLECTING INFORMATION

Using samples

When applying evaluation methods, it may not always be feasible, necessary or good business practice to involve all learners. Instead, an appropriate sample of learners, managers, customers or work results can be determined and used to inform the evaluation.

Samples should be large enough to be credible and to give a fair representation of different groups and types of learner but be small enough to avoid placing a burden on the business. You might decide, for example, to involve 'representative' learners from different departments, different grades, or different levels of experience in your evaluation activity rather than every learner.

SOME TIPS FOR COLLECTING INFORMATION

- Stick to the information that is relevant to your evaluation purposes.
- Be prepared to adapt your methods as you go along, if necessary.
- Be careful not to make assumptions or react to one striking piece of information without checking out how valid it is.
- Treat the respondents in your evaluation activity with respect – they may not be obliged to provide the information you need.
- Handle information with sensitivity – what may be interesting evaluation data to you may be someone else's individual work results or feedback on their performance.

Handling information appropriately and in line with legislation

As above, information collected for evaluation can include sensitive data – learners' performance results, learners' opinions of others, others' opinions of learners – and therefore it is crucial that good practice is followed in terms of collection and storage of information.

There should always be a good reason for collecting particular information and it should be collected and stored in line with data protection legislation. Think carefully about whether information can be collected anonymously rather than linked to specific individuals – and take great care about how and where evaluation information is stored. For more information about this topic you may want to refer to Chapter 3: Using, recording and analysing L&D information, or follow up the references at the end of this chapter.

ANALYSING INFORMATION

The availability of software programmes for analysing, manipulating and presenting data has made data analysis an increasingly user-friendly and interesting activity to undertake.

Survey programmes and spreadsheets allow us to analyse, organise and view data in different ways, and to establish, for example:

- ratings applied to different 'reaction factors' – the training approach, the venue, the learning experience
- ratings relating to levels of learning or transfer of learning to the workplace
- ratings relating to improvements in performance.

All these ratings and scores can then be 'sliced', further analysed and compared to give us information such as:

- average scores for different learner groups
- average scores for groups attending training at different times
- average scores for learners attending training events delivered by different trainers
- key learning outcomes in relation to different groups, contexts or training delivery factors

- percentage improvements in performance for an individual, for a group of learners, for learners who work to a particular manager or who used a particular learning method
- comparison of work results between trained groups and control groups (who have not had the training)
- areas of knowledge or skill where improvement levels are greatest or lowest
- areas where learning is still required
- areas where learning is high but has not been transferred to the workplace
- a timeline of how skills have improved in a certain area over a particular period
- patterns in learning or of learner satisfaction with training activities
- unusual or inconsistent 'scores' requiring further investigation.

REFLECTIVE ACTIVITY

Select any five items of information from the list above and consider how each item of information could inform improvements to learning activities.

This kind of information enables us to draw important conclusions about the effectiveness of learning approaches and learning events; further learning needs, potential skills or knowledge gaps and future requirements of the L&D function; the performance of individual trainers and the support provided by managers; the relative costs of different training initiatives and the benefits of training in relation to costs incurred. We then have a sound basis from which we can determine and justify improvement action and make our recommendations.

Of course, evaluation also reveals L&D's successes and the contributions made by L&D towards the achievement of business objectives.

> Evaluation information provides some great 'sound-bites' to promote further programmes.
>
> Wendy Strohm, Wendy Strohm Associates Ltd

PRESENTING FINDINGS AND MAKING RECOMMENDATIONS

We can present our findings in the form of:

- a short report
- a presentation at a meeting
- tables of statistics
- charts, graphs and images.

Using visual representations will make data more accessible and interesting, and make patterns, trends and deviations more easily apparent.

A good structure to follow for an evaluation report or a presentation is the one underpinning this chapter:

- what was evaluated (scope)
- purposes of the evaluation (evaluation objectives)
- how evaluation was undertaken (methods, participants, timing)
- findings (key conclusions from the analysis)
- recommendations.

If you are presenting information to different stakeholder groups, you might want to emphasise information relating to their particular area of interest and any improvement or ongoing actions that are required from them.

For learning sponsors:

- the benefits gained from their time/money/emotional investment
- the case for continuing funding and support for the same training
- the case for supporting new/other training and development.

For line managers:

- benefits – justifying release of team members for learning
- ways in which managers can support team members' learning
- the case for more management involvement in learning
- the benefits of encouraging and promoting training to staff.

For learners in the programme:

- clarification of learning achievements
- how they may have influenced further developments
- further training opportunities for them.

For future/potential learners:

- benefits of the programme and reasons for signing-up
- how to prepare for the programme to get the most from it.

For the training team:

- confirmation of 'successes'
- required changes and updates to the programme content
- proposed changes and updates to training style and methods.

For course organisers:

- required changes to admin procedures
- changes to venue and domestic arrangements.

WHAT NEXT ?

EVALUATION

Here are some activities you could consider to further develop your practical evaluation skills:

1. Research your organisation's evaluation process:
   - Do they have one?
   - What level does the evaluation go to?
   - How is the evaluation data collected?
   - How has that data been used?

2. Make a proposal in favour of introducing an evaluation strategy into your organisation. You could think about:
   - the benefits that it would bring
   - the costs involved
   - who would be involved.

3. Design an evaluation strategy for a piece of learning that you are undertaking (your CIPD qualification, or reading this book, for example):
   - What impact do you want it to have?
   - How will you measure that impact?
   - How will you know you have achieved?

4. Research alternative approaches to evaluation in other organisations, or in other parts of the world:
   - How else can it be done?
   - What could you do that is different?

5. Finally, have a look at the case study below and consider:
   - how this example relates to your situation or practice
   - what you can take forward from the example for your own evaluation practice.

CASE STUDY 7.2

EVALUATION

As L&D Manager for a large utility company, the question of evaluation was always an area of concern and embarrassment. We understand the theory, but getting it done in a meaningful way was difficult. Like most trainers, my team used questionnaires at the end of each programme and these provided little other than a general reassurance that the learners were leaving without major complaint. We had in place a policy that said managers would meet with their staff before and after their courses, however, I was acutely aware that its effectiveness was patchy. Some of our managers would do it solely to keep me off their backs or to be seen to be doing what they should, others would say that 'this time I didn't but it's the first time I haven't, honestly', while others were overcome by time. And if we are being honest, even I, Head of the Learning Department and with a passion for development that underpinned my career since 1990, did fail to conduct any meaningful evaluation with my own staff!

When in 2002 we decided to spend a large (very large) amount of money on a senior management development programme the process of 'hit and miss' evaluation could not continue. Rightly we needed to show both a healthy return on investment and that the competency gap identified in our management population was reducing. The need for the programme was clear – we had managers who were subject experts and had long levels of service within the company. They did, however, struggle with leading our staff through the cultural and organisational changes that we needed to make. The transition from being a public service to a commercial business was the goal and this required us to change a well established 'jobs for life' parental culture to one that focused on performance and cost efficiency. I also believed that if we could integrate evaluation properly into the managers' own development, we stood a better chance of impacting how they evaluated other learning in their teams – for me there was something about showing the managers how to do it so that they would do more of it themselves.

So how did we make this happen? Inherent within the management development programme was the message that 'review' was important and was the key to improved performance. At the end of each module, a group exercise was set asking learners to review the module using 'what went well and what didn't go well'. Emphasis was placed on the importance of being able to say 'why' and 'ideas for next time'. This provided the first reaction level of Kirkpatrick. The data collected was more valuable because learners weren't just completing a questionnaire at the end of the day; they were undertaking a group activity as part of two or three days together when they had got into the mode of questioning and probing each other and recording it for others to understand.

During the month after the programme, I made a point of seeing all the programme participants myself and asking them about their experiences. These 'meetings' were often informal and therefore less threatening; usually more of an 'interested chat', often when I needed to see them about something else. This meant that my building a personal relationship with each

of them, I was able to get their honest personal view. Yes, time consuming, as we put over 100 people through the programme, but I do believe that by showing interest and support, it helped me understand what was gained from the programme and also provided the individuals with the opportunity to think about what they needed in order to use their learning in their every day work.

Three months after the programme we sent out a pro-forma questionnaire to participants' line managers asking them to feedback to us observed improvements and changes in the participants' performance following the course. This was successful because my training managers also started to have meetings with the heads of each department on a quarterly basis. The agenda for these meetings was:

- L&D undertaken in the last quarter
- improvements observed in performance of individuals and teams
- development needs for the next quarter and beyond
- general feedback and discussion on how L&D department can support you.

Initially the information from these meetings was patchy; however, once the directors and heads of department realised what we wanted, they began to gather information prior to our 'get togethers'. We included a summary of this information on our regular reports to the board.

Summary

This chapter has explored:

The value of evaluation activity

- Evaluation enables us to ensure that learning is meeting learning objectives and to continuously improve learning provision.
- It builds learner, manager and organisational confidence in the L&D function and helps engage learners and their managers in learning activity.

The definition of evaluation and some related terms

- Evaluation takes a wider view of learning programmes than validation.
- Validation is concerned with establishing whether learning has met its stated objectives.
- The main focus of evaluation is often validation, but may include other factors such as value for money.
- Assessment, testing, monitoring and review activities can all contribute to evaluation.
- Models of evaluation include 'return on investment' and 'return on expectation'.

Some key theories and thinking on evaluation

- Our thinking on evaluation has been informed by several writers and practitioners including, Donald Kirkpatrick, Mark Easterby-Smith, Jack Philips and CIPD contributors.

Different evaluation methods

- Methods include 'reactionnaires', pre and post testing, self-assessment and line manager assessment, surveys, focus groups and desk research.
- We should consider the timing of applying evaluation methods.
- We can develop our own questionnaires, surveys or assessment sheets to aid evaluation.

Key factors to be considered in the collection and analysis of information

- We can collect quantitative as well as qualitative information in evaluation activities.
- To minimise the costs of evaluation and avoid it being disruptive we can use samples of respondents rather than involving everyone.
- We must be aware of and compliant with data protection laws.

Key factors to be considered when reporting evaluation findings and making recommendations

- We can select from a range of different communication methods to deliver our findings.
- We should clarify what we have evaluated, what our evaluation objectives were, how we evaluated, what our findings are and what our recommendations are.
- We should target our communications for particular audiences.

EXPLORE FURTHER

BOOKS:

Anderson, V. (2007) *The value of learning: from return on investment to return on expectation*. London: CIPD.

WEBSITES:

CIPD factsheet on evaluation:

www.cipd.co.uk/subjects/lrnanddev/evaluation/evatrain.htm

CIPD factsheet on data protection:

www.cipd.co.uk/subjects/emplaw/dataprot/dataprotec.htm

Free (or partially free) on-line access to evaluation information or tools:

www.businessballs.com

www.businesslink.gov.uk (select employment and skills)

On-line survey providers (free for basic level usage):

www.freeonlinesurveys.com

www.surveymonkey.com

www.smart-survey.co.uk

CHAPTER 8

Developing Coaching Skills for the Workplace

INTRODUCTION

This chapter begins with a look at the popularity of coaching and a full definition of its meaning. We go on to consider different types and styles of coaching and some activities which are 'similar but different' to coaching. The chapter moves on to explore the processes, roles, responsibilities and skills required within the coaching relationship and some coaching models which can support a typical coaching conversation. Finally, the chapter considers the key factors involved in implementing coaching activity in the workplace and the benefits that can be derived from this.

LEARNING OUTCOMES

When you have read this chapter you should be able to:

- define different types and styles of coaching
- discuss the roles and responsibilities of a coach and a coachee
- explain some main coaching models and techniques
- describe the potential benefits of coaching
- discuss factors which affect the implementation of coaching.

THE POPULARITY OF COACHING

The CIPD 2008 Annual Survey of Learning and Development described coaching as 'the shining star of the L&D portfolio' with seven out of 10 respondents believing it to be an effective tool.

By the time of the 2010 Survey, the percentage of respondents' organisations using coaching had risen still further:

> Coaching takes place in four-fifths (82%) of organisations. Although this is consistent across sectors, bigger companies are more likely to use it (86% of organisations with more than 250 employees compared with 62% of SMEs).

It is also more likely to happen in organisations with a specific training budget (84% compared with 72% of those who do not have one).

CIPD Annual Survey of Learning and Talent Development 2010

These findings are echoed in the heightened interest in coaching from L&D professionals, the ever-increasing profile of coaching in the L&D media and the growth of training, accreditation and qualification systems for coaches.

DEFINING COACHING

Although the term coaching is one of the most popular and widely used terms in the world of learning, coaching has developed so much as an activity that the term can often mean different things to different people.

In straightforward terms, coaching, whatever its label or variation, usually refers to an interaction between two people, a coach and coachee, aimed at developing the performance of the coachee in some aspect of their life:

> a process that enables learning and development to occur and thus performance to improve.

> Parsloe 1999

However, the definitions above can be applied to many L&D interventions – so what makes coaching different? There are several answers to this, still to be explored in this chapter, but, essentially, the difference is the emphasis coaching places on building a coachee's understanding of their own performance and their confidence and ability to manage and develop this for themselves.

Two definitions which particularly capture this aspect of coaching are:

> Coaching is centred on unlocking a person's potential to maximise his or her own performance…, improving the individual with regards to performance and the development of skills.

> Gallwey 1986

And very simply:

> The purpose of the coach is to raise awareness in the coachee.

> Downey 1999

We started this section by saying that coaching can often mean different things to different people. Indeed, as coaching has developed as an activity, with an array of emerging types, models, approaches and techniques, it has become more complex to capture in a single definition.

TYPES OF COACHING

Sports coaching: initially the term and activity of 'coaching' came from a sporting context in which a 'player' was helped to develop their skills in their particular sport by a 'coach', who used a range of skills and techniques to do this.

Workplace coaching/performance coaching: following the example of sport, and influenced by texts, particularly, 'The Inner Game of Tennis' by Timothy Gallwey, and the various works of John Whitmore, coaching was gradually taken up by the business world and moved into the workplace. Some writers and organisations refer to coaching in the workplace as 'performance coaching', a term generally attributed to John Whitmore, emphasising the focus of this type of coaching on developing a coachees' work-related performance.

Coaching in the workplace often takes place between staff member and their line manager, but may also be between staff member and colleague or staff member and training professional. It is undertaken with a view to developing performance in a specific area of work, and quite often, the coach has expertise in the area of work being coached and may sometimes use this expertise to advise the coachee.

Workplace coaching is less defined than some other types of coaching, and therefore is generally seen to embrace a wide mix of approaches and techniques.

More recently we have seen the emergence of some more specifically defined types of coaching, with their own codes of practice and specialist training, qualification and accreditation structures for coaches. For example:

Executive coaching: executive coaching is often provided for Senior Managers by professional coaches who are external to the organisation. The coach may not have expertise in the Executive's area of work, and will, therefore, follow a mainly non-directive approach.

Career coaching: career coaches work with clients who want to improve their job satisfaction, change jobs, or make a career change. They will help to identify the coachees' skills and talents and help them to prepare for the job search, application and selection process.

Life coaching: life coaching is usually provided by independent freelance coaches, for an agreed fee, in response to a personal application from the potential coachee. Like executive coaching, life coaching tends towards being non-directive and has a high focus on assisting a coachee to define goals and maintain the motivation to achieve them.

DIRECTIVE AND NON-DIRECTIVE COACHING STYLES

Above we have used the term 'non-directive' when comparing different types of coaching. Coaches can tend towards a directive or non-directive style or anywhere in between.

By directive, we mean how much the coach inputs their own view, expertise and advice into the process, as opposed to how much they stand back and resist inputting to the process, leaving the coachee to take responsibility for decisions and selection of activities.

We can consider 'directiveness' as a scale, from highly directive to non-directive:

Highly directive ⟵——————————————⟶ **Non-directive**

If a key purpose of coaching is, as discussed, to develop a coaches ability to take responsibility for developing their own performance, then it is fair to say that all coaching activity has, or should have, a strong leaning towards being non-directive. However, there will also be occasions when more directive interaction is also appropriate.

This scale of 'directiveness' is well illustrated by Myles Downey (*Effective Coaching*, 1999) who shows how the use of various coaching skills and techniques link to directive and non-directive approaches to coaching.

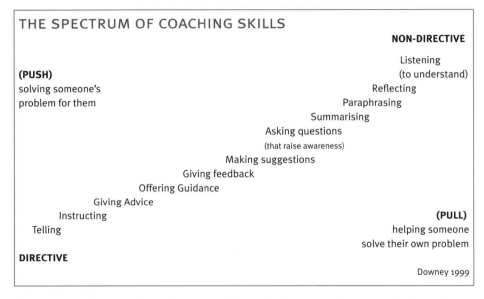

Because coaching involves these variables, it is important for individual coach–coachee pairs to give some thought to how they will work together, and maybe, whether their individual styles are compatible and conducive to a positive coaching relationship.

Equally, it is sensible for organisations and managers of coaching programmes to consider the model of coaching they want to operate.

Here is what the NHS Institute for Innovation and Improvement say about their executive coaching programme:

What is Leadership Coaching at the NHS Institute?

There are many definitions of coaching, some of which are contradictory. The NHS Institute has worked hard to agree what the term 'coaching' means for us so that leaders, employees and external coaches can share a common language.

… For us, coaching holds the philosophy that, the individual is a talented, competent individual with many strengths and that, through coaching, we help the individual to unlock that potential to maximise their performance/behave more effectively in achieving their goals. The focus is on supporting individuals to learn rather than teaching them.

To be congruent with this view of coaching, coaches will draw more on non-directive skills which help individuals to solve their own problems, empowering them to take responsibility for their own performance and development. Coaching will support individuals to learn by understanding themselves more, reflecting on their work, challenging their assumptions and supporting them to experiment with new behaviours and attitudes. Coaching facilitates learning from experience and reflection and is less concerned with new models or theory.

And from a large organisation about the implementation of coaching practice within the line-management structure:

(Our approach is to) ... include the development of coaching skills in our management development programmes (as one of many valid management techniques) so that we equip managers with the knowledge and ability to coach their staff, when this is appropriate, within usual management practice. For us, coaching is another tool in a manager's 'kit-bag'.

COACHING IN PRACTICE

SIMILAR BUT DIFFERENT

Coaching has substantial cross-over with many other developmental activities.

REFLECTIVE ACTIVITY

Can you think of at least one similarity and one difference between coaching and each of the following:

- Training?
- Delegating?
- Counselling?
- Mentoring?

In the reflective activity above you may have considered a number of factors, for example:

Training: like coaching, training on a one-to-one basis involves two people working together with the aim of developing the trainee. It can involve a number of different communication techniques – such as questioning, giving advice, instructing and giving feedback.

Less like coaching, one-to-one training tends to be more directive than coaching and it is generally assumed that the trainer will know about the subject that is being trained.

Delegating: like coaching, delegating generally gives responsibility for undertaking a task or activity to the person being delegated to, and it can be a developmental activity, if implemented in that way.

However, unlike coaching there is a sense of greater detachment between delegator and person being delegated to, and may not include any element of support. Also, delegation is often used for reasons other than development, and there is often an assumption that the person being delegated to is already competent.

Counselling: counselling focuses on personal issues, often where the person being counselled has undergone difficult experiences and seeks a therapeutic intervention or where they need help to cope with a current reality. To do this counselling often tends to look backwards at personal experiences and issues.

Workplace coaching tends to focus on specific performance issues and is forward looking, i.e. how something can be performed in a better way. Although coaching can bring out emotions it does not seek to unravel deep emotional issues in the way that counselling does. The two disciplines are quite different in this aspect and it is important that coaches are very aware of this and do not stray into areas where a therapeutic solution, and professional counsellor, would be more appropriate.

Mentoring: perhaps the activity which is considered to have most in common with coaching is mentoring. Many of the skills, and approaches, used by a mentor in the mentoring process are the same as those used by coaches in a coaching process. However, there are also significant differences. Table 8.1 highlights some of the similarities and differences between workplace coaching and mentoring.

Table 8.1 **Comparison of workplace coaching and mentoring**

	Workplace coaching	**Mentoring**
Context/areas addressed	Work/task performance issues	Work issues Ongoing career issues Personal issues
Relationship between coach and coachee	Often coach is coachee's line manager, but could be peer or trainer	Usually a more experienced, senior work colleague, from outside the mentee's immediate work team or location
Coach expertise	Coach may or may not have experience in the area being coached	Mentor usually has general knowledge and experience of the mentee's work area

Coach/mentor approach	Coaches are encouraged to, at least, limit the giving of advice and focus on assisting coachees to find their own solutions	Greater acceptance of the mentor acting an advisory capacity, allowing mentee to share and learn from mentor's experience
Typical nature of meetings	Focussed, agreeing goals and reviewing progress towards them	General and informal discussion around work, personal and career issues
Frequency of meetings	Regular, programme of meetings usually agreed in advance	May be more ad-hoc or called, when needed, by mentee
Duration of arrangement	Usually short term – until goals achieved (task related)	Can last for a long period of time (career related)

To suggest that these differences make training, coaching, mentoring, and counselling quite different activities would be wrong. There is much similarity between them and it can therefore be difficult to decide which intervention is most appropriate. Whilst coaching is an effective and useful intervention for many occasions, the information above shows it is not always the only, or best, solution. Other types of training approaches, as well as mentoring, counselling and general performance management will sometimes be much more effective in improving work performance.

REFLECTIVE ACTIVITY

Consider the following four situations and whether coaching is likely to be the most effective intervention to enhance or improve work performance. If not, what might be?

1. A new recruit to a job of which they have little or no prior experience.

2. A team member who is known to be competent but who's standard of performance has dropped significantly over the last few months.

3. A team member who knows and performs their job well, but who could undertake more complex tasks and contribute more to the team – and advance themselves within the team.

4. A very competent team member who is able to undertake all the tasks within the team and is seen as the most senior and expert by the rest of the team.

Whilst coaching might be effective in any of the scenarios above, a new recruit to a job is likely to need to build up some basic skills and knowledge before they can really benefit from coaching. A more directive approach to their early development might therefore be more efficient and effective.

A significant change in a team member's performance suggests that there are problems to explore – and it would be unwise for a manager to take any particular developmental approach without exploring what the problems might be. Ultimately, this is more likely to about general management and support than a straightforward development intervention. An established relationship with a mentor could also prove very useful here.

Example 3 above seems an ideal scenario for coaching to take place. The team member seems to have the basic skills and knowledge required but needs to build confidence and expertise in more complex tasks. Doing this in their own way and at their own pace, supported by a more experienced coach might be an ideal intervention here.

A very competent and experienced team member might find performance coaching unnecessary, even patronising, unless it was highly non-directive. A more appropriate development method here might be the full delegation of new responsibilities which will stretch and challenge them.

Another scenario to consider is when a coaching process starts to shift into other areas. Consider the example below.

CASE STUDY 8.1

A coach was working with a member of staff on aspects of managing a section of a small retail outlet. When exploring the coachee's difficulties in dealing with customer complaints (part of the team leader's job role), the coachee became emotional and began to relate her response to angry customers to a difficult relationship in her personal life. At further coaching meetings, the staff member brought up the personal situation more frequently and became very upset about it. The coach, in this scenario, felt uneasy about some of this discussion and unable to keep the sessions to a work context. He suggested that they have a break in the coaching relationship and that the coachee may want to consider accessing the company counselling service.

REFLECTIVE ACTIVITY

Do you agree with the course of action taken by the coach here?

If you were the coach, how would you take this situation forward?

COACHING AND THE ORGANISATION

So far we have focused on the coaching experience from the points of view of the coach and the coachee. However, in any workplace based or funded programme there is always a third and very important agenda to consider, that of the organisation.

In a life coaching scenario, the coachee will most likely be able to select their own coach and determine goals based purely on their own needs, concerns and preferences. In a workplace coaching scenario, contexts and boundaries may be set by the organisation or the dimensions of the particular coaching programme. Whether this is done formally or not, both coach and coachee have a responsibility to consider the wider context of the organisation in setting and working towards coaching goals.

Consideration of the organisational context and organisational goals and objectives should inform:

- **Individual coaching goals:** in Chapter 3 we discussed the importance of individual and team development goals being aligned with organisational goals. In determining goals for coaching, coachees should be encouraged to consider what their key performance requirements are and what their priority areas for developing performance are. If there is a tension between what the coachee would like to work on and what the organisation needs the coachee to work on, then the coach has a responsibility to the organisation to challenge and encourage the coachee to set aligned objectives that will benefit the organisation, as well as the individual. Having such discussions not only assists in the achievement of organisational goals but also helps heighten staff awareness of, and engagement with them.

- **Links between coaching and other L&D activities:** to be most effective and return most benefit to the organisation, coaching needs to complement, support and enhance other L&D initiatives. For example, coaching may be positioned as a follow up activity to more directive training, allowing learning to be positioned in an individual context and extended through supported practice. Such an arrangement would assist an effective transfer of learning to the workplace and further consolidate the initial learning provision. Taking a strategic view in this way minimises wasted efforts and expenditure and enables the organisation to gain maximum benefit from L&D expenditure.

- **How coaching is positioned:** coaching within the management line, may be the most cost and time effective way for an organisation to address specific individual needs. Developing line managers to be able to provide coaching on an ad-hoc, as required basis for their team members can maintain a level of individual competence and therefore effectiveness within the team, whilst reducing the need for formal, and more costly, learning interventions. This local and spontaneous contribution to the maintenance of competence levels will help teams respond more easily to business change.

Whilst any coaching activity which helps make staff more competent will have a positive impact on the organisation, coaching which is aligned to organisational context and goals is likely to contribute much more to organisational success.

THE COACHING PROCESS

A typical coaching process has four main stages (see Table 8.2).

Table 8.2 **Coaching process**

Stage	When	Coach role and responsibilities
Preparation and set-up	Before coaching starts	Coach training and preparation Familiarisation with overall approach, parameters and procedures of coaching activity in the organisation Making contact with coachee or agreeing the coaching partnership within the management line Initial relationship/rapport building Arrangement of initial coaching meeting
Contracting	Initial meeting	Contracting with coachee. This will have differing degrees of formality depending on any existing coach–coachee relationship and the context of the coaching activity, but should include discussion and agreement of: • meeting timings • meeting locations • roles and responsibilities • 'ground rules' and risk factors • main areas or 'themes' to work on • general success measures Agreements would usually be recorded (see example agreement document below)
Coaching activity	Ongoing meetings	Ongoing relationship/rapport building and creation of a positive climate, conducive to coaching. Assisting and motivating the coachee to: • determine and set goals • identify courses of action • identify and fulfil specific learning needs • review progress towards goals • explore obstacles and set-backs • review, clarify, refine and re-set goals • influence the nature of the coaching process Again, key points of coaching meetings may be recorded, to inform ongoing review (see example document below)
Exit	Final meeting	Usually undertaken when objectives have been achieved, but may be appropriate at an earlier stage A final meeting would usually include: • review and recognition of achievement • identification of any areas for ongoing development • review of the coaching process – to inform further coaching activity and practice

Figure 8.1 shows a typical example of an initial coaching agreement, and Figure 8.2 shows a coaching meeting record.

Figure 8.1 Coaching agreement

COACHING AGREEMENT

Between (1) Coachee and (2) Coach: Date:
(1)
(2)

Background to meeting:

General goals and desired outcomes:

Agreed support arrangements:

Working together agreements:
  We have both agreed to:

- Honour meeting arrangements

- Fulfill undertakings between meetings

- Take responsibility for our own decisions, actions and development

- Honour confidentiality needs

- Discuss any concerns about the coaching process

Agreed _____   _____

Figure 8.2 Coaching meeting record

COACHING MEETING NOTES

Participants: Session No: Date

Key Notes from today:

Agreements for next time:

Agreed:_____   _____

COACHING SKILLS

"Coaching is helping someone to achieve their goals by themselves, though not on their own."

In order to fulfil the responsibilities of the coaching process, coaches need a particular range of knowledge, skills and attributes. These include:

- *An understanding of coaching principles and processes.* Without an understanding of how coaching seeks to build a coachee's awareness of their performance and ability to self-improve, through the use of non-directive coaching approaches, busy managers and trainers could easily fall back on wholly directive approaches which may seem quicker and easier in the short term. Even more importantly, coaches need to be aware of the boundaries of coaching and when other interventions are more appropriate. Knowledge of coaching processes and recording systems will also enable coaches to operate efficiently and in-line with other coaching practice in the organisation.

- *Relationship-building skills.* Coaches need to be able to help coachees feel relaxed, be willing to experiment, and to explore their own behaviour. Coachees will only be able to do this if they feel comfortable in the coach–coachee relationship and believe that their coach has their best interests at heart. This is partly about the personal stance of the coach and their honest interest and concern for their coachee, and partly about learnable skills such as use of body language, listening skills and conversation skills. Coaches may also find useful techniques within Emotional Intelligence (EI) and Neuro-linguistic Programming (NLP) texts.

- *Communication skills*, particularly techniques which support non-directive coaching approaches, such as questioning, active listening, paraphrasing, summarising and reflecting back. The role of the coach within a coaching discussion includes assisting the coachee to identify and specify coaching objectives. In order to do this, coaches need to ask questions which help coachees reflect on their experiences, break through their personal thinking boundaries and be creative in considering the possibilities. As well as active listening and questioning skills, coaches need to be confident in challenging unhelpful assumptions and limitations and in inspiring creative thinking.

- *An understanding of organisational goals and priorities* and how these cascade into team and individual requirements. This knowledge is essential if coaches are to help coachees determine appropriate and useful coaching goals which support wider organisational objectives.

- *A genuine respect for the coachee* and recognition of the coachee's ability to find the best solution for themselves – and the patience and discipline not to fall into a directive style inappropriately.

- *An awareness of opportunities and facilities* a coachee can access to improve their own performance and how they can do this. This might include other

L&D opportunities such as courses, e-learning, or workbooks, as well as peer-mentoring and work based opportunities to take on new activities and projects. One advantage of a line-manager coach is the access to and easier allocation of relevant work activities to assist coachee development.

- In some cases, and where it is appropriate to the type of coaching, some *expertise in the subject being discussed* in order to feed in relevant ideas and suggestions, when it is helpful to do so and requested by the coachee.

- *A willingness to understand what motivates a particular coachee* and to use this knowledge to encourage them to experiment and maintain progress towards their goals

- *The ability to manage the coaching discussion*, keeping it on track and ensure it addresses the areas and issues the coachee needs to address. Knowledge of some coaching models (see some of these in the next section) will substantially help a coach to do this, although models are not a requirement of coaching.

- *Knowledge of any recording procedures* and an understanding of the right balance in keeping coaching records (sufficient information to inform the process without becoming a burdensome or even non-compliant data processing activity) and the requirement for confidentiality.

In many ways, and as with other L&D roles, we can think of the role of the coach as being to assist coachees to move around the learning cycle as developed by David Kolb. This involves, encouraging coachees to experiment/have experiences, to reflect on these experiences, to have new ideas about how they could do things differently, and then to try out these new ideas/experiment, and so on, moving round and round the cycle and continuously developing.

Ref to ELP 2 – Experiential learning cycle

> "I keep six honest serving-men
> (They taught me all I knew)
> Their names are What and Why and When
> And How and Where and Who."
>
> Rudyard Kipling

COACHING MODELS

There are many different coaching practice models available to coaches, each with a related acronym title, representing a framework or guide to structuring a coaching session. A search on the internet will find several of these, some known and used generally, and others belonging to specific branded coaching programmes or individual coaches.

Some examples of coaching models and their acronyms follow.

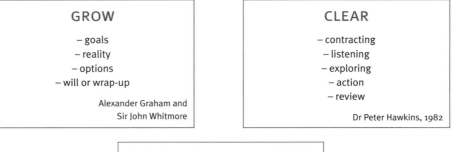

GROW

– goals
– reality
– options
– will or wrap-up

Alexander Graham and
Sir John Whitmore

CLEAR

– contracting
– listening
– exploring
– action
– review

Dr Peter Hawkins, 1982

COACH

– current competence (assessing)
– outcomes (setting)
– action (agreeing and taking)
– checking (feedback and review)

Ian Fleming and Allan J D Taylor

STAR

– situation
– task
– actions
– results

WINA

– where are we now?
– investigate the options
– name the outcomes
– Agree the action

REFLECTIVE ACTIVITY

Which of the above are you familiar with?

What other coaching models do you know?

Do you find any particular model immediately easier to understand and relate to than the others?

USING THE GROW MODEL

Probably the best known coaching model, GROW was originally developed by Graham Alexander. However, it was later championed and made popular by John Whitmore.

Ref to ELP 10 – GROW

GROW stands for:

Goals: what does the coachee want to achieve and why, what does that mean in very specific terms and how will success be measured, by when do they want to achieve their goals, who else might be involved or have an influence on this, what would be the consequences of achieving these goals.

Reality: what is happening now, the current reality, what are the helpful factors, what are the unhelpful factors, what issues or barriers are there to overcome, who is involved, how did the current situation arise, what is real and what is opinion or assumption, what has already been tried, what have been the results.

Options: what possibilities are there for moving forward, what options are available, what other options might there be, what options could there be if there was more money, time, energy, resources, confidence, support available or if the context was somehow different or the situation seen through someone else's eyes (these questions being used to stimulate new ideas and thinking). What is possible? What really are the options?

Wrap up or will (way forward): what is/are the best options and what specific action will be taken. What obstacles may be encountered and how will these be addressed. What support is needed to stay on track?

Being aware of GROW or similar coaching models can be very helpful for the coach in keeping the conversation flowing in a way that is productive and useful and results in some agreements to take forward.

Here is a simplified version of how a GROW conversation might go:

Coach – *'What area would you like to discuss?'* (Topic)

Coachee – *'I'd like to get better at time management.'*

Coach – *'What, in particular, would you like to achieve?'* (Goal)

Coachee – *'I'd like to leave on time at least three times a week.'*

Coach – *'How often do you leave on time at the moment?'* (Reality)

Coachee – *'Only about once a week – I work over by at least 30 minutes most days.'*

Coach – *'What options could you consider to help you achieve that goal?'* (Options)

Coachee – *'I could cut down the time that my team meetings take. Or I could ask my deputy to do the end of day reporting. Or I could learn to say 'No' a bit more often.'*

Coach – *'And which of those options are you most committed to?'* (Narrowing options)

Coachee – *'Delegating the end of day reporting would be the easiest and might give me more time to draw up a plan for the other things.'*

Coach – *'OK, so what will you do between now and our next meeting?'* (Will)

Coachee – *'I'll arrange a meeting with my deputy to plan the handover and monitor how much time I can save.'*

In reality, the conversation is likely to be more complex with options taking longer to define and being explored in more depth, and goals and reality being revisited, before a final option is declared

GROW does not need to be used in the order of the acronym. In practice, coaching conversations move backwards and forwards around goal setting, current reality and options, and may make several 'u-turns' before arriving at an agreed course of action. This is natural and how GROW should be used – ie it is not meant to create a strict four stage conversation but to help guide the conversation and ensure that all important areas are covered.

THE ROLE OF THE COACHEE

Earlier in this chapter we considered when it might or might not be appropriate to use a coaching intervention. For example it may not be appropriate for a team member who is very inexperienced or for someone whose work is affected by personal problems. Equally coaching cannot be imposed on an unwilling or passive 'subject'. By its very nature, and emphasis on developing coachee responsibility, coaching requires the coachee to take an active part in the process.

For coaching to be effective, a coachee will need to be honest about their hopes, mistakes and uncertainties as well as their achievements. A coachee has to be prepared to take responsibility for setting their own goals and following through on these. Whilst a coach will help motivate and encourage, it is the coachee's responsibility to complete agreed actions – or not.

Coaching can be a challenging process for coachees, pushing them out of their comfort zones and requiring them to take on new challenges and personal change. To cope with this, coachees will need to have a level of work skills and abilities to be able to do new tasks, without direct support.

Trying out new work activities will not always be successful and coachees need to be able to take a positive view and not give up too easily. Equally, there are limitations to what coaching can achieve and it is important that expectations of the process are realistic.

A coachee will also need to listen actively and ask questions within their work practice, in order to bring back meaningful information to the coaching session. They may also have to research and undertake opportunities for learning which support the coaching and development process.

Finally, just as the personal stance of the coach is crucial to the coaching relationship, the stance of the coachee can make or break the success of coaching. Respect for the coach and appreciation of the coach's intention to help is essential to a good relationship, along with the recognition that the coach is also human and will make mistakes along the way.

> "I am always ready to learn, I am not always ready to be taught."
>
> Winston Churchill

Consideration of the requirements of a coachee, for an effective coaching relationship, makes it even more evident that coaching is not the right solution for every learner. Coachees need to be willing to, and capable of, playing their part in the process if it is to be successful.

IMPLEMENTING COACHING IN THE ORGANISATION

Potential benefits

Considering the many potential benefits of coaching, it is unsurprising that so many organisations have introduced or extended coaching practice in the last decade. These benefits include the following.

For the coachee:

- dedicated time to focus on own performance and development needs
- support to reflect on and challenge limiting assumptions
- clarification of thinking and ability to set goals
- a safe context to make mistakes, ask 'silly' questions and be given honest feedback
- increased confidence
- honing of (self-awareness and self-management) skills which transfer to other aspects of life
- increased learning – consolidation of other learning
- reduced frustration and stress as a result of being able to discuss disappointments and concerns
- improved relationship with line-manager
- greater understanding of role requirement and of own contribution to the organisation.

> "I found the process gave me a greater insight into the details of … (the task) … and greatly increased my confidence."
>
> A coachee

For the coach:

- an increased connection with team members
- greater awareness of team strengths and learning needs
- a more effective team
- a greater understanding of the organisation's work and systems
- constant learning from coachee's experiences and reflections
- development of own ability to set goals and reflect on own experiences
- continuous improvement of communication and coaching skills
- increased confidence and self-esteem from developing skills
- satisfaction in coachee achievements
- professional recognition/accreditation.

> "Although the 'agenda' is the coachee's and the aim of our sessions is the coachee's development, I also get a real 'buzz' from our coaching conversations and always come away with new ideas for my coaching practice."
>
> A coach

For the organisation:

- enhanced staff competence
- enhanced management capabilities and manager engagement in team development
- improved relationships
- greater awareness of and engagement with organisational goals
- greater transfer of learning to workplace and consolidation of other learning increasing returns on L&D expenditure
- more measurable results of learning (tangible and recorded outcomes from implementing agreed actions)
- a move towards a 'learning organisation' culture.

> "Coaching has been seen as a benefit to the individual but it also has considerable benefits to the organisation. At its core coaching is about awareness and responsibility. Employees who accept awareness and responsibility are better focused to deliver. Employees who are focused on goals, allied to the appraisal system and aligned to the organisational strategy can learn better, manage relationships better, be better team members and deliver better performance."
> Taking the temperature of coaching, CIPD, 2009

Coaching programmes

Any L&D professional charged with introducing a coaching programme or formalising coaching provision within their organisation has a number of options to consider. Primarily involving:

1. The overall model of coaching to be implemented?

2. How will coaching be established and managed?

1. The overall coaching model

Whatever model of coaching is implemented, it should always be the best fit for the organisation. A best-fit model or programme would be appropriate to the size, culture and resources of the organisation and be designed with a main aim of bringing organisational, as well as individual, advantage. To help identify the best coaching model for an organisation, it is helpful to consider:

Who will be coached?

Coaching may be provided across the organisation, or for specific groups. Specific groups may be selected because they are seen to have the most pressing need or as 'pilot group' prior to further implementation.

Specific groups offered coaching on a needs basis may for example be, senior managers, in an executive coaching programme, reasonably newly competent staff needing to develop skills in the workplace, or teams facing particular challenges or new developments.

Who will be the coaches?

Coaches can be internal or external to the organisation, experts or non experts, line managers, L&D professionals or peers, and there are good reasons for selecting any or all of these. External coaches can give the programme a greater formality and perhaps because they are also more costly, increase a coachee's commitment to honouring meetings and completing agreed actions. Also, some coachee's may find discussing experiences, issues and concerns about their work easier with an external person, who has no influence over their future prospects, than with a line-manager or peer. However, external coaches are costly, and are only likely to be feasible for small-scale use. They are also likely to have less understanding of the organisational context than internal coaches.

Internal coaches will have an understanding of the work and the organisation, which may be an advantage in helping individuals set honest, realistic and organisationally aligned goals. Equally, internal coaches, with expertise of the work area, may be more able to assist a coachee's reflection on their performance at work, give feedback, and be better equipped to provide new knowledge and ideas where helpful and requested by the coachee. On the other hand this can, of course, bring with it a potential for a directive stance, unless coaches are well trained in the art of coaching.

One of the most popular implementation models emerging is for line managers to deliver coaching for their team members, and for them to be supported in this by L&D specialists. Responsibility for design of coaching systems and for training and supporting line-managers rests with L&D, possibly working with external specialists. Some of these models have the further addition of leadership/executive coaching provided by the external specialists.

The use of internal coaches is likely to assist the embedding of coaching into the organisation and help create a greater learning culture. It also allows for a greater integration of coaching with performance management systems and can improve workplace relationships. However, a key factor to consider in the use of internal coaches is the capability of managers or other internals to take on the role, and implementers have to be careful that coaching is not seen as just another demand on busy managers.

The nature of coaching practice

It is good practice to clarify from the outset what coaching means within the organisation and how it will be implemented. As we have already discovered, there are many variables to coaching and a clear statement about what is expected will benefit all involved and help standardise practice across the workplace. Parameters to consider here include:

- directive or non-directive approaches
- formal coaching sessions or integration into other management techniques
- regular planned sessions or spontaneous as required
- pre-set duration or as required
- location of meetings if not at immediate workplace.

Links to other L&D initiatives

Coaching for all its popularity is just one development method and will work best when it is part of a wider provision. Coaching complements other methods and is a very useful addition to the portfolio, along with courses, one-to-one training, e-learning, peer learning, self-directed learning and mentoring.

In implementing coaching it is important to consider how coaching will link to other learning and development in the organisation and where it fits within an overall L&D strategy.

> In the CIPD 2009 Learning and Development Survey 55 per cent of respondents positioned coaching within management development initiatives, and 44 per cent offered coaching as part of leadership development programmes. Whilst 26 per cent had formally written coaching into the learning and development strategy, 28 per cent said coaching was a 'stand-alone' process with no established links to wider learning and development.

2. How will coaching be established and managed?

Issues to consider here are:

- How will coaches be trained and prepared for carrying out coaching?
- What ongoing support will be provided for coaches?
- What supporting systems, eg recording systems, are required?
- How will coaching be evaluated?

If managers are to carry the responsibility for coaching others then the organisation has a responsibility to prepare and equip them for this, and whether coaches are line-managers or not, a programme is only likely to be successful if it has line-manager 'buy-in'.

Training will be required in the knowledge and skills areas identified earlier in this chapter and this should be followed up with some form of on-going support and supervision for coaches. Ideally all coaches should be afforded the opportunity to experience coaching for themselves, as coachee.

Supporting systems, such as recording systems, if they are to be used, are best designed and provided centrally to cut down the burden on coaches and to encourage a standardised approach. Whilst some recording may be essential the amount of this should be appropriate to the type of implementation and always avoid becoming bureaucratic.

Finally, as with any other L&D approach, thought needs to be given to how coaching will be evaluated. Coaching requires effort, commitment and resources and the provision of these can only be justified if the results of coaching can be seen.

> The CIPD 2010 Annual Learning and Talent Development Survey showed that, of the 82 per cent of organisations using coaching as a development tool, only 36 per cent had a system of evaluating it. The most commonly used systems were: post event evaluations (58 per cent), individuals' testimonies (56 per cent), assessing impact on KPIs (44 per cent), and measuring return on expectation (40 per cent).

> "I never cease to be amazed at the power of the coaching process to draw out the skills or talent that was previously hidden within an individual, and which invariably finds a way to solve a problem previously thought unsolvable."
>
> John Russell

WHAT NEXT

COACHING

1. Have a go. If you have not formally coached or been coached, now is the time. Identify a peer or colleague who would benefit from a coaching exercise, and on the basis that you are both experimenting, try out a coaching conversation.

2. Reflecting on all the information offered by this chapter, consider how coaching could best be used within your organisation and draw up a plan for how it could be implemented.

3. Have a look at the case study below and consider:

– What the actual conversation between coach and coachee may have been (maybe expressing this as an outline coaching 'script').

– This example involves an external coach working with the manager. How might it have been different with an internal coach?

– What are your own feelings about this coaching example and what can you learn from it for your own practice?

CASE STUDY 8.2

COACHING A MANAGER WITHIN AN INTERNATIONAL LIQUID NATURAL GAS COMPANY

The problem

The manager of the site fire brigade had brought his staff (of local nationals) to a good level of capability. However, the plant around them was under redevelopment and his supervisors were finding it difficult to keep the teams in a high state of readiness and capability, in this period of relative inactivity. He was worried that if this continued it would seriously undermine the ability of the site fire brigade to deal with any emergencies.

The coaching

We began by using open dialogue to talk through and help the manager define the problem. In the course of the coaching it became clear that a key issue was maintaining the motivation of the fire fighting teams in a period of intense change. Various approaches had already been tried but everyone was feeling stuck and deflated with the potential lack of readiness of the teams and this was a critical issue for emergency response.

For a while we explored several possible approaches to solving the problem, most of which had been tried already and found wanting. However, discussing the nature of the problem helped create the space needed to set current worries to one side and focus on potential solutions.

We stimulated a discussion to explore what was known from previous management experience in other areas. Asking open questions took the manager back in his career and he started to talk about managers he had worked for and really admired. This prompted memory of a previous boss who had used games to motivate his staff.

This led the manager to realising that he had been trying too hard to motivate his staff and had ended up micromanaging them which was counterproductive. The harder he tried, the worse the problem with the staff became. This realisation allowed him to think differently and he came up with the idea of creating a series of competitions rather than using a dictatorial style.

The results

This change of attitude turned the problems facing the site into something challenging and fun that the staff could engage with. A series of competitions were devised around the essential processes and activities that had to be done and the skills that had to be practised and honed. Things that were previously considered 'a chore' became key events in the day of the fire fighters. The manager also had the idea of mixing teams to include experienced staff with new recruits in order to achieve a transfer of learning and skills to the newer staff – something he particularly wanted to achieve.

Going back later it was great to see the teams' new enthusiasm and their almost incidental skills development as they competed against one another in a friendly way.

This is a lasting change and continues to this day. The team is developing and maintaining a high standard of readiness and a consistently high level of motivation. The manager of the fire brigade now reports that he is freed from the day to day micromanaging and can step back to take a more proactive, strategic leadership role.

Adrian Nixon, Nixor Limited

SUMMARY

This chapter has explored:

The definition of and different types and styles of coaching

- Coaching is an interaction, usually between two people (coach and coachee), aimed at developing the coachee's performance in a certain area. This is achieved by raising the coachee's awareness of their performance and exploring options for improvement.
- Different types of coaching include sports coaching, performance coaching, executive coaching and career coaching.
- Coaching can be performed by internal or external coaches, who may or may not have experience of the subject being coached (subject experts or process experts) using different degrees of directiveness.

- Coaching is similar to, but different from other development approaches. It is best suited to a coachee who has some degree of knowledge, skill and willingness to develop.

The roles and responsibilities of coach and coachee

- The role of the coach includes preparing for the coaching relationship and contracting with the coachee.
- A coach will assist and motivate a coachee to determine and set goals, identify courses of action, identify and fulfil specific learning needs, review progress towards goals, explore obstacles and set-backs and review, clarify, refine and re-set goals.
- A coach may also be required to keep records of meeting outcomes.
- A coachee is responsible for setting their own goals, following through on these and taking equal responsibility for the coaching process.
- Roles and responsibilities can be captured in a 'coaching agreement' between the parties.

Some main coaching models and techniques

- Coaches can make a range of interventions, from the highly directive (telling/advising) through to non-directive (listening/reflecting). The ideal is to lean mostly to the non-directive.
- Coaches can make use of a range of coaching 'models' such as GROW, which can help guide the coaching discussion.
- Coaches also need the skills of active listening, effective questioning, agreeing objectives, giving feedback and sometimes, problem solving.

Describe the potential benefits of coaching

- There are numerous potential benefits of coaching.
- For a coachee, these include: dedicated time to focus on own performance and development needs, support to reflect on and challenge limiting assumptions, clarification of thinking and ability to set goals.
- For a coach: ongoing learning from coachee's experiences and reflections, development of own ability to set goals and reflect on own experiences, continuous improvement of communication and coaching skills.
- And for the organisation: enhanced staff competence, enhanced management capabilities and manager engagement in team development, and greater staff awareness of and engagement with organisational goals.

Factors affecting the implementation of coaching

- Organisations which want a culture of coaching can take steps to train managers/coaches, identify coaching needs, identify coachees, and set up processes to implement and evaluate the process.
- Coaching needs to be aligned to the needs of the organisation, as well as to the needs of the coachee.

EXPLORE FURTHER

BOOKS:

Whitmore, J. (2002) *Coaching for performance*. London: Nicholas Brearley Publishing.

Downey, M. (2003) *Effective coaching: lessons from the coach's coach*. 3rd edn. London : Texere Publishing.

Thorpe, S. and Clifford, J. (2003) *The coaching handbook*. London: Kogan Page.

Starr, J. (2007) *The coaching manual: the definitive guide to the process, principles and skills of personal coaching*. 2nd edn. New Jersey USA: Prentice Hall.

WEBSITES:

On-line guidance and resources relating to coaching:

www.cipd.co.uk

www.coaching-at-work.com

www.trainingzone.co.uk

On-line articles relating to workplace coaching:

Chartered Institute of Personnel and Development: www.cipd.co.uk

People Management: www.peoplemanagement.co.uk

CHAPTER 9

Developing Mentoring Skills for the Workplace

INTRODUCTION

This chapter begins with an exploration of the meaning and purpose of mentoring and the nature of different mentoring relationships. We consider similarities between mentoring and other approaches and when mentoring is most appropriate. Having identified the potential benefits that mentoring has to offer, we move on to explore the further implications and key questions involved in implementing mentoring within a workplace. We conclude the chapter by exploring the mentoring process in more detail, looking specifically at the mentor role and some mentoring techniques

LEARNING OUTCOMES

When you have read this chapter you should be able to:

- understand and explain the meaning and purpose of mentoring
- describe the potential benefits of mentoring
- discuss factors which affect the implementation of mentoring
- describe the role of a mentor in the mentoring process
- identify and explain some techniques for use in mentoring.

A MENTORING RESURGENCE?

It would be fair to say that mentoring has existed in the shadow of coaching for some time. The popularity of coaching continues to soar and coaching continues to be a main theme in the learning and development (L&D) media.

Some would say that this is because coaching has a more exciting image, or that the benefits of coaching have been more explicitly reported or even that the term 'coaching' implicitly includes mentoring. It is also undoubtedly because coaching is now a profession of its own, in which people earn their living, network and gain accreditation, and so the ongoing promotion of coaching is essential to, as well as being an outcome of, this growing industry.

However, just a small amount of research shows that mentoring is very much alive and well and seemingly increasing in popularity. In the 2008 CIPD Annual Learning and Development Survey, 36 per cent of respondents reported an increasing use of mentoring and buddying systems, and mentoring schemes are now reported as operational in the Health Service and other areas of the public sector, the finance industry, the voluntary sector, education, armed forces, charities, social initiatives and a wide range of business organisations.

Mentoring has always been around and brought benefits, and many of us will be lucky enough to have had people in our lives we think of, however informally, as our 'mentors'. Perhaps, though, we are now seeing the resurgence of the popularity of mentoring and an increased recognition of the potential benefits mentoring can bring to the workplace:

> From our point of view mentoring seems to have become exceedingly popular. Back in the days when we first set up, mentoring was not well known but it seems to be all over the place now.
>
> Jan West, MentorSET, quoted in TrainingZONE.co.uk

DEFINING MENTORING

The original Mentor is a character in Homer's epic poem The Odyssey. When Odysseus, King of Ithaca, went to fight in the Trojan War, he entrusted the overseeing of his son, Telemachus, to Mentor.

As with most L&D approaches, there are several variations of mentoring, and therefore the term can mean different things to different people. In its simplest form, *mentoring is about two people coming together with a view to helping one of them progress more easily through work, life or whatever context the mentoring is taking place in.* However, to get a fuller definition of mentoring, we first need to explore this activity and some of its variations in a little more detail.

PURPOSES OF MENTORING

The various purposes of mentoring include:

- to provide a role model – someone who a mentee can look up to and base their own behaviour on
- to provide a sounding board – someone with whom the mentee can discuss ideas, problems and concerns within a safe environment
- to provide a source of advice from someone who has already 'been there' and has real experience of the issues likely to be faced by the mentee
- to enable work-related development – someone who can directly or indirectly help the mentee to develop their work related skills and knowledge

- to provide an advocate – someone who can help support, represent and champion the mentee when needed

- to provide contacts and access to opportunities – someone who can 'open doors' for the mentee (sometimes called 'sponsorship')

- to enable personal development – someone who can help the mentee to become more adept at managing themselves and their relationships and at achieving personal and career goals.

In reality, a mentoring relationship is unlikely to be restricted to any one of these, with one of the main benefits of mentoring being that there are fewer assumed restrictions. It is accepted that mentors and mentees will work together in different ways to suit their particular needs at any time.

REFLECTIVE ACTIVITY

Looking at the different purposes of mentoring above, who are the people who have provided these things in your life?

Have you thought of these people as your mentors?

DIFFERENT MODELS OF MENTORING

In the very broad definition above, we talked about 'two people coming together'. Whilst this arrangement remains the most popular, there are also various models of mentoring which involve more than two people coming together – and indeed some where no one physically comes together at all.

Group mentoring

Where there are several potential mentees in an organisation and fewer potential mentors, it is possible for groups of mentees to work together with one or two mentors facilitating the group. The group might discuss a variety of issues from all mentees or concentrate on a particular issue at each meeting. This arrangement can allow a greater number of mentees to benefit from mentoring and, where available, different mentors may be asked to attend the meetings, enabling everyone to benefit from the different specialist experience of individual mentors.

Group peer mentoring

This another type of group mentoring. Here, groups come together because they have a common interest, usually a similar work role, for example, new managers or owners of small businesses. Rather than have a lead mentor, the group operates in a self-directed way, in which all group members operate as both mentees and mentors.

A typical format for peer mentoring is for individuals to take it in turns, perhaps at successive meetings, to talk about challenges and aspects of their work, and for the rest of the group to focus on that person's situation, helping them to clarify issues, find new ideas – inspired by the suggestions and experiences of other group members – and determine potential solutions.

This type of mentoring arrangement, also referred to as 'action learning sets' and championed by Reg Revans (1971, *Developing effective managers*), brings forward a multitude of different experiences and allows all group members to learn from each other.

Online mentoring

The Internet has brought a new way for mentors and mentees to find each other and work together. An increasing number of sites allow potential mentors to register and offer their services, and mentees to find and communicate with selected mentors. This is a voluntary arrangement in which mentors are offered the satisfaction of passing on their wisdom to others and mentees have a safe and confidential (anonymous, if they choose) context in which to discuss concerns and uncertainties. Whilst many online mentoring schemes are positioned within specific contexts and professions, others are open to all. Certainly there may be safety considerations about use of some of these sites, but there is no doubt that the Internet has widened access to mentoring, and access to specialist mentors, for many more people.

One-to-one mentoring

Returning to the more traditional mentoring arrangement, of one mentor and one mentee, there are further variations possible in the type of relationship between the two. Typically a mentor in the workplace is:

- a more experienced person
- in a senior position in the organisation, industry or sector
- not connected to the mentee's management line (ie not the mentee's manager or their manager's manager)
- who may or may not have been trained as a mentor (although increasingly training is provided)
- who is motivated to assist the development of a 'junior' person in their organisation or industry.

Variations on this traditional arrangement are where the mentor is a mentee's peer or colleague, rather than being in a senior position, or where the mentor actually is the mentee's line manager.

One-to-one peer mentoring

The term 'peer mentoring' has already been used above to refer to a form of group mentoring, but it can also refer to mentoring between two people, where the mentor is a peer, rather than someone of designated senior position in the organisation. In this arrangement mentoring may be one-way or two-way, with each of the pair taking mentor and mentee roles as required. This arrangement allows the two to learn from each other, share the challenges of the workplace and perhaps feel less isolated. It can also open up access to mentoring for a greater number of team members.

Line manager mentoring

This is an accepted model and no doubt happens informally all the time. However, discussing issues and uncertainties can be more sensitive within a management line relationship and could inhibit honest discussion and resolution of problems. On the positive side, managers may have greater insights into work situations and be able to facilitate more relevant and useful thinking, but the arrangement does require some careful and flexible shifting of roles by both manager and mentee.

CASE STUDY 9.1

GROUP PEER MENTORING

The example here is of a group peer mentoring session or action learning set, supported by a facilitator (whose role is not to act as a mentor but to facilitate the peer mentoring process). The six participants are all owners of small businesses who meet every four to six weeks as part of a 10-month peer mentoring programme. The number of meetings was determined to ensure that every participant could have a meeting devoted to their particular issues; plus an introductory meeting and a final review meeting.

The facilitator, an L&D professional, explains about setting up the group:

> When I started the peer mentoring group I couldn't decide if there ought to be two groups – one for very new businesses, and one for established businesses. The question I had was: 'What would start-ups have to contribute to the learning experience of more established businesses?' I could see the value that the established companies could potentially add to the new ones but was unsure how much value would be added in reverse. I wanted the sessions to be of equal benefit to everyone and I was concerned that the more experienced ones would do all the talking, limiting the participation of the newer ones – and also that the

more experienced ones might feel that there was not much learning from the sessions for them.

Here's what I've found so far from the five sessions that have already run:

- Indeed the new owners are keen to learn and ask lots of questions, and they listen. They have no previous experience so are very open to 'thinking differently' because everything *is* different. They respond well to anecdotal input and real examples, and the conversation flows easily with little input from me. The new owners leave the sessions with lots of new thinking, ideas and learning.

- However, the established business owners are also learning a lot from the sessions. Some of the established owners have been 'stuck and struggling', thinking the same thoughts and using the same ways of solving their problems even though the world has changed. The 'new guys' naive questioning has made them think about what they did in the past, what worked, what didn't and why. These questions cause them to re-live past issues and so reflect on their own behaviour patterns, taking them to another level of learning.

- When the new ones ask completely open questions such as: 'What do you *think* you could do about X?' it is because they have no idea themselves and are looking for suggestions, not because they are trying to be mentors and stimulate learning – but that is definitely the effect!

  Christine James, Chris James Learning

DIFFERENT STYLES OF MENTORING

There are probably as many different styles of mentoring as there are mentors. One of the benefits of mentoring is the greater acceptance of different approaches to working together than, say, in a coaching context. However, we can categorise mentoring styles to some extent.

In the previous chapter on coaching, we explored the concept of directive versus a non-directive approach. By 'directive', we mean how much the coach inputs their own opinion, suggestions and advice into the process, in contrast to how much they stand back and desist from inputting to the process, leaving the coachee to take responsibility for decisions and selection of activities.

We considered 'directiveness' as a scale, from highly directive to non-directive. This scale of approach applies equally to mentoring, with non-directive activities including:

- listening
- reflecting back
- paraphrasing
- summarising
- asking questions to raise awareness.

More directive approaches are:

- making suggestions
- giving feedback
- offering guidance
- and ultimately, instructing or telling.

In *Everyone needs a mentor: fostering talent in your organisation* (Clutterbuck 2008), David Clutterbuck refers to another dimension of mentor approach, a scale of 'stretching through to nurturing'. On this scale mentoring can be geared towards stimulating greater learning through challenging and stretching the mentee or towards the perhaps more comfortable position of being supporting, encouraging and nurturing.

The style taken by the mentor will depend on their personality, the training they have received and any parameters set for the programme in which they participate.

There will be many times when it is appropriate to be non-directive, to encourage the mentee to explore their experiences and enhance their understanding of their own behaviour. Non-directive mentoring encourages mentees to find the answers within themselves, which in turn impacts positively on their confidence and self-esteem. Equally the more ownership the mentee has of any potential solutions, the more likely they are to follow through on agreed actions and be committed to making improvements.

As for coaches, there are a number of models available to mentors which can assist a non-directive style of conversation, for example, the GROW model, and these are discussed in the previous chapter on coaching.

Ref to ELP 10 – GROW

GROW

Goals
Reality
Options
Wrap up/**W**ill

There will also be times when it is appropriate to be a directive mentor. Mentees often need mentors to help them negotiate workplace challenges or politics, help them find accurate solutions quickly and point them in appropriate directions. A mentor who only asks questions is likely to frustrate the mentee rather than meet the pressing need.

> "Learn from other people's mistakes, you don't have time to make all of them yourself."
>
> Source unknown

Equally there will be times when mentees need to be challenged and other times when they will just need re-assurance and support.

So is there one correct approach? No. Ideally a mentor will move around the different styles finding the best way to support their mentees as they experience different challenges, performance results, emotions and, consequently, differing needs.

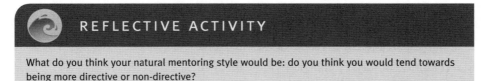

REFLECTIVE ACTIVITY

What do you think your natural mentoring style would be: do you think you would tend towards being more directive or non-directive?

What kind of circumstances would make you adopt an approach further towards the other end of the scale?

The potential benefits of mentoring

Some of the potential and reported benefits **for mentees** of a mentoring relationship or programme are:

- increased confidence and self-esteem
- an opportunity to reflect and focus on personal situations
- improved ability to reflect, analyse and find solutions to problems
- increased motivation from being encouraged and the desire to have 'achievements' to report back to the mentor
- broadened horizons and raised aspirations
- reduced isolation and availability of a 'sympathetic friend'
- increased learning and knowledge
- a supported opportunity to develop a career plan
- faster orientation to the organisation for new recruits
- increased understanding of the wider organisation
- insights into the thinking patterns of more senior management
- links with a figure who is respected within the organisation
- a role model for success within the organisation
- a better understanding of, and help to build, professional networks
- a chance to discuss issues that straddle the boundary between work and personal (work–life balance, job insecurity, work pressures, work relationships) with someone who understands the workplace but is off the management line
- reduced stress as a result of being able to discuss challenges and frustrations.

And **for mentors**:

- an opportunity to make use of hard-earned knowledge and experience
- the satisfaction of helping someone else and seeing their development
- an opportunity to learn from others
- enhanced communication skills
- enhanced skills relating to the development of others
- insights into other areas and aspects of the organisation
- the satisfaction of helping the organisation, through contributing to the development and effectiveness of the workforce
- recognition of mentor contribution by the mentee
- recognition of mentor contribution by the organisation.

And **for organisations:**

Where mentoring is part of an organisational programme, there are also benefits to be had for the organisation as a whole. These can include:

- greater transfer of knowledge and learning
- a more competent workforce
- potential for improved productivity
- enhanced understanding of learning needs and skills gaps
- greater individual ownership of development
- greater retention of knowledge within the organisation
- enhanced atmosphere of trust and respect
- stronger links across hierarchical levels
- stronger links across different areas of the organisation
- greater employee understanding of the wider organisation
- increased individual engagement with the organisation
- better working relationships, with issues being addressed in a safe context, before they grow in significance
- enhanced staff well being
- improved staff retention rates
- helps build an organisational identity
- enhanced image of organisation for staff and externally – which can impact on, for example, recruitment and marketing
- potential recognition of the organisation's efforts by staff and possibly others (external awards and accreditations).

MENTORING – A SUMMARY

We have now explored different aspects of mentoring, including purpose, types, styles and benefits, and discussed some of the main variations of mentoring practice. Despite these variations, we can extend our earlier definition of mentoring to:

> a relationship between mentee(s) and mentor(s), aimed at helping to ease the progress of the mentee through work, career or life generally, depending on the context of the mentoring, in which mentors can employ a wide range of different styles and approaches (including listening, encouraging reflection and self-learning, sharing experiences, giving advice, coaching and assisting with networking) to support mentee progression.

We could also add:

> whilst also meeting particular needs and motivations of the mentor, and potentially bringing organisational benefits, where mentoring is part of a supported organisational programme.

MENTORING IN PRACTICE

MENTORING, COACHING AND OTHER APPROACHES

Undoubtedly, there is substantial confusion between mentoring and coaching, and often the two are combined together into a single approach labelled 'coaching and mentoring' or just labelled 'coaching', even though mentoring is included.

This confusion and combination is understandable. There is much crossover in the two approaches, particularly in the type of techniques used by coaches and mentors. Both are encouraged to listen in depth and use open questions and strategies which enhance self-reflection, and both seek to enable development and progression.

Also, as both coaching and mentoring can appear in different variations, there is every chance that one organisation's mentoring programme may be very similar to another organisation's coaching programme – whilst two programmes with the same title could actually be quite different in practice.

Mentoring does have much in common with coaching and other L&D and even some therapeutic interventions, but there are also many differences. In the chapter on coaching we presented a chart showing differences between coaching and mentoring; this has been extended to include counselling, which is also sometimes confused with mentoring, and re-presented in Table 9.1.

Table 9.1 Comparison between workplace coaching, mentoring and counselling

	Workplace coaching	Mentoring	Counselling
Context/areas addressed	Work/task performance issues	Work issues Ongoing career issues Personal issues	Usually very personal issues, sometimes going back in years
Relationship between coach and coachee	Often coach is coachee's line manager, but could be peer or trainer or an external coach	Usually a more experienced, senior work colleague, from outside the mentee's immediate work team	Usually a professional relationship, in which counsellor is paid to provide a therapeutic service
Coach expertise	Coach may or may not have experience in the area being coached, and may or may not be trained as a coach	Mentor usually has general knowledge and experience of the mentee's work area. May or may not be trained as a mentor	Professional counsellors must be trained and qualified. Some are subject specialists – eg bereavement

Coach/mentor approach	Coaches are encouraged to, at least, limit the giving of advice and focus on assisting coachees to find their own solutions	Greater acceptance of mentors taking a more directive, advisory role, allowing mentee to share and learn from mentor's experience	Different styles of counselling – but tend towards being non-directive in approach
Typical nature of meetings	Focused, agreeing goals and reviewing progress towards them	General and informal discussion around work, personal and career issues	Often slow and intense exploration of experiences, feelings and emotions
Frequency of meetings	Regular, programme of meetings usually agreed in advance	May be more ad hoc or called, when needed, by mentee	Regular, planned meetings
Duration of arrangement	Usually short term – until goals achieved (task related)	Can last for a long period of time (career related)	Duration depends on need – can be short or longer term

We can also compare mentoring with other approaches such as direct training, which is likely to be more focused on one particular theme, more directive, delivered by qualified L&D professionals and possibly subject specialists, and shorter in duration than mentoring, possibly a one-off or series of specific initiatives.

All of the above approaches have their uses and the main consideration is that the approach selected is most appropriate and will bring the most benefits for the individuals involved and, importantly, for the organisation in which they operate.

IMPLEMENTING A MENTORING SCHEME

In view of the potential benefits of mentoring, it is unsurprising that it appears to be growing in popularity. However, implementing a scheme does require significant resources and expenditure, for example, possible work down-time costs of participants, the provision of training for mentors, and the costs of co-ordinating and supporting a scheme, and so it is important that mentoring is implemented in a way which ensures potential benefits are realised.

As well as financial considerations, thought should also be given to how appropriate the introduction of formal mentoring would be to the existing culture of the organisation.

REFLECTIVE ACTIVITY

Consider the contrasting organisational culture features in Table 9.2 and how these would help or hinder the implementation of a new mentoring programme.

Table 9.2 **Contrasting oganisational features**

There is very little training activity already within the organisation and appraisal activity is left to individual managers to implement as they choose	The organisation supports all staff to undertake learning relevant to job role and monitors this via regular performance and development review
The organisation does not have a specific budget for learning and development	The organisation has a specific learning and development budget and reviews this at least annually
The organisation has a macho culture with little acceptance of error or slower/poorer performance	The organisation has an open culture where acceptance of some mistakes is considered an acceptable price to pay for continuous development and improvement
The organisation has a very formal hierarchy, with little interaction between different levels	There is an informal and relatively 'easy' interaction between managers and staff
Most staff see their work as just a means of earning a living and have little respect or affection for their workplace	Staff are proud to be associated with their organisation, and have a sense of personal investment in the organisations success
The organisation has little experience of any initiatives beyond the usual routine work activities	The organisation has a history of involvement in community, social and developmental initiatives for staff and the local community
Senior management had no interest or commitment to a mentoring programme	Mentoring was supported from the top down as part of an overall L&D strategy
If anyone wanted to mentor anyone else in the organisation it would be up to them to find the time and capability to do this and organise it for themselves	Mentoring would be a designed initiative, where mentors were supported by the organisation and their efforts recognised, by some flexibility of work conditions, professional respect and internal celebrations

If mentoring is to be introduced then there are key questions to consider, including:

1. In relation to the format and design of mentoring:

- What are the aims of introducing mentoring and how does it fit into the wider organisational L&D strategy? What are the specific purposes of mentoring? In order to give clear guidelines and parameters to participants, organisations need to be clear about why they are introducing a mentoring scheme and the specific purpose(s) of the scheme. The answer to this question will inform the answers to all the remaining questions about the design of any mentoring scheme.

- Who will have access to mentoring? Will it be open to anyone or targeted at specific groups? This is, of course, a business decision, but most advice from those already involved in managing mentoring schemes is to start small and build up numbers slowly, as processes are snagged and mentoring becomes an established initiative.

- What form of contact will be used, will all mentoring be face to face, all by e-mail or online, or a specified combination of these? Or will contact arrangements be left for the mentor and mentee to decide? Factors to be considered here are availability of mentors, geographical locations, access to IT equipment, IT skill levels, safety and ethical considerations and availability of appropriate meeting places.

- Where and when will mentoring meetings be held – during normal work time or not, within organisational premises or not? To a great extent this is a business decision – but there are also safety and ethical factors to consider. From our research most workplace mentoring schemes allow mentoring sessions to take place within work time and require them to be held on work premises. Careful thought should be given to safety considerations if schemes are to operate outside of these boundaries.

- What will be the frequency of meetings, duration of meetings and duration of relationship? Much of this is best left to mentee and mentor to decide, within business constraints, but in terms of guidelines, typical schemes involve meetings of approximately one to two hours held every four to six weeks. Scheme duration varies, but with quite a few found to be for a one-year period.

- What safety and ethical guidelines are required? Areas to consider here include:

  - arrangements for matching mentoring pairs

  - scope and boundaries of mentoring activity (eg are discussions ring-fenced to work and performance issues?)

  - guidelines regarding means of contact (see above)

  - 'ground rules' for working together

  - confidentiality arrangements

  - arrangements for ceasing unsuccessful relationships or for changing mentors.

- What will be the position of the mentee's line manager in the mentoring arrangement (assuming they are not the mentor)? Most arrangements do not formally involve the mentee's line manager in the relationship, other than them knowing a relationship is in place. Some of the more formal schemes do include an update from mentee to their line-manager about progress made within the mentoring arrangement.

- To what extent, and how, will mentoring be recorded? A usual scenario is for mentoring pairs to complete an agreement often referred to as a 'mentoring agreement', 'mentoring contract' or 'mentoring plan' (see example agreement at Figure 9.1). After that, the amount of recording of ongoing meetings varies, depending on the formality of the scheme. For some, recording is seen as a possible inhibitor or burden and so there is no requirement, whilst others include completion of a standard summary document, usually just detailing key discussion points and agreed actions, which then informs discussions at the next meeting.

2. In relation to the initial implementation of mentoring:

- How will the scheme be promoted and volunteers attracted? As well as promotion on intranets and notice-boards, it is usual to offer an information session before expecting people to volunteer.

- Will there be selection criteria for mentors? Different mentees suit different mentors, so there is unlikely to be one description of the ideal mentor. However, a general list of qualities reflecting a good mentor candidate might be someone who:
  - wants to be a mentor and volunteers for the role
  - genuinely respects, likes and cares about others
  - is respected in the organisation
  - has relevant professional experience, knowledge and skills
  - has reasonable people skills
  - is generally supportive of organisational change and progression
  - is open to different viewpoints and new learning
  - has time to commit to mentoring
  - agrees with the purpose, guidelines and ethics of the mentoring scheme.

- How will mentoring be integrated into existing job roles? Some organisations make the role a formal part of a job description, thus ensuring time is allocated and allowed for the activity, within the working month. Other schemes are less formally integrated but promote a culture of general support for mentoring activity.

- How will mentors and mentees be matched and allocated? More informal and on-line schemes leave mentors and mentee's to self-select. Where allocation is undertaken by a third party, such as the L&D function, different approaches can be taken (working on a like-with-like basis or bringing together different types to increase difference of thinking), and different factors considered, for example: location, style, gender or common areas of interest.

- What training should be provided for mentors? Mentors should be made fully aware of the purpose and processes of mentoring and are likely to benefit from some training to refresh techniques such as using questions effectively, active listening, problem-solving, setting objectives and giving feedback.

3. In relation to the ongoing management of mentoring:

- What ongoing support is required for mentors? Some organisations offer supervisory support for mentors, usually provided by L&D staff or external providers. This may take the form of ad-hoc advice as needed or formal mentor meetings, where mentors can discuss issues and participate in ongoing development activities.

- How will mentoring be monitored and evaluated? Finally, as with any other L&D approach, thought needs to be given to how mentoring will be evaluated. Evaluation results (however intangible outcomes may be) will inform the design of further programmes and should be essential to the ongoing justification of expenditure on a mentoring programme.

Figure 9.1 An example mentoring agreement form

MENTORING AGREEMENT

Mentor: Mentee: Date:

Arrangements for meeting or contact:
How:
When:
Where:

Agreed main aims of mentoring (*add as many as required*):
(1)
(2)
(3)

Ground rules for working together (*add as many as required*):
(1)
(2)
(3)

After each meeting (mentee) will update the mentoring record with any actions agreed and e-mail to (mentor).

Agreed: _____   _____

AN EVOLVING EMPLOYEE MENTORING SCHEME

One local authority has long recognised the benefits of mentoring and made a commitment to making the resources available to ensure a successful in-house scheme.

Their initial scheme involved establishing mentoring relationships which were set to last for a one-year period. The scheme involved initial training for mentors and mentees who were then 'matched' together using information such as learning styles and interests.

Mentoring pairs went on to hold monthly meetings of about an hour and a half, with mentees setting the agenda and objectives for each meeting. There was a structured evaluation process for the scheme, involving groups of mentors and mentees, and the year was topped off with a mentoring ceremony.

This scheme ran quite successfully for several years and was used as a model by other organisations, but eventually seemed to 'run out of steam'. There were fewer volunteers coming forward, and it seemed that staff's needs of a mentoring scheme were changing. Consequently the authority is now trying out some new approaches.

The main change is that the new scheme is less formal and standardised than the previous one. Although there is still some initial training for both mentors and mentees, participants now select each other from a list on the scheme's web pages. Once contact is established, the pair decides the frequency and timing of the mentoring and the form of contact they will have. Whilst some 'mentoring pairs' still choose to have regular face-to-face meetings, many communicate more casually, making use of workplace facilities such as e-mail, tele-conferencing and video-conferencing, as well as social media such as Facebook.

REFLECTIVE ACTIVITY

Looking at the case study above:

- What do you think caused the downturn in the initial scheme? Does this tell us anything about the life-cycle of mentoring schemes?

- How might this case study influence the way in which you would introduce a mentoring scheme?

- What level of formality of scheme would best suit your organisation?

THE MENTORING RELATIONSHIP

The beauty of the mentoring relationship is that it is not prescribed but that it evolves with the needs and requests of the mentee. However, all ongoing mentoring relationships will have an introductory phase, a phase of mentoring activity, and an exit phase, each of which requires different activities and skills of the mentor.

MENTORING ACTIVITIES AT EACH STAGE OF THE MENTORING RELATIONSHIP

Introductory stage

Making initial contact with mentee and arranging first meeting.
Relationship/rapport building, introductions.
Facilitation of initial meeting, to include:

- ensuring mentee's understanding of purpose and processes
- exploring mentee's motivations and needs of process
- sharing and aligning expectations of process
- establishing a commitment to work together (or not)
- agreement of how to work together, both in terms of guidelines and ground rules as well as logistics about where, when and how communication will take place.

Agreements would usually be recorded in a mentoring agreement, contract or plan – see Figure 9.1.

Active mentoring stage

Depending on the needs and preferences of the mentee, and the nature of any mentoring programme, the mentor's role will include any or all of the following:

1. Assisting the mentee to reflect on, analyse and fully understand work progress, challenges and issues, through:

   - reviewing progress towards objectives and goals
   - actively listening
   - using open questions to stimulate thorough reflection
   - reflecting back, to clarify own and mentee's understanding
   - challenging assumptions and perceptions
   - providing different perspectives
   - discussing and debating
   - clarifying work requirements
   - helping to identify and explore obstacles to progress
   - giving honest and constructive feedback.

2. Assisting the mentee to find appropriate solutions and best courses of actions, through:

   - drawing out mentees ideas
   - encouraging mentees to find own solutions
   - making suggestions and giving advice from own experience
   - sharing technical knowledge
   - sharing knowledge about the organisation
   - providing 'nuggets' of direct training, coaching or teaching
   - signposting mentees to useful resources or contacts
   - helping convert thoughts into specific objectives for action
   - arranging introductions or access to useful contacts.

3. Assisting the mentee to become more self aware, more self-directing and to develop personal effectiveness skills, through:

- helping the mentee to recognise and understand their own behaviours, communication styles and learning styles
- summarising and reflecting back to aid self-awareness
- challenging assumptions and limitations to help develop greater self-responsibility
- providing encouragement and reassurance to help build confidence
- encouraging mentees to set the agenda for meetings and to 'drive' the mentoring process.

4. Assisting the mentee to plan and progress their overall career, through:

- reviewing career aspirations and goals
- developing a career plan
- reviewing the different requirements of different career stages and how the mentee can prepare for these
- exploring and identifying development needs
- exploring and identifying development opportunities
- signposting or enabling access to opportunities.

5. Assisting the mentee to build their professional networks, through:

- role-modelling behaviour
- coaching in networking skills

6. Managing the mentor's own role in the mentoring process, through

- monitoring own responses to mentoring, for example ability to stay objective, comply with guidelines and ethics, honour confidentiality
- monitoring own effectiveness and enjoyment of the role
- recognising own learning and support needs and fulfilling these
- ensuring compliance with any process requirements, such as record keeping or participating in process evaluation.

Exit phase

The mentoring relationship may come to a natural end when it is no longer useful or when situations change. Equally the relationship may change to a more distant one of friendship, based on the sharing of previous experiences, but no longer be a formal mentoring relationship.

Where there is a set end to mentoring – because a programme or particular context has come to an end, eg the programme is a one-year programme or is linked to a particular phase of the mentee's work or career progression, say the first the year in the job or until a particular qualification is gained – then it is useful to formally close down the relationship. Useful activities here are:

- reviewing progress and learning from the relationship
- exploring how this can be taken forward into new aspects of work, and life generally
- identifying further areas for and ways of developing
- recognising and celebrating achievement.

SOME MENTORING TECHNIQUES

There are so many ways in which mentors can assist mentees to work through issues and develop their abilities. Some have already been discussed, and some are detailed below. If you would like to explore some of these techniques further, some references have been provided in the Explore Further section at the end of this chapter.

ACTIVE LISTENING

- try to eliminate other distractions and focus on the speaker
- show your concentration physically (with body language) so the speaker feels they have your attention
- avoid interrupting
- summarise and reflect back to check your understanding.

USING QUESTIONS EFFECTIVELY

Questions can open up or close down a conversation. They can be used quite simply to draw out information:

> **'What did you do next?'**

Or to inspire deeper thinking:

> **'Why did you choose to do that particularly?'**

Or to consider different viewpoints:

> **'Why do you think they might have responded in that way?'**

Or to challenge assumptions:

> **'How do you know for sure that X feels that way?'**

They can also be interesting, creative and engaging:

> **'Has this situation occurred before, and how was it resolved then?'**
> **'If you could do anything you wanted in this situation, what would you do?'**
> **'How would (celebrity, hero, person admired by the mentee) deal with this?'**

Open questions usually require more than a few words by way of a response and so can help open up a conversation or derive greater amounts of information:

> **'How are things going at work?'**

Probing or clarifying questions seek to find out a bit more about specifics to clarify or extend understanding:

> **'Can you say a bit more about what X involves?'**

Reflective questions help the speaker to check that their words are reflecting their real thoughts and the listener to check that they have properly understood:

> **'So, you feel that they did that intentionally?'**

Closed questions can usually be answered with one word (often 'yes' or 'no') or just a few:

> **'Do you have any ideas about what to do next?'**

PROBLEM-SOLVING TECHNIQUES

Brain storming
Force-field analysis
Edward DeBono's six thinking hats
Pros and cons

AGREEING SMART OBJECTIVES

Specific
Measurable
Achievable
Relevant
Timebound

GIVING FEEDBACK

- Be honest – (unless you have a very, very good reason not to be)

- Be gentle – none of us take negative criticism well

- Be balanced – the good as well as the not so good

- Be specific – otherwise it may be general encouragement rather than feedback

- Be constructive – help the recipient to see ways of moving forward

WHAT NEXT

1. Building on the responses to the first two reflective activities in the chapter, consider what sort of mentor you would be... or are you already?

2. Find out if there are any mentoring schemes in operation near you and see if you can visit to find out more. Also, have a look at some of the on-line mentoring sites, easily found via a search engine.

3. Look at the mentoring techniques mentioned in the chapter, and carry out your own further research of these and maybe other mentoring skills and techniques. Some further references are provided in the Explore Further section at the end of this chapter. Then, using this material, design a training session you could deliver to new mentors.

4. If there are no organisational opportunities immediately available to you, you might consider finding out about and applying to one of the many social programmes, seeking mentors, eg there are schemes for young people in care, for young offenders and for people setting up new businesses.

5. Finally, have a look at the case study below and, considering this and all the information offered by this chapter, think about:

   - how mentoring could be useful to your organisation

   - the kind of mentoring programme that would best suit your organisation

   - how you would make a case to implement a mentoring programme.

CASE STUDY 9.3

ONE-TO-ONE MENTORING

This example is from a primary school, where an experienced teacher, Suzanne, is acting as mentor to a newly qualified teacher (NQT), Rachael, during Rachael's probationary year of teaching. The purpose of the mentoring scheme is to ensure that Rachael meets work standards and expectations whilst being supported with any difficulties or challenges that may arise. Suzanne and Rachael describe their work together as follows:

We began with an initial discussion to understand Rachael's current experience and areas to focus on during the year. As our mentoring is part of a wider programme, we have specific documents to complete (an 'initial discussion record' and an ongoing checklist ('calendar') showing completion of various required activities by Rachael, over the year). These standard documents ensure consistency of information and process for all NQTs.

We meet approximately six-weekly (half-termly) to reflect on the progress made during that time and to find solutions to any problems encountered. We also discuss Rachael's development since our last meeting and update her calendar.

A typical meeting takes place at an appointed time and usually begins with Suzanne asking how things have progressed since the last meeting, which then forms the basis of our discussion. Any minor problems are considered and solutions found together. For instance, when Rachael found that her PE skills needed developing, Suzanne referred her

to an NQT PE course with lots of hands-on experience. After the course, Suzanne was able to link Rachael to the local gymnastics coach, who then supported her in some lesson delivery. This has proved to be very successful, with Rachael now having increased confidence in developing more stimulating and interactive lessons for the children.

If Rachael has a problem that cannot wait until the next planned meeting, she can always contact Suzanne and a suitable time will be found to discuss her concerns. It is times like this when a mentor's advice and support can be most valuable. As an experienced teacher, Suzanne has a wealth of ideas and methods of dealing with behaviour and relationships in schools, which is of great help to Rachael. On one occasion, Rachael had issues that both she and Suzanne felt needed to be taken to a higher level and Suzanne was able to support Rachael in this and accompany her to a meeting to discuss the problem, where it was quickly resolved.

As the mentoring is part of a formal development scheme, Suzanne is required to give formal feedback on Rachael's progress, which contributes to Rachael's achievement of full teacher status. Although the year is only half way through, both find the mentoring arrangement extremely helpful and satisfying and look forward to Rachael's success at the end of the year.

Provided by Suzanne Copley, mentor, and
Rachael Beech, mentee

SUMMARY

This chapter has explored:

The meaning and purpose of mentoring:

- Mentoring is essentially about two (or more) people coming together with a view to helping a mentee progress more easily through, work, life or whatever context the mentoring is taking place in.

- Mentoring exists in many variations, including one-to-one and group mentoring arrangements.

- Mentoring can have several different purposes, including the sharing of experience, the provision of advice, the development of professional networks and the facilitation of learning.

- The nature of a mentoring relationship will depend on the styles of the personalities involved and the parameters of the mentoring programme in which they operate.

The potential benefits of mentoring:

- The benefits of mentoring for mentees can be both personal, for example, increased confidence and reduced stress, and work related, such as new ideas and learning and a greater understanding of the workplace.

- Whilst mentoring is primarily intended to benefit the mentee, it also offers a range of potential benefits to the mentor and to the employing organisation.

Factors which affect the implementation of mentoring:

- Implementing mentoring programmes requires organisational commitment and resources, and so it is important to spend some time working out the best and most suitable type of programme for the organisation.

- Factors to consider include: how mentoring would fit with other L&D initiatives, the level of formality of the programme, the actual design of the programme, how to get mentoring started and how to co-ordinate mentoring on an ongoing basis.

The role of a mentor in the mentoring process:

- The mentor role includes: helping to establish the mentoring relationship, undertaking mentoring activities during the relationship, and when the relationship has run its course, helping to bring it to a successful conclusion.

- Helping to establish the relationship involves building rapport, clarifying roles and agreeing main objectives.

- The nature of mentoring means that mentoring activities can be very diverse, from non-directive approaches such as active listening and reflecting back to highly directive approaches, such as advice giving, and direct training.

- The mentor's role is to work with the mentee, finding the approaches which best meet the mentee's needs as they emerge.

Mentoring techniques:

- Because the range of approaches used in mentoring is so wide, mentors can benefit from developing a whole range of skills and techniques.

- Some useful skills and techniques are rapport building, active listening, effective questioning, giving feedback constructively, agreeing objectives and facilitating problem solving.

- Mentors will already have many of these skills and use them in other areas of their work and lives – but they can be enhanced and contextualised through specific training for mentors.

EXPLORE FURTHER

BOOKS:

Alred, G., Garvey, B. and Smith, R. (2006) *Mentoring pocketbook*. 2nd edn. Alresford: Management Pocketbooks.

Clutterbuck, D. (2008) *Everyone needs a mentor: fostering talent in your organisation*. 4th edn. London: CIPD.

De Bono, E. (2000) *Six thinking hats*. 2nd rev edn. London: Penguin.

ILM and Mana (2007) *Solving problems and making decisions super series*. 5th edn. Oxford: Pergamon Flexible Learning.

Revans, R.W. (1983) *ABC of action learning*. Kent: Chartwell-Bratt.

WEBSITES:

On-line guidance and resources relating to mentoring:

www.cipd.co.uk

www.cipd.co.uk/subjects/lrnanddev/coachmntor/mentor.htm

www.cipd.co.uk/qualifications/choose/foundation/ccm.htm

On-line articles relating to in-company mentoring and mentoring networks:

www.trainingzone.co.uk

Free (or partially free) on-line access to problem solving techniques:

www.businessballs.com

www.mindtools.com

Essential Learning Pages

Training cycle

THE BIG PICTURE

A popular model, showing a four stage process, which provides the basis for learning and development activity in many organisations.

BACKGROUND

The concept of a cycle is common throughout many business theories and models (for example a buying cycle – consumers recognise that they have a need, research their options, reach a decision and make a purchase).

The Training Cycle, although not attributable to any one writer, is commonly recognised as a 'good practice' process underpinning effective L&D activity. Following the cycle guides L&D professionals to ensure that: training needs are identified, interventions are designed to meet needs, the right learning content is delivered and evaluation is carried out to ensure that needs have been met.

ESSENTIAL DETAIL

The training cycle can be illustrated diagrammatically as in Figure ELP1.1:

Figure ELP1.1 Training cycle

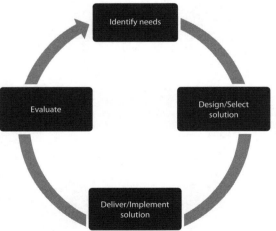

The fours stages are:

1. Identify needs. This will involve any of the methods of learning needs analysis that are covered in Chapter 4. Sometimes learning/training needs will become apparent by themselves – maybe as a result of customer complaints, new

initiatives etc. But most L&D professionals will have proper systems in place to identify and anticipate needs.

2. Design. Chapter 5 deals in depth with training design. This design stage could also include commissioning/selecting training from outside sources, or choosing the best option from an existing portfolio of solutions.

3. Delivery. This could include the running of a training course, but could equally encompass the implementation of a solution or putting an action into practice.

4. Evaluation. This provides the link back to the original needs and answers the questions 'has that need been met?' Evaluation also gives us the impetus to begin the cycle again by asking 'what else is needed, or what is needed next?'

Some writers add an extra stage of (individual) **assessment** in between delivery and evaluation, to acknowledge that assessment activities often take place between delivery and evaluation – and can feed into the evaluation of training activity.

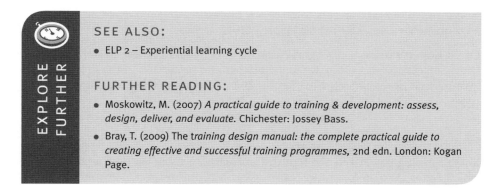

SEE ALSO:

- ELP 2 – Experiential learning cycle

FURTHER READING:

- Moskowitz, M. (2007) *A practical guide to training & development: assess, design, deliver, and evaluate.* Chichester: Jossey Bass.

- Bray, T. (2009) The *training design manual: the complete practical guide to creating effective and successful training programmes,* 2nd edn. London: Kogan Page.

EXPLORE FURTHER

Experiential learning cycle

THE BIG PICTURE

A four-stage 'learning cycle' which helps to explain how people learn in different ways. A 'complete' learning experience needs to cover all four stages of the cycle.

BACKGROUND

Having developed his theory over many years, David Kolb published his learning styles model in 1984. In his publications Kolb acknowledges the early work on experiential learning by others in the 1900's, including Rogers, Jung, and Piaget. In turn, Kolb's learning styles model and experiential learning theory are today acknowledged by academics, teachers, managers and trainers as seminal works: fundamental concepts towards our understanding and explaining human learning behaviour, and towards helping others to learn.

David Kolb is Professor of Organisational Development at Case Western Reserve University, Cleveland, Ohio, where he teaches and researches in the fields of learning and development, adult development, experiential learning, and learning styles.

ESSENTIAL DETAIL

Kolb's learning theory sets out four distinct learning styles (or preferences), which are based on a four-stage learning cycle. In this respect Kolb's model is particularly elegant, since it offers both a way to understand individual people's different learning styles, and also an explanation of a cycle of experiential learning that applies to us all.

Kolb includes this 'cycle of learning' as a central principle in his experiential learning theory, typically expressed as four-stage cycle of learning, in which 'immediate or concrete experiences' provide a basis for 'observations and reflections'. These 'observations and reflections' are assimilated (absorbed and translated) into 'abstract concepts' which the person can actively 'test and experiment' with, and which in turn enable the creation of 'new experiences'.

Kolb says that ideally (and by inference not always) this process represents a learning cycle or spiral where the learner 'touches all the bases', ie., a cycle of experiencing, reflecting, thinking, and acting.

Kolb's model works on two levels – **a four-stage cycle**:

- Concrete Experience – (CE)
- Reflective Observation – (RO)

- Abstract Conceptualization – (AC)
- Active Experimentation – (AE)

and a **four-type definition of learning styles**, (each representing the combination of two preferred styles, rather like a two-by-two matrix of the four-stage cycle styles, as in Figure ELP2.1), for which Kolb used the terms:

- Diverging (CE/RO)
- Assimilating (AC/RO)
- Converging (AC/AE)
- Accommodating (CE/AE).

Figure ELP2.1 Experiential learning cycle

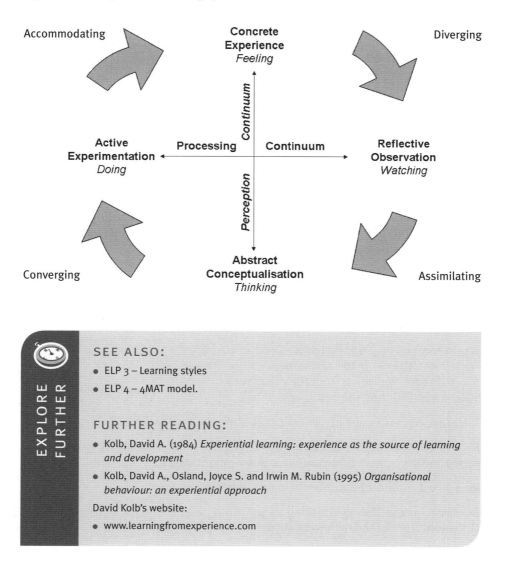

SEE ALSO:
- ELP 3 – Learning styles
- ELP 4 – 4MAT model.

EXPLORE FURTHER

FURTHER READING:
- Kolb, David A. (1984) *Experiential learning: experience as the source of learning and development*
- Kolb, David A., Osland, Joyce S. and Irwin M. Rubin (1995) *Organisational behaviour: an experiential approach*

David Kolb's website:
- www.learningfromexperience.com

Learning styles

THE BIG PICTURE

A model of the different ways in which people prefer to learn.

An understanding of different learning styles is essential to ensure that you design and deliver effective learning and development interventions.

BACKGROUND

In the 1970s Peter Honey and Alan Mumford looked at the earlier work of David Kolb. They worked for around four years with groups of managers looking at how they used Kolb's theory, and establishing whether individual managers had preferences for different styles of learning.

They define learning styles as 'a description of the attitudes and behaviours that determine an individual's preferred way of learning'.

They first published their findings in *The manual of learning styles* in 1982 and *Using your learning styles* in 1983.

They have also developed a questionnaire to help individuals to ascertain their own preferred learning style, which is available via www.peterhoney.com

A MORI survey in 1999 showed that Honey and Mumford's Learning Style Questionnaire (LSQ) was the most popular method of determining learning styles in the public sector.

ESSENTIAL DETAIL

Honey and Mumford describe learning as a continuous lifelong process, which constantly involves moving around four stages as in Figure 3.1:

Stage One: Having an experience
Stage Two: Reviewing the experience
Stage Three: Concluding from the experience
Stage Four: Planning the next steps.

A learner can start anywhere on the cycle, because each stage feeds into the next.

Each of the four stages plays an equally important part in the learning cycle. Most people, however, have preferences for one or more stages.

Honey and Mumford describe these preferences or styles as:

Activists – prefer the experiencing stage
Reflectors – prefer the reviewing stage

Theorists – prefer the concluding stage
Pragmatists – prefer the planning stage

Figure ELP3.1   Four-stage learning cycle

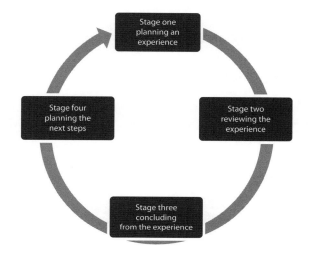

Activists

Activists involve themselves fully and without bias in new experiences. In a learning situation they respond well to:

- action learning
- business game simulations
- discussion in small groups
- job rotation
- outdoor activities
- role playing
- training others.

Reflectors

Reflectors like to stand back and observe experiences from many different perspectives. In a learning situation they respond well to:

- e-learning
- learning reviews
- listening to lectures and presentations
- observing role plays
- reading
- self-study and self directed learning.

Theorists

Theorists think problems through in a vertical, logical way and like to understand models and principles. In a learning situation they respond well to:

- analytical reviewing
- exercises that have a 'right' answer
- listening to lectures
- self study and self directed learning
- solo exercises
- talking-head videos.

Pragmatists

Pragmatists are practical and down to earth, and they like to know how things will work in the real world.

In a learning situation they respond well to:

- action learning
- discussion about work problems
- discussion in small groups
- group work with tasks where learning is applied
- problem solving workshops
- project work.

Applying your knowledge of learning styles can help considerably in designing and delivering effective learning programmes that will appeal to everyone.

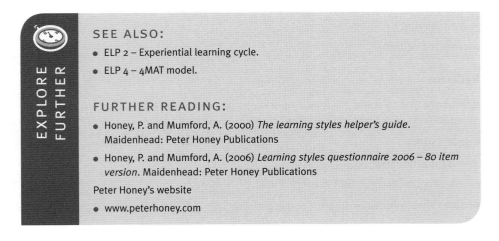

EXPLORE FURTHER

SEE ALSO:
- ELP 2 – Experiential learning cycle.
- ELP 4 – 4MAT model.

FURTHER READING:
- Honey, P. and Mumford, A. (2000) *The learning styles helper's guide*. Maidenhead: Peter Honey Publications
- Honey, P. and Mumford, A. (2006) *Learning styles questionnaire 2006 – 80 item version*. Maidenhead: Peter Honey Publications

Peter Honey's website
- www.peterhoney.com

4MAT model

THE BIG PICTURE

4MAT is a model for brain-based design and delivery which addresses the needs of all learning styles to increase engagement and learning transfer.

BACKGROUND

Bernice McCarthy is an American teacher and writer. She developed this model of learning in 1980 after having researched many different theories of learning, including those of Kolb (the experiential learning cycle), and Honey & Mumford (learning styles). Widely used in schools, the model has been successfully adapted and used by corporate and government organisations.

ESSENTIAL DETAIL

The 4MAT Model identifies four distinct preferences in how individuals prefer to take in and process information, referred to as 'learning styles'. Preferences in learning style determine where an individual prefers to linger in the learning process. The 4MAT model teaches how to design and deliver training that addresses the needs of all styles. More importantly, the model delivers a framework that moves every learner through four essential steps of the learning cycle. Each step answers a unique question, 'Why?', 'What?', 'How?' and 'If?' The suggestion is that each learning style focuses on one question more than others. However, each question must be answered for complete learning to occur, regardless of style preferences.

Table ELP4.1 Essential questions about learning style

Learner style	Description	Best trainer style
Favourite question: Why?	People who ask the 'why?' question are imaginative learners. They learn from feeling and watching, need to understand the reason to learn, and are interested in the personal meaning of learning. They like to work and learn with other people. They look for meaning.	Facilitator – engage through meaningful dialogue, reflection on personal experiences and sharing of stories, creating a personal interest in the learning content. Method: reflection and dialogue. Activities: stories, reflection exercises, Simulations and other experiential activities.

Favourite question: What?	Learners whose key question is 'what?' learn by watching and thinking. They are analytic learners. They enjoy independent research and lecture. They like models, theories and analysing data. They look for concepts.	Teacher and information giver – enable the participants to find out the facts and understand the key concepts and topics. Method: presentation. Activities: lecture, teach-back activities, learner note-taking, visual metaphors.
Favourite Question: How?	People who ask the 'how?' question learn by thinking and doing. They are common-sense learners who need activities and hands-on tasks. They need to know how things work and like to experiment and apply their own ideas. They look for skills.	Coach – allow participants to do something practical with what they have learned, adding something to it for themselves. Method: hands-on practice. Activities: case studies, simulations, role-plays, field work.
Favourite question: What if?	'What if?' learners learn by feeling and doing. They are dynamic learners who like to explore and learn by trial and error. They rely on their own intuition and they like independent study. They are risk-takers and enjoy active learning. They look for adaptations.	Evaluator – help participants to pull everything together, adapt the learning to their world and assess their application for future improvement Method: assessment. Activities: critiquing practice, self-assessment, scaling criteria, action planning, learner commitments.

EXPLORE FURTHER

SEE ALSO:

- ELP 2 – Experiential learning cycle.
- ELP 3 – Learning styles.

FURTHER READING:

- McCarthy, B and O'Neill-Blackwell, J (2007) *Hold on you lost me!: Using learning styles to create training that sticks.* Virginia USA: ASTD Press.
- The 4MAT for business website: www.4mat4business.com.

Multiple intelligences

THE BIG PICTURE

A theory that there are eight different forms of intelligence, and how an understanding of this can help to make the design and delivery of learning and development more appealing and memorable.

BACKGROUND

Howard Gardner is a developmental psychologist based at Harvard University in the USA. He first published his theory of multiple intelligences in 1983 after extensive research and synthesis of information.

He defined intelligence as 'the capacity to solve problems or to fashion products that are valued in one or more cultural setting'. In his research, he looked for all attributes that could be judged to be a separate form of intelligence using eight criteria or 'signs' of intelligence:

- potential isolation by brain damage
- the existence of exceptional individuals demonstrating the intelligence
- an identifiable core operation or set of operations
- a distinctive development history, along with a definable set of 'end state' performances
- an evolutionary history and evolutionary plausibility
- support from experimental psychological tasks
- support from psychometric findings
- susceptibility to encoding in a symbol system.

To be called 'an intelligence', each attribute had to satisfy a range of these criteria and must include, as a prerequisite, the ability to resolve 'genuine problems or difficulties' within certain cultural settings. Gardner himself is quoted as saying that making judgements about this was 'reminiscent more of an artistic judgement than of a scientific assessment'.

ESSENTIAL DETAIL

Gardner initially formulated a list of seven intelligences, divided into three key categories:

- traditional **academic** intelligences – Verbal/linguistic, logical/mathematical
- **arts** intelligences – auditory/musical, bodily/kinaesthetic, visual/spatial
- **personal** intelligences – interpersonal, intrapersonal.

In 1999, Gardner added an eighth intelligence to the list – naturalistic.

Verbal Linguistic	Likes wordplay, stories and discussions Has a wide vocabulary Quality of language is important
Logical Mathematical	Likes logical analysis and problem solving Works well with numbers and statistics Logic and structure are important
Musical Auditory	Likes music and well-pitched sounds and tones Has good musical pitch Quality music and appropriate voice tone are important
Visual Spatial	Likes visual imagery and design Visually creative and able to make things Shape, form, texture and colour are important
Physical Kinaesthetic	Likes movement and physical activity In tune with the needs of the body Physical well-being, health and fitness are important
Interpersonal	Likes interacting with others to share ideas Able to build relationships Sharing of ideas and experiences is important
Intrapersonal	Likes personal development High levels of self-awareness Personal reflection time and relating theories to own experiences are important
Naturalistic	Likes the natural world Able to identify and classify natural and man-made objects Time spent in the natural world is important

People have a unique blend of intelligences. Gardner argues that the big challenge facing the deployment of human resources 'is how to best take advantage of the uniqueness conferred on us as a species exhibiting several intelligences'.

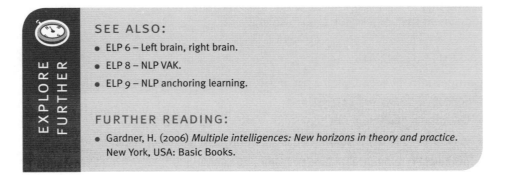

EXPLORE FURTHER

SEE ALSO:

- ELP 6 – Left brain, right brain.
- ELP 8 – NLP VAK.
- ELP 9 – NLP anchoring learning.

FURTHER READING:

- Gardner, H. (2006) *Multiple intelligences: New horizons in theory and practice.* New York, USA: Basic Books.

Left brain, right brain

THE BIG PICTURE

An understanding of how the brain functions, which helps give us a simple model of 'brain friendly learning' – ie making sure that we design and deliver L&D activities that engage and stimulate both sides of the brain.

BACKGROUND

Research into the functions of the two hemispheres of the brain (or, to be more precise, the neo-cortex) has been progressing since the 1960s when Roger Sperry first presented his split-brain theories.

ESSENTIAL DETAIL

It is well established that the neo-cortex has two distinct hemispheres. These are commonly called the left brain and the right brain. The key differences between the two hemispheres are:

LEFT HEMISPHERE	RIGHT HEMISPHERE
• starts with the pieces first	• sees big picture then the pieces
• looks at parts of language	• looks for language comprehension
• syntax and semantics	• images, emotions and meanings
• letters and sentences	• rhythm, flow and dialect
• numbers	• images
• linear analysis	• intuition and estimates
• differences	• similarities
• controls feelings	• free with feelings
• planned and structured	• spontaneous and fluid
• sequential thinking	• simultaneous thinking
• language-orientated	• feelings/experience orientated
• future-orientated	• present-orientated
• 'technical' interest in sports	• 'holistic' emotional interest in sports
• 'technical' interest in arts & music.	• 'holistic' emotional interest in arts & music.

The concept of 'whole brain learning' is so important because, in order to learn most effectively, we need to engage both hemispheres of the brain to enable us to absorb and interpret information, find meaning and relevance in it and then store it our long-term memory in a way that enables us to retrieve it quickly and accurately.

It is a fallacy to say that an individual is either left brained or right brained. Whereas we all have a certain brain dominance, it is extremely rare for someone to be wholly left or right brained.

Within each hemisphere of the brain, there are six levels of processing that take place. We will have a preference for processing style at each level. Understanding these helps us to understand the degree of brain dominance (left or right) that an individual has and enables us to structure learning activities that cater for all preferences and processing styles.

Table ELP6.1 **Left brain and right brain processing**

Left brain processing	Right brain processing
Linear Processes information in a linear way, from part to whole. Takes all the pieces, lines them up in a logical order then draws the conclusions.	Holistic Takes a holistic approach, from the whole to its parts. Starts with the answer and sees the big picture before the details. Needs to understand an overview of what is happening before engaging.
Sequential Processes information in sequence. Makes lists plans and schedules. Starts at the beginning of a task and works through to until completion. Focuses upon one thing at a time.	Random Processes information randomly. Tends to rebel against schedules. Flits between a number of tasks, completing bits of all of them. Has multiple focuses.
Symbolic Processes symbols such as letters and mathematical notations easily. Likely to memorise spellings and mathematical formulae.	Concrete Prefer to work with 'real' things that they can see, hear or touch. Don't always see the relevance of symbols and likely to work things out by using case studies and real examples.
Logical Processes facts and data in a sequential order to draw logical conclusions. Decisions based upon 'proof' – the assimilation of factual evidence. Reaches the answer by piecing together the information. Pays attention to accuracy.	Intuitive Bases decisions on intuition and trusts in gut reaction. Sometimes reaches an answer but cannot explain how the answer was reached. Pays attention to coherence and meaning and whether something 'feels' right to them.
Verbal Can work from purely verbal information without the need to write it down or make associations. Remembers the details of what they hear.	Non-verbal Finds it hard to remember verbal information on its own. Prefers to write things down or make associations to aid memory.

Reality-based	Fantasy-orientated
Deals with things as they are now – ie current reality. Adjusts to the environment they are in. Follows rules and keeps to deadlines/schedules set by others.	Deals with things as they could be. Tries to change their environment to meet their needs. Not always aware of rules and consequences. Tends to think creatively.

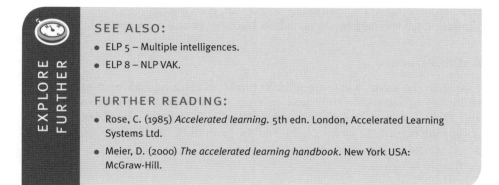

EXPLORE FURTHER

SEE ALSO:

- ELP 5 – Multiple intelligences.
- ELP 8 – NLP VAK.

FURTHER READING:

- Rose, C. (1985) *Accelerated learning.* 5th edn. London, Accelerated Learning Systems Ltd.
- Meier, D. (2000) *The accelerated learning handbook.* New York USA: McGraw-Hill.

Principles of adult learning

THE BIG PICTURE

A set of learning strategies used by adults that, if considered by L&D professionals, will help to engage adults into the process of learning.

BACKGROUND

Most educationalists had centred their studies on teaching and learning for children – or 'edagogy' ('child-leading' from the Greek *peda* – child). In the 1970s and 1980s, however, Malcolm Knowles looked at theories of adult learning and coined the word 'andragogy' ('man-leading' from the Greek *andro* – man).

ESSENTIAL DETAIL

Knowles emphasises that, unlike child learners, adults are self-directed and expect to take responsibility for their own decisions. He argues that this must be taken into account when designing any form of adult learning programme.

Andragogy means that instruction for adults needs to focus more on the process and less on the content being taught. Strategies such as case studies, role playing, simulations, and self-evaluation are most useful. Trainers should be more like a facilitator than a lecturer.

Knowles makes six assumptions about the motivation of adult learners:

1. Adults need to know the reason for learning something (*need to know*).
2. Experience (including mistakes) provides the basis for learning activities (*foundation*).
3. Adults need to be responsible for their decisions and involved in the planning and evaluation of their instruction (*self-concept*).
4. Adults are most interested in learning subjects which have immediate relevance to their work or personal life (readiness).
5. Adult learning is problem-centred rather than content-oriented (*orientation*).
6. Adults respond better to internal, rather than external, motivators (*motivation*).

In his book, Knowles provides an example of using andragogy principles to the design of computer training:

- There is a need to explain why specific things are being taught (eg certain commands, functions, operations etc.).
- Instruction should be task-oriented instead of memorisation – learning activities should be in the context of common tasks to be performed.

- Instruction should take into account the wide range of different backgrounds of learners: learning materials and activities should allow for different levels/ types of previous experience with computers.

- Since adults are self-directed, instruction should allow learners to discover things for themselves, providing guidance and help when mistakes are made.

EXPLORE FURTHER

SEE ALSO:

- ELP 2 – Experiential learning cycle.
- ELP 3 – Learning styles.
- ELP 4 – 4MAT.

FURTHER READING:

- Knowles, M., Holton, E. and Swanson, R. (2005) *The adult learner: The definitive classic in adult education and human resource development.* Burlington USA: A Butterworth-Heinemann.
- Knowles, M. (1984) *Andragogy in action: Applying modern principles of adult learning.* New Jersey USA: Jossey Bass.

NLP – Visual, auditory, kinaesthetic

THE BIG PICTURE

An explanation of some of the different ways in which people take in, store and recall experiences and information. Understanding this can help us to design and deliver L&D activities that are appealing and memorable for all learners.

BACKGROUND

Neuro-linguistic programming (NLP) was created in the early 1970s by Richard Bandler, a computer scientist and Gestalt therapist, and Dr John Grinder, a linguist and therapist. Bandler and Grinder invented a process known as 'modelling' that enabled them to study three of the world's greatest therapists: Dr Milton Erickson, father of modern hypnotherapy; Fritz Perls, creator of Gestalt therapy; and Virginia Satir, the mother of modern-day family therapy. They wanted to know what made these therapists effective and then to train others in their methods. What is known today as NLP is the product of this modelling process.

Their early work showed that humans process information through our 'representational systems'. The main 'rep' systems are visual, auditory and kinaesthetic. To a smaller extent we also make use of our olfactory (smell) and gustatory (taste) systems too.

ESSENTIAL DETAIL

The VAK learning styles model shows that there are three main preferences that people use when learning. None of these styles are right or wrong, and most of us have access to all three. Many people, however, tend to favour or use one style more readily than the others. For example, when asked to spell a word, someone might visualise the word written out on a page, someone else may hear the letter spelt out in their mind, whilst others may construct the spelling by applying a series of logical rules:

- Someone with a **visual** learning style has a preference for things that they can see or watch, such as pictures, diagrams, demonstrations, displays, handouts, films, flip-charts, etc. These people will use phrases such as 'show me', 'let's have a look at that' and will be best able to perform a new task after watching someone else do it first. These are the people who will work from lists and written directions and diagrams.

- Someone with an **auditory** learning style has a preference for the transfer of information through listening: to the spoken word, sounds and noises. These people will use phrases such as 'tell me', 'let's talk it over' and will be best able to perform a new task after listening to instructions from an expert. These are the people who are happy being given spoken instructions over the telephone, and can remember all the words to songs that they hear!

- Someone with a **kinaesthetic** learning style has a preference for physical experience – touching, feeling, holding, doing, practical hands-on experiences. These people will use phrases such as 'let me try', 'how do you feel?' and will be best able to perform a new task by going ahead and trying it out, learning as they go. These are the people who like to experiment, hands-on, and never look at the instructions first!

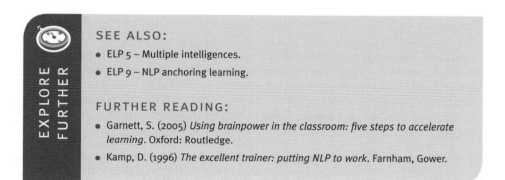

EXPLORE FURTHER

SEE ALSO:
- ELP 5 – Multiple intelligences.
- ELP 9 – NLP anchoring learning.

FURTHER READING:
- Garnett, S. (2005) *Using brainpower in the classroom: five steps to accelerate learning*. Oxford: Routledge.
- Kamp, D. (1996) *The excellent trainer: putting NLP to work*. Farnham, Gower.

ESSENTIAL LEARNING PAGE 9

NLP – anchoring learning

THE BIG PICTURE

A tool that helps learners to remember their learning in a positive way by making visual, auditory or kinaesthetic links.

BACKGROUND

Neuro-Linguistic Programming (NLP) was created in the early 1970s by Richard Bandler, a computer scientist and Gestalt therapist, and Dr John Grinder, a linguist and therapist. Bandler and Grinder invented a process known as 'modelling' that enabled them to study three of the world's greatest therapists: Dr Milton Erickson, father of modern hypnotherapy; Fritz Perls, creator of Gestalt therapy; and Virginia Satir, the mother of modern-day family therapy. They wanted to know what made these therapists effective and then to train others in their methods. What is known today as NLP is the product of this modelling process.

NLP is widely used in a variety of settings, from physcotherapy to business planning. Many parts of NLP are extremely useful in the field of learning and development, and one of the most useful (and easy to master) is the simple act of creating anchors.

ESSENTIAL DETAIL

An 'anchor' can be described as 'the process by which we make associations between experiences', for example, hearing a particular piece of music and immediately feeling happy because of the pleasant association with a happy event.

Anchors happen naturally all of the time, but a skilled designer or deliverer of learning and development activities can make sure that positive anchors happen for the benefit of their learners.

In the training room you can use anchors in a number of ways to enhance the learning experience. For example:

Spatial anchors
- Use different parts of the room for different activities so that learners associate one area with group work, another with reflection etc.
- Use different parts of the room for your own delivery of the session. Standing at the front signifies expert input, sitting at the side signifies group discussion and so on.

Sound (auditory) anchors

- Use the tonality of your voice to emphasise key points. Use repetition. Use it consistently so that you deepen the understanding of the audience.
- Use music or other sounds to establish learning patterns, bring groups back from breaks or to energise the group.

Visual anchors

- Use your mannerisms or body language to help your audience associate your main points. Think about your clothes, or have something visually different in the room that people will remember and associate with your session.
- Use your visual aids wisely – use colours to signify the journey through the training, or use diagrams, pictures etc to reinforce the learning.

Kinaesthetic anchors

- Design and use activities. People will remember 'doing' what they learned.
- Make wise use of 'emotional' anchors. People will remember how they felt about the learning. They will remember feeling happy when they solved a problem or sad when they saw a video about the dangers of fire.

Remember to use your anchors consistently – mixing them will cause confusion, but compounding them will add depth and association to your event.

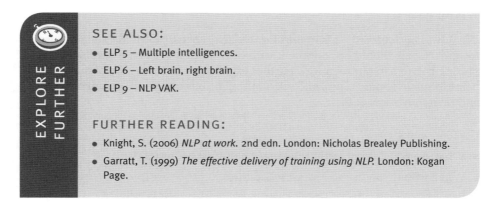

EXPLORE FURTHER

SEE ALSO:
- ELP 5 – Multiple intelligences.
- ELP 6 – Left brain, right brain.
- ELP 9 – NLP VAK.

FURTHER READING:
- Knight, S. (2006) *NLP at work*. 2nd edn. London: Nicholas Brealey Publishing.
- Garratt, T. (1999) *The effective delivery of training using NLP*. London: Kogan Page.

GROW Model

THE BIG PICTURE

A simple model of coaching which uses a series of questions to guide the person being coached towards a suitable set of actions to help them identify and achieve their goal.

BACKGROUND

The GROW model, originally devised by Graham Alexander, was developed and popularised by John Whitmore and colleagues, and published in the book *Coaching for Performance* (1996). John Whitmore's first career had been as a British racing driver in the late 1950s and early 1960s. He then became a sports psychologist before moving his coaching interests and talent into the world of business. He is now the executive chair of Performance Consultants International.

ESSENTIAL DETAIL

GROW is a four-stage model.

G is for goal(s)

What is to be achieved? It is important to clarify specific (SMART) goals to work towards. Goals should be congruent with our values otherwise we will keep putting barriers in our own way. Further exploration of the reality of our goals helps to uncover our values, and self-limiting beliefs and goals are often refined and revised in view of this.

Goal questions

- What are you aiming for in the long/medium/short term?
- When would you like to have reached this?
- What would you like to achieve by the end of this session?
- How will you know when you have achieved this?
- What will it look/feel/sound like?

R is for reality

What is the *truth* about the situation? The current situation is explored and the facts are established. During this phase it is important to encourage the client to use *descriptive* and not evaluative statements. It is also helpful for the coach to ask challenging or searching questions and to probe beneath the surface in order to get the client to examine their thoughts and to raise awareness. Questions in this phase are usually prefaced by *'what'*, *'where'*, *'when'*, *'who'* and *'how'*, which help the client to think creatively and to draw out the facts of the situation.

Reality questions

- What is happening at the moment around this issue?
- What have you done so far towards this goal?
- What is your main concern around this goal/issue?
- What resources do you have to help you with this?
- What might be holding you back?

O is for options

What *choices* exist to change the reality and reach the goal? What *alternatives* are there? Generating options is a creative process that is stimulated by the coach asking the right kinds of open questions, by inviting the client to suspend all judgement and self-criticism, by maintaining interest and by challenging the client just when they think they cannot come up with another idea. Often the best ideas come after the point when the client thought they were finished.

Options questions

- What could you do to move yourself one step forward to achieving your goal?
- What are all the different ways you could approach this?
- What else could you do?
- What if you knew you couldn't fail?
- If you could think of three more things, what would they be?

Evaluating each option narrows down the choice to which one or ones feel right and achievable for the client, this leads into the final stage.

W is for 'What will you do?'

Which option *will* the client really enjoy doing because it is part of the life they want? Which one are they willing to do, regardless of how much work it takes? Which one will they actually do, because it will take them nearer their goal or their dream? This is where *commitment* comes in. This is the step just before *action* or implementation. The next steps are agreed with a timetable and a commitment from the client.

Will questions

- Which of your options feels best/seems best/looks best/sounds best?
- Which would take you nearest to your longer term goal?
- Which would give you the most satisfaction?
- When will you do this?
- Tell me specifically what actions you will take and when to carry this out?

EXPLORE
FURTHER

FURTHER READING:

- Whitmore, J. (2002) *Coaching for performance*. London: Nicholas Brearley Publishing.
- Downey, M. (2003) *Effective coaching: Lessons from the coach's coach*. 3rd edn. London: Texere Publishing.
- Thorpe, S. and Clifford, J. (2003) *The coaching handbook*. London, Kogan Page.

John Whitmore's website:

- www.performanceconsultants.com

Levels of evaluation

THE BIG PICTURE

A model that provides four levels at which learning or training can be evaluated within an organisation.

BACKGROUND

Donald Kirkpatrick first published his ideas on evaluation in a series of articles for the *Journal of the American Society of Training Directors* (ASTD) in 1959. Kirkpatrick was president of that society in 1975.

In his book, *Evaluating training programs* (1994), he pulled together his previous works about the four levels of evaluation.

Kirkpatrick's four level model is the most widely used model of evaluation and is usually thought of as the 'industry standard' model.

ESSENTIAL DETAIL

The original four levels of Kirkpatrick's evaluation model measure:

1. The reaction of the learner – what they thought and felt about the training

2. The learning itself – the resulting increase in knowledge, skill, attitude or capability

3. The change in behaviour – the extent to which the learning has been transferred to the workplace, and

4. Results – the effects on the business resulting from the change in performance.

Kirkpatrick recommends that full and meaningful evaluation only takes place when the learning and its impact are measured at all four levels.

Table ELP11.1 Kirkpatrick's eevaluation levels

Level	What is measured	Description	Methods and tools
1	Reaction	How the delegates felt about their training or learning experience	'Happy sheets' Feedback forms Verbal reaction Post-training surveys or questionnaires On-line evaluations Feedback collected via trained observers

2	Learning	Measurement of the increase in knowledge or skill (before and after)	Assessments and tests either before and after, or after the training Interview Observation
3	Behaviour	The extent to which the learning is applied back at the workplace	Observation over time Interviews and self-assessment 360° Feedback Work review Regular monitoring
4	Results	The effect that the changed behaviour of the trainee has on the business or the environment	Key performance indicators Results measured in via existing management information systems Anecdotal evidence

Generally speaking, the lower levels of evaluation are the most commonly measured, and are generally less costly than level three.

Levels Three and Four need more planning and it is not always easy to determine whether a change can be directly attributed to a piece of learning and subsequent reinforcement.

It is, nonetheless, essential to have a system of evaluation that measures the extent to which the learning objectives of the intervention have been met.

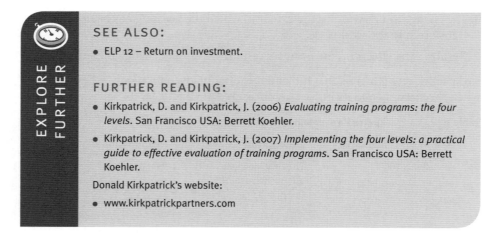

EXPLORE FURTHER

SEE ALSO:
● ELP 12 – Return on investment.

FURTHER READING:
● Kirkpatrick, D. and Kirkpatrick, J. (2006) *Evaluating training programs: the four levels*. San Francisco USA: Berrett Koehler.
● Kirkpatrick, D. and Kirkpatrick, J. (2007) *Implementing the four levels: a practical guide to effective evaluation of training programs*. San Francisco USA: Berrett Koehler.

Donald Kirkpatrick's website:
● www.kirkpatrickpartners.com

Return on investment

THE BIG PICTURE

Return on investment (ROI) tells you the financial impact that a piece of training (or other learning activity) has had on the bottom line of the business. It tells you the percentage return that your organisation has made over a given period of time by investing in a training programme.

BACKGROUND

ROI was popularised by Jack Phillips and is often seen as a 'fifth level' of the levels of evaluation.

Every activity that takes place in an organisation involves a cost – staff wages, production costs, overheads etc.

Assuming that the overall aim of an organisation is to make a profit (or at least to operate within a budget) then it is important that all costs are managed and understood.

Every activity undertaken within an organisation should contribute towards the goals of the business – so every pound that is invested in training should, in theory, produce at least a pound's worth of return (in terms of increased profits or reduced costs).

Calculating ROI is the way in which an organisation checks that the investment that is making in learning and development activities is paying off.

ESSENTIAL DETAIL

In order to calculate the ROI you will need to be able to assess the costs of providing the training, and also be able to measure the financial impact (benefits) of the training.

Training costs could include:

- development costs
- delivery time (trainer and learner wages)
- materials
- venue and domestics
- opportunity cost (how much a learner could have been contributing if they had not been attending the programme)
- evaluation costs.

Benefits may include:

- cost savings
- productivity increases
- income generated.

For example, here are the simplified training costs for a customer care programme (one-day programme for 10 staff):

Table ELP12.1 **Training costs for a customer care programme**

	Cost (£)
Design and development	1500.00
Admin costs	200.00
Venue and domestics	1250.00
Learner costs	1200.00
Opportunity cost	1000.00
Materials	50.00
Evaluation	200.00
Total costs	£5400.00

The value of benefits might be:

Table ELP12.2 **Benefits from the customer care programme**

Increased cross-sales over first six months	2500.00
Cost savings due to reduced number of customer complaints	3500.00
Total benefits	£6000.00

In this example therefore, the calculation of ROI is

(Benefits ÷ costs) × 100

(£6000.00 ÷ £5400.00) × 100 = 111.11 per cent

In other words, the return on investment in a six month period after the training delivery is 111 per cent.

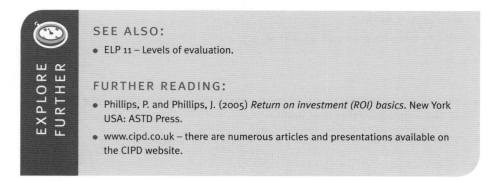

EXPLORE FURTHER

SEE ALSO:
- ELP 11 – Levels of evaluation.

FURTHER READING:
- Phillips, P. and Phillips, J. (2005) *Return on investment (ROI) basics*. New York USA: ASTD Press.
- www.cipd.co.uk – there are numerous articles and presentations available on the CIPD website.

Index